CAPE
FLORIDA
LIGHTHOUSE

KEY
BISCAYNE

SOLDIERS
KEY

STILTSVILLE

PUNCH
BOWL

LA
VIZCAVA

BISCAYNE
BAY

JACK'S
BIGHT

THE BARNACLE

THE KAMPONG

POOL

PLYMOUTH CONGREGATIONAL
CHURCH

FAIRCHILD TROPICAL
GARDEN

ABLES HOUSE

CAROL GARVIN,
1990

BILTMORE HOTEL

MIAMI, U.S.A.

For Marie M. Long,
my lifelong friend whom
I just met in person.
With affection and may
we meet again — Soon!

Helen Muir

Coconut Grove, Florida
14 November 1992.

MIAMI, U.S.A.

Helen Muir

Photographs by Masud and Najam Quraishy

The Pickering Press

The Pickering Press, Inc.
2575 S. Bayshore Dr., #3-A, Miami, FL 33133

Photo Credit: ©1990 by Masud and Najam Quraishy
All photographs are reprinted by permission of the
photographers Masud and Najam Quraishy

Design by Matthew Pimm
Typeset by Bessas & Ackerman
Photography by Masud and Najam Quraishy
Endpapers illustrated by Carol Garvin
Color separations by Professional Graphics, Inc.
Printed by Malloy Lithographing, Inc.

Library of Congress Cataloging-in-Publication Data

Muir, Helen, 1911—
        Miami, U.S.A. / Helen Muir : photographs by Masud and Najam
    Quraishy. — 2nd ed.
                p.   cm.
        Includes bibliographical references.
        ISBN 0-940495-19-8
        1. Miami (Fla.)—History.   I. Title.
    F319.M6M83   1990
    975.9'381—dc20   90–6908
                                        CIP

Front Cover Photograph: El Jardin, built circa 1918

For Mary and William Torbert Muir who march in the growing company of native-born sons and daughters of Miami and in memory of Melissa who lived and died under the warm sun.

Acknowledgments

Without the recollections of the people who helped build Miami this record could not have been compiled. Men like fire chief Henry R. Chase and Henry H. Filer gave generously of their time. So did Miss Cornelia Leffler, Mrs. Ben Shepard, whose father was Old Judge Worley, and Mrs. Henry E. Tuttle, the widow of Julia Tuttle's son.

J. E. Lummus and I spent mornings going over the early days in Miami, and C. W. Chase, Jr., was of assistance with maps and stories of the Miami Beach days. J. Arthur Pancoast gave photographs and Mrs. Russell Pancoast, Collins family history.

Mrs. Thomas W. Hutson, who was born in Miami as the daughter of Miami's favorite physician, Dr. James M. Jackson, was a deep well of information. So was John Frohock, who as sheriff had so much to do with the early Miami. Carl Holmer, Jr., gave me free use of valuable papers and Josiah F. Chaille took time off from gardening to go over the early days. Mrs. R. M. Davidson, daughter of S. Bobo Dean, and Mrs. E. Hugh Duffy, daughter of Cap'n Charlie Thompson, were generous with time and interviews, and so was Dan Hardie. When, after several interviews, Mr. Hardie died, advancing into the operating room with the same courage he exhibited on his trips into the 'Glades in search of criminals in hiding, it was a personal sorrow. Dan Hardie made a million dollars in Miami and died in a financial state that men of wealth would describe as "broke." Dan Hardie was never broke. He was always alive and full to the brim with color and warmth and humanness and experience.

Miss Hattie Carpenter was a constant and valuable source of information. So were Charlie Oxar, Wirth Munroe, who offered the Commodore's photographs, and Mrs. E. A. Waddell, who when this book was first written thirty-seven years ago, still resided in her old home in the middle of downtown Miami, apparently undisturbed by the encroachment of hotels and business houses.

For scientific assistance I am indebted to Nevin Hoy of the United States Geological Survey, whose brow I unwittingly furrowed with my unscientific approach to drainage; to Daniel Sullivan, who put me straight on more than one occasion on the subject of crime; and to Charles M. Brookfield, whose knowledge of the birds and bees of the region helped me set the pre-railroad landscape accurately.

Others whose time and memory store I confiscated were Miss Maude Brickell, Mrs. George Brickell, Mrs. Charles Brickell, Mrs. Gaston Drake, Adrian McCune, Frank Malone, Roby Wetmore, Mrs. Mabel Dorn, S. P. Robineau, Miss Julia Fillmore Harris, Mrs. George Merrick, J. W. Watson, Jr., W. Cecil Watson, Ernest R. Graham, Mrs. Charles Blair, and C. Townsend Ludington.

George Worley, Jr., permitted me to borrow the transcript of the case of the FEC Railroad vs. George Worley et al.; Miss Lois Gilbert of the Miami *Daily News* was cooperative in searching out old copies of the *Metropolis*.

For the new edition, as always, I have the library to thank, especially Lillian Baker, Marguerite Carden, Sam Boldrick and Sylvia Wahrburg of the Main Library. Assistant director Carden offered special assistance on occasion. Sue Browning and her staff at the Coconut Grove Library Branch were as usual helpful.

I appreciate the time given me by so many of those interviewed and particularly Monsignor Bryan O. Walsh, with whom I discussed endlessly the refugee problems, and Arva Moore Parks and Dr. Thelma Peters. The latter two have produced much information in the field of Miami history since 1953 when the first edition of this book was issued. They were generous in sharing it with me whenever requested to do so. They also were good enough to review and comment on the first edition.

My appreciation goes to Dorothy J. Fields, founder of Black Archives, History and Research Foundation of South Florida, Inc. and to members of the Coconut Grove community: Leona Cooper, Millard Roberts, Thelma Gibson, widow of Canon Theodore Gibson, and to Dolly Lauderdale, who typed the manuscript with such careful attention.

I wish to acknowledge the assistance of Mark Seibel, who took time out from running the foreign desk of the Miami *Herald* to serve as editor for The Pickering Press in the matter of this book. He helped in the selection of the material at hand, which, both written and unwritten, constituted a mountain. He was unfailingly good-humored and patient and earned both respect and affection.

I deeply regret the many subjects that had to be deleted for lack of space and wish to thank my fellow journalist-turned-banker Jeanne Bellamy for the time spent in conversation about the Greater Miami Chamber of Commerce. She was the first woman to head that group and understood my approach to what was going on there.

Talks with Allen Morris in Tallahassee were helpful and so were those with Charity Johnson of Pickering Press.

Richard Plumer, Lisa Hardeman and Randy Nimnicht, director of the Historical Association of South Florida, gave time and information. So did Louis J. Hector, Frank Scruggs, Marjorie Donohue, and Leona Cayton, and my thank-you goes to all of them.

To all these and many others goes my appreciation.

H. M.

Coconut Grove, Florida

Table of Contents

Part Five

New Growth, Old Problems

Part Six

Living in Miami 1953—1990

Foreword

On a number of occasions people have assured me that Miami has no soul. My response usually has been that Miami has a number of souls. Just as another city I love, New York, has a number of souls.

My mother was born in New York, a city in decline.

My three children were born in Miami, a city still in the process of being created. As for souls, I happen to know a thing or two about souls. I believe there is a soul hovering over Miami. I believe I know what it is.

It is a soul made up of survivors, those who did not flee to the hills when assaulted by crime and senseless violence, uprootings and displacement, irrational politicians or mere hurricanes that wiped them out but set them to forging new paths.

Today, Miami is hot and we don't mean climate. Miami is a hot property. Editors and writers of books, magazines and newspapers arrive in a steady stream for the purpose of gathering material to tell the world exactly what Miami *is*.

Interpreting Miami has become something of an international pastime.

All over the world when one travels, whether in London, Paris or a German village, when it becomes known where you live the question is asked: "What is it *like* living in Miami?"

A flippant answer might be: "It is like proceeding through rubble and occasional high water on a pogo stick" or even "riding a roller coaster while playing lookout for bullets and bombs," but they would only be partially true.

Try emphasizing the natural beauty of one's home place, the excitement, the richness and satisfactions of overcoming seemingly insurmountable problems and eyes glaze over.

Miami is actually a great northern city transplanted to the sub-tropics. It has the lure of a tropical country, but it's strictly American, with all the good and bad ingredients that America can produce.

It has been called everything from the new Casablanca to Paradise Lost. In thirty years it suffered waves of immigration, a virtual invasion by people of another culture. Citizens of the entire world are knocking at Miami's doors, indeed knocking down the doors, in their hurry to flee revolution, poverty or mere boredom and seek a richer life.

Cubans and Haitians still arrive on makeshift rafts, but wealthy Europeans and Asians jet in as well.

Everybody appears eager to visit, to invest, to sniff the atmosphere.

A persistent Florida myth is that long ago a race of giants dwelt on the sun-washed peninsula. There is no basis in archaeological fact for this notion. Florida, one of the earliest spots discovered in North America and, paradoxically, one of the latest to be developed, was inhabited by Indians before Columbus. The giants who came in the twentieth century were financial giants and they changed the face of the land.

Everything modern and familiar about Miami is man-made or man-juggled. Miami grew carelessly, in fits and starts, then leaps and bounds. There was never any distinguishing rhythm to its growth, only an overnight suddenness on the order of the fairy-tale beanstalk that Jack climbed to get to the giant's palace.

Miami will be one hundred years old in 1996. In that time many people came and stayed, worked and left, died, got rich or went broke.

Some came merely to get rich and for them the beauty of the region was lost. In order to love one must first look and see and come to understand. Others, from the beginning, appreciated the region, fought to keep it unspoiled, lost the fight nearly always.

In its rush toward the twenty-first century, it is hoped that Miami may be ready to drop its youthful preoccupation with its image. Admittedly, that has not happened as yet and may still be a long way off.

In Miami, the slogan is still the first step and the amazing thing has been that so often the slogan introduces the picture that eventually comes to pass. William Butler Yeats wrote, "Seek out reality, leave things that seem." In Miami it has seemed to work in reverse.

Exotic is the word frequently employed to describe Miami and Miami

Beach. The dictionary offers as a synonym "foreign." I prefer another definition: "Belonging as a flower, to another part of the world."

This book which speaks of Miami's past can serve as a mere kaleidoscope; but if it tells something of how it was at each of its fast-changing periods, perhaps it will have served a purpose.

1 | THE BEGINNING OF THE DREAM 1875–1911

The Era of the Bay

YOU HUNG A FISH LINE OVER THE SIDE, and if you didn't like what you caught, you threw it back in and tried again. There was a fish at the end of every one cast in glittering Biscayne Bay.

The shallow waters were so clear you could see the sandy bottom alive with turtle and crawfish. Green turtle soup was mighty tasty, and so were chicken and loggerhead turtle steaks. Live green turtles shipped to Key West brought a cent a pound in the shell, and from there they were shipped alive to New York to tickle the palates of big-city epicures.

The shores of the southbay settlement known as Coconut Grove were a breeding place for the green turtle, and families kept them imprisoned in "crawls" nearby their weathered primitive homes for use when they needed them. Until Edmund Beasley and later John Pent built the first wooden houses, people were contented with shelters of palmetto leaves thatched over a frame. Everybody cooked out of doors over a chip fire.

North on the bay in the settlement known as Lemon City, people thought so highly of the green turtle as food that they made special turtling trips to a tongue of land between the bay and the Atlantic Ocean, a land of crocodiles and raccoons known vaguely as "the beach"—but which later would carry the name Miami Beach.

Hordes of mosquitoes and sand flies inhabited this half-swampland during the summer months. It was then, by the light of the moon, that the turtles laboriously crawled up on the sand to dig holes and lay their eggs. Groups from Lemon City would sail over in the late afternoon, then divide the beach, walking barefoot as the moon rose, two by two, so as not to miss one green turtle. Once they sighted their prey, they would tie a rope on the turtle's flipper and drag it to the bayside. The women always demanded turtle eggs for cake-baking. They were lighter than hen's eggs but gave the cakes a slightly salty taste.

Down at Elliott Key green turtle were so plentiful an old Conch had a system of his own: he would stick a pole down in the water to attract a turtle, then peg it on the order of gigging a fish.

Some early settlers were called Conchs and later others were called Crackers. Conchs were men who lived by the sea, and Crackers were inland people, both mainly English. Conchs came by boat from the Bahamas, and Crackers came south via the land after the American Revolution.

Conchs lived on seafood and pigeon peas, "sours and dillies," the colloquial names for limes and sapodillas. Conchs used a squizzle of lime juice on everything they ate, and when they got cuts and insect bites, they used a squizzle of lime to cure those. The test of a true Conch was whether he put a squizzle of lime in his morning coffee. There was a "limey" quality to pronunciation in many cases as well, and it would be up to the courts to untangle the deeds to some of this land by ordering one name changed from "Hagan" back to "Egan."

Crackers were not really content unless they had cowpeas and collards, mustard greens or white bacon, Georgia style.

Some Conchs on the mainland and down on the Florida Keys, those tiny tropical islands which curved south and west like a broken path to the thriving city of Key West, were quite scholarly and were said to be descendants of the Eleutherian Adventurers, a band formed in London in 1647 who settled in the Bahamas in order that "every man might enjoy his own opinion or religion without control or question." They moved from England to Bermuda and then to the Bahamas where they settled on an island which they named Eleuthera. Sympathetic New Englanders sent food to the freedom-loving band, and in return, the Adventurers shipped back loads of brasiletto wood to New England. People said the money realized on this wood was donated to the institution now known as Harvard University.

There was a black settlement in Coconut Grove known as Kebo, made up mostly of Bahamians with their strong British accents, although southern American blacks were there, too, some the descendants of runaway slaves.

A Bahamian named Rose came often to a home overlooking the bay

4

with offers to "help," but always ended up standing at a window looking mournfully across the water. Questioned, she said, "I was lookin' at Nassau." Nassau was a good hundred and fifty miles across the ocean.

They sailed over, cutting through the blue-black waters of the Gulf Stream, and when they got lonesome, they sailed back again. There was an even flow, back and forth, between the colonies.

And when they came they carried in their pockets the seeds that would glorify the Florida dooryards: soursops, sugar apples, Barbados cherries, trees that transformed the rocky sandy tip of the U.S.A. into a West Indian land.

Sometimes the seeds were blown over by hurricanes or drifted in the Gulf Stream. One way or another they got to the mainland of the Florida peninsula and settled into the porous rock, oölitic limestone it was, good soil for tropical trees.

This land, flat as a tabletop, rock and sand covered with curly-top Caribbean pines and palmetto scrub as far as the eye could see, rose slightly as it neared the bay and formed a hammock, the tropical name for forest. There, live oaks, ironwood trees, the gumbo limbo, the strangler fig crowded each other, making a jungle cool and pungent away from the piercing rays of the constant sun. Its dense tangle of tropical growth and fallen trees made entrance impossible without the aid of a machete.

The sun was part of the earth and sea, showering its hot yellow-white rays over the surfaces of both, tinging the sea grapes and coco plums which lined the uneven shore, changing the bay's color with each spark from blue to green, now dark, now light, filtering through the hammock to spatter delicate pink on tree trunks and the tea-colored forest floor. In this hammock, moths and spiders and snakes and scorpions lived their hidden lives. Birds were absent, and there was at once a terrible quiet and an image of great busyness.

The land on which the settlers lived was a rock ridge, a rim of rock with the sea on one side and the watery expanse of the Everglades on the other. The land was a mere backdrop for the action which took place on the water.

Biscayne Bay, broad and brimming with fish, was the highway on which the people moved in their small sailing craft under shifting starch-white clouds while great blue and great white herons, American egrets, and roseate spoonbills dipped and wheeled and came to rest in the shallows along the shore.

Across the bay, Miami Beach, a spit of land fastened to the mainland, was preceded south in the curved march of islands by Key Biscayne, which had its own history. Some say that in the shadowy past, Don Pedro (el) Biscaino lived there and gave the bay its name. He was a Basque who had held the title "Keeper of the Swans" at the court of Spain.

Outside the Keys lay the Florida Reef, a string of coral rock ledges and shoals which spelled disaster to many a Spanish galleon caught in a storm or guilty of faulty navigation. Wreckage strewn through the centuries told that tale. Wreckage still played its part in supplying the needs of the bay people, who led a free, barefoot life in a world of blue water by day and moonlight shining through Bear Cut at night, a track of glistening silver from Biscayne Bay to the Atlantic Ocean.

Until 1896 South Florida might as well have been an island joined to the Bahamas by sailboat and custom, separated from the rest of the state by miles of swamps and rivers. Mail came by sailboat twice a month from Key West and was also carried by barefoot mailmen who walked the wild beaches from Lake Worth on the north to the Bay, a stretch of nearly seventy miles. Men bound on Dade County business, tax assessors and the like, made the trip the same way. It was either that or risk your life in an open boat in water often too rough for small boats—or go hundreds of miles around by Key West in a seagoing vessel.

In those early times the oldest of the Brickells' seven children, Miss Alice, was postmistress, and if she felt like it, she would give out the mail. If she didn't, you went without mail that day. The mailman dumped it on a long table, and sometimes Miss Alice sorted it and sometimes she didn't. People came in and out to buy necessities—flour, sugar, salt, blue denim overalls and shirts, kerosene, and shoes. Anyone walking the rocky paths away from the water would need shoes. They wore out mighty fast on the ragged rock.

If you asked for a size-ten shoe and the size tens were high up on a shelf, Miss Alice would look you in the eye and say she didn't have any size tens, but would offer eights that were closer by. If you pointed out the tens, clearly marked, on the upper shelf, Miss Alice would look you in the eye and say, "Who's running this place, you or me?"

You took the eights and cut the toes out to fit. Pieces of leather came in handy for making washers for pitcher pumps, and most men's shoes had round holes showing at the ankles, proof they had recently been engaged in a pump repair job.

You dug down ten or fifteen feet and ran into all the fresh water you wanted for your pump. The thing that made the bay country was fresh water. Tequesta Indians, discoverers, pirates, seamen of all description, had been sailing up the Miami River to stock up on fresh water for centuries.

You could dip a tin cup in the Miami River and bring up a crystal-clear drink, and there were places in the bay itself where fresh cold water bubbled up. Fishermen knew where these places were and used them to stock up on drinking water without coming ashore.

South of Brickell Point, where the Brickell home stood, there was a spring six or eight feet across, like a big bowl at the edge of the bay and known as the Devil's Punch Bowl. Some said the water had special qualities, really was the Fountain of Youth Ponce de León was said to have been seeking. Others pointed to strange carvings on the live oaks, marks like Masonic symbols, and whispered that pirates had made them to denote where they had put away their treasure.

Indians had been poling up and down the river in their cypress dugout canoes for centuries. Now they were a mixed band, part Creek, known as Seminoles, the name generally meaning "separatists." The pole was used because a paddle never would have cut through the tough saw grass of the Everglades, which lay beyond the river.

Seminoles made Brickell's business. They came in their canoes over the rapids of the Miami from their camps at the edge of the Everglades, bringing alligator and deer and otter skins, egret plumes, and the inevitable coontie or comptie starch which white men, too, had been making for years. A species of *Zamia*, the coontie was also known as Florida arrowroot and sold to biscuit companies.

In exchange for these offerings, the Indians would carry away sugar and alarm clocks and hand-powered sewing machines, which the women doted on, and beads, beads, beads, for the rows they wore, collar-like, around their smooth brown necks. They demanded solid beads about the size of a small pea and preferred the colors red and turquoise.

One day, a Seminole squaw consented to have her beads weighed at Brickell's trading post, and they tipped the scales at twenty-five pounds.

Calico, the brighter the better, was in demand, and with it the women made their skirts, edging them in bright color. Below the long-sleeved, emblemed waists, their bare midriffs made a pleasing break in the color splashes.

The women either wore their sleek black hair in bangs or in a forward pompadour. The men, too, wore bangs and knee-length shirts, sometimes belted. It was a wonder to the white man that these shirts never blew up in the wind. They might quiver a bit, but never did they rise above the knee. Embroidered jackets were often worn over the shirts, and, occasionally, a Seminole wore deerskin leggings and moccasins as well as a bright turban. The latter was in reality a shawl, usually red, a practical garment which, twisted and knotted, served as a head covering by day and unfolded to make a cover by night.

Indians said they wore red to attract the deer.

The Seminoles who came to Brickell's trading post did not actually barter. They demanded cold cash for their wares, but as soon as Brickell laid it on the line they willingly handed it back, piece by piece, for the things they wanted. Certain coins they kept and made into jewelry.

If a Seminole made friends with a white family, he would feel free to enter their kitchen and make a cup of coffee, whether there was anyone about or not, since in their tribes they had communal kitchens. But no white man in his right mind would leave the sugar around if he expected an Indian caller. One Seminole could empty a sugar bowl in no time at all.

One winter night an Indian entered the house of Adam Richards and crawled in with the sleeping children. "Cold," he explained briefly when they found him there next morning.

The Indians knew their friends. Any number of them had been present the day Adam Richards took Rose Wagner for his bride in the little Catholic mission that was the first official church of the region, located out at William Wagner's Grove near Allapattah Prairie (the early settlers said it per-rarry).

The youngest squaw of Chief Cypress Tiger came to the Brickell home one early evening to borrow a cooking pot, which she filled at the outdoor pump before retiring into the hammock. Later, the light of a campfire shone through the swift-falling night where the river poured into the bay. In the morning, the squaw came to return the vessel, twin newborn babies clasped in her arms. One of them she named Princess Miami, for the winding river.

8

These Indians lived in the Everglades in thatched huts and cooked their fish and venison, ibis, turkey, and deer outdoors. They raised beans and squash and made a soup-like dish of ground coontie called *sofkee*.

Often on Sunday mornings, the Seminoles came to stand in the garden which Old Man Brickell, who had a green thumb, had planted with frangipani and Jamaica apple, breadfruit and grapefruit, oranges and oleander, to listen to the bay people sing their white men's songs. Hymns they called them, and the one the Indians liked best was called "Onward Christian Soldiers." Miss Alice played the piano and sang in a clear sweet voice, and people came from way down on the Keys for these Sabbath morning services according to the late Maude Brickell, interviewed in the early 1950s.

Before coming to the bay, William Barnwell Brickell had been a member of the Presbyterian Church. His English wife, born Mary Bulmer in Yorkshire, was an Episcopalian. The older children were given their choice of either religion back in Cleveland, Ohio.

"I am a Republican and a Presbyterian," their father told them. "Any man who changes either his religion or his politics is a mugwump."

In the general church service of the bay all creeds were welcome. A Sunday school was begun and the women, whose visiting was usually tied up with helping nurse a stricken neighbor, saw to it that everyone turned out. Because of distances, this operation involved feeding the young physically as well as spiritually. Scrubbed and dressed in their best, everybody looked forward to Sunday school. The men wore shoes and coats and trimmed their beards or mustaches. The women smoothed down their long-sleeved calicoes and got out frilly bonnets for the current baby.

The women saw to it that the Sabbath was kept. They felt they had things to be thankful for, and they also knew they needed each other. One of the early bay tales is of the woman who came as a bride and kept a sunbonnet on, in and out of the house, for the first month in order to hide her tears from her husband. It was the loneliness the women had to fight at first. Another early settler thanked her husband for the black-striped lawn dress he had brought her from Key West and then went into the hammock and bawled because she had hoped for a "morning-glory pink-striped dress." They were busy and contented enough, but most of the time they longed for the company of other women.

They learned to use guava syrup as the principal sweetening for pies and cakes. They made johnnycake, "sweet and plenty of it," stewed venison, ash-baked sweet potatoes, roast wild hog, gypsy stew (usually made from wild hog, turtle or manatee), coontie pudding, and coontie pancake. Their children never saw milk but they ate the Indian *sofkee* for gruel and the boiled Seminole squash, reef bean soup, turtle fry, and fried chicken. Most families had a few chickens, but if you did, you paid the price by fighting off coons and wildcats and possums. If you planted vegetables, the deer and rabbits became your enemies. What with wild duck and quail in the hammocks, there was always plenty to eat. The women made good use of fruits like the hog plum, coco plum, sea grape, and custard apple as well as the sapodillas, guavas, limes, and the few pomegranates.

In order to get that nearly unknown commodity known as cash, the people of the bay manufactured coontie starch, which brought from three to eight cents a pound at the Key West market. So did the Crackers homesteading back "in the sticks," as the pineland away from the water was called. A family of three or four operating a mill could without much effort make one barrel or two hundred and fifty pounds of starch in a week. This brought a nice little income of twelve dollars and fifty cents in a medium market. In comparison with the rest of the U.S.A., which had hit financial bottom after the panic of 1873, the subsequent closing of the Stock Exchange, and the railroad strikes and widespread poverty, the bay people were well off.

Some families operated their starch mills by mule or horse power, grinding the roots, which looked like giant sweet potatoes (and which in their raw state were poisonous), washing them, setting them out to bleach, then packing them in barrels.

There was one drawback to the industry: the root as it decomposed gave off a powerful stink, and the steady trade winds upon which the great sailing ships had so long depended were no less valuable in blowing away the fumes from the coontie mills.

The schooner from Key West, which every six weeks picked up the starch, also brought groceries, so the operation amounted to barter. But a man could get along fine without ever seeing cash money. If he found himself with a pocketful, he celebrated by buying jawbreakers for the children when the Key West schooner dropped anchor. If you felt like eating venison but didn't feel like killing a deer, you might effect a barter with an Indian. Fifty oranges were considered a fair exchange for half a deer. Twenty-five would bring a couple of hams. And if a man had a bit of luck and ran into a school of kingfish on the Cape Florida sand bores or off Bear Cut buoy, he would lay aboard all he could hold and sail home blowing the conch shell to call the settlers to come and share the haul. The blast of the conch, that for years meant "wreck" off the Florida Reef, held the same promise of treasure washed ashore to the people of the bay, but it meant other things as well. It might mean that Argyle Henry had driven his cattle from Titusville to Lemon City, slaughtered them, and was bound south on the bay to sell choice beef. He called it "boating beef." Or it might mean that Old Ned Pent had got hold of a jug of cider or whisky and was in a mood to strike up a fiddle for a square dance either at Coconut Grove or Lemon City. In that case, the babies were bundled up and the whole family got in their sailboat and headed for the fun. It goes without saying that a man sailing in the direction of the dance would sound the conch at each place along the water to see if anybody wanted a ride. Some men could make music, wild, strange, sweet music, pour out of an old conch shell.

The bay fed and housed and clothed its people. It cast up via the wrecks off the Reef everything from a grand piano to silk shawls and a fancy carriage. Nobody was ever surprised, only pleased, at what the sea washed in. Into the sun-splashed isolation one day floated a railroad freight car. The people of Cutler, south of the Grove, eyed it speculatively, then turned it into a post office.

A woman with her first-born son in her arms said to her husband, "I wish you'd go over to the Cape and see if you can't find a cradle."

He did and he brought it back, and when it was painted French gray and mended, it was her joy.

If you wanted to build a house, you mentioned it around, and a party would organize to sail over to Cape Florida to hunt up timber. They'd make a raft of the stuff and float it in with the tide. People were beginning to disparage thatched roofs, but if you wanted shingles, you'd have to order them from Key West, along with the nails.

Summer was the same as winter, only in wintertime it sometimes got uncomfortably chilly, and then you piled on extra clothes and huddled around the outdoor cooking fire waiting for it to get warm again, putting up a windbreak, Indian fashion, against the chill breezes.

11

Nobody had screens against the mosquitoes and horseflies, and out in Coconut Grove when Henrietta Trapp lit her oil lamp as a beacon for sailors, the bugs were so thick she often had to close the windows. Summer and winter, the light burned steadily in her window nonetheless.

Hurricane weather was a pure lark. A good hurricane would wash in plenty of wreckage: cheese and candles, soap and bags of flour, fine old wines and whiskey. The popular wreck cry was "Providence, bad machinery, and worse navigation sent us one." While the men were "off wrecking" the women got together for company. The preferred wreck was the one that brought "canned foods, dry goods, household furniture, and baby carriages," and the one they cared for the least was a ship loaded with stuffed olives.

On one occasion there was so much champagne floating around the bay that one old fellow filled a tin tub with the bubbly stuff and took baths in it to see if it would help his rheumatism. A Seminole named Johnny Jumper found bottles marked "Beef, Iron, and Wine" and consumed quarts of it. His three anxious squaws, unable to either rouse or move him, built a thatch of palmetto over his turbaned head and left him to the soothing play of the trade winds while they set about cooking pancakes in the Vaseline that had providentially floated in.

You never knew when you got up in the morning what the bay would wash in before the sun went down.

If you got a toothache, you headed for Brickell's and the toothache drops that never failed to ease the pain. Any other disability was taken care of at home by your wife or mother. If she and the rest of the women called into consultation couldn't cure you, they loaded you on a sailboat and prayed for a good wind to get you to Key West.

If the woman of the house took sick there was real consternation. One woman who fell ill was sent to Key West for medical attention by her insistent husband and sons, and while she was gone they considerately put away all the sheets and pillowcases so they would not be "dirtied up." On her arrival home a month later, the poor woman was faced with having to wash the heavy blankets they'd used instead of sheets as well as the bed ticking in both mattresses and pillows.

If you died, your coffin would be fashioned from driftwood. One homemade casket about to be loaded aboard the boat for Key West and thence bound north with the remains of a bay woman who had escaped her conventional children in life was discovered at the last moment to show the words "Mumm's Extra Dry" printed across the lid. The boat waited while the bay people hastily covered the words with white paint. Later, the captain reported that when it dried the words shone through just the same.

Old Ned Pent, who built boats when he wasn't walking the beaches with the mail or acting as bay pilot for a Northern wrecking company or playing the fiddle, made shipshape coffins, painting them with copper paint and lining them with white muslin. But he was unpredictable. Often it was necessary for the family of the deceased to lock Old Ned in his workshop with a bottle. In the morning, the bottle would be empty and the coffin completed.

The last coffin Old Ned built things didn't go right. In the early morn in that still moment before the wind was up when the family went to claim the casket they found Old Ned sleeping as per expectations, only he had equipped the coffin clear down the middle with a centerboard.

In a rhythm as natural as the tides, people were born and people died. People laughed and people cried. But nobody locked their doors, nobody ever hurried, everybody had time to laugh. Nobody kept track of dates. What happened today was gone tomorrow.

Fort Dallas

O N THE OTHER SIDE OF THE RIVER from Brickell's trading post, surrounded by coconut palms and limes and royal poinciana trees, stood the remains of Fort Dallas. Traditionally referred to as an abandoned army post, the remaining buildings actually represented the residence and slave quarters begun by William F. English of Columbia, South Carolina, in 1849.

The army post known as Fort Dallas had been there all right, but the low stone structure referred to as "the barracks" originally had been quarters for the slaves English borrowed from his mother in order to clear land and build. The two-story structure known as the "officers' quarters" was built as his home.

English followed his uncle to Biscayne Bay. The latter, Colonel Richard Fitzpatrick, had been an energetic Dade County territorial delegate; a decade after the United States claimed Florida, he had purchased the Miami hammock including tracts of land on both the north and south banks of the river. His slaves cleared three miles of jungle along the river, a sizable piece of jungle even with good sharp machetes and the trade winds blowing, then planted cotton, sugar cane, and limes.

The start of the Seminole Wars interrupted his operations, and he evacuated to Key West before embarking on a state mission "to the island of Cuba to purchase bloodhounds for the purpose of employing them against the Seminoles." His experiences in accomplishing this mission make a story in themselves, involving near-shipwreck and costing the state of Florida more than four thousand dollars. Nevertheless, he returned with thirty-three bloodhounds and five reluctant Cubans as dogkeepers. For his services he received one thousand dollars.

It was at this time that Fort Dallas was established on the north bank of the river. It was named for a navy man, Commodore Alexander James Dallas, who was in charge of the United States naval forces in the West Indies in the first days of the Seminole Wars. (His brother George later became vice-president under James K. Polk.)

The post was opened in 1838, the year Dade County was created by an act of the Territorial Legislative Council and named for Major Francis L. Dade, who had been massacred the year before by Indians in Sumter County, his death signaling the start of the war.

Actually the main naval post was at Key Biscayne, which offered a better command of the approaches from the West Indies or the Atlantic, and was called Fort Bankhead and again Fort Russell. By any name, the navy was on the lookout for the landing of arms for the Seminoles by Spanish traders and sympathizers.

Two years later, the navy withdrew from Fort Dallas to Key Biscayne, and in 1839, the army took over Fort Dallas. It was January when Company B, Third Artillery, moved in and the next month when Fort Miami, which had been established in the Everglades, was disbanded. Thirty-nine men of Company I, Second Infantry, who had been stationed at Fort Miami, canoed down the river to join the others. Along the coco-plum-fringed banks of the Miami just south of the rapids, Seminoles, fully armed, lay in wait and attacked with a sudden volley of fire. The first volley failed to reach the mark, and Captain S. L. Russell ordered his men to row for the opposite bank. Springing to shore, he turned to issue an order and fell dead from a shot that found its mark there in the southern wilderness. After an hour's exchange of fire, the Indians withdrew, and the party, with some injured, proceeded downstream to Fort Dallas.

The buildings at Fort Dallas at that time were temporary affairs, unlike the substantial rock buildings put up later by English, whose slaves did expert work. William English followed in his uncle's footsteps as a member of the state legislature and for a time resided at Indian Key. Happily, he was not at home the morning of August 7, 1840, when Indians attacked and murdered

16

Dr. Henry Perrine, the former doctor-turned-diplomat who harbored the dream of introducing large-scale tropical planting to subtropical America.

The government had granted Perrine a township of land on the mainland along the bay in unsurveyed territory for this purpose, and while he was waiting for the "Indian trouble" to subside Perrine had moved his family to the settlement at Indian Key. A mile to the north at Tea Table Key there was a naval station and a small detachment of soldiers and it was considered safer than the mainland.

On Indian Key a ruthless and unscrupulous wrecker named Jacob Housman ruled the roost, which was elaborate and included the Tropical Hotel for visitors and a mansion where Housman dwelt with his ill-gotten gains and his beautiful common-law wife. He was a scamp who in his early youth had stolen in Staten Island, New York, a vessel belonging to his father and headed for the West Indies.

When Dade County was created and Indian Key was made the county seat, a shout went up from Monroe County on the south that it was a clever stunt to remove Housman's machinations from the Monroe County courts and permit his highhanded method of dealing with wrecks to continue.

At this time there were more than twenty vessels, some from Connecticut and New York as well as Key West and Indian Key, engaged in the legitimate business of wrecking. There was no Coast Guard to watch the remote shore, and the two hundred miles from Key Biscayne to the Dry Tortugas were patrolled in sections by the captains of these vessels, men familiar with the Florida Reef, whose first job was to save lives and whose second was to save the ship. Their third aim was salvaging the cargo. The wreckers got their reward in shares administered by the courts.

The peak of wrecking rewards came in the 1850s when five hundred vessels valued at sixteen million dollars hit the coral ledges of the deep. But a decade earlier, Jacob Housman was doing very well, his warehouses bulging with salvaged goods in a business that brought him as much as thirty thousand dollars a year. Finally, his wrecking permit was taken from him after incidents of obvious brazenness in which he continued to ignore the code of salvaging.

Looking about for new fields to conquer, Housman then proposed to the United States government that it pay him two hundred dollars a head to catch or kill all the South Florida Indians. The offer went untaken, but some said the attack on August 7 was part of the Indian reply to that offer.

It was typical of life's injustice that Housman and his wife escaped out the back door in their bare feet and night clothes and made a getaway by sea when the hundred or more Indians, augmented by runaway slaves and Spanish freebooters, rushed through the front door, while Perrine, who was wrapped up in his dream of continuing the plant investigations begun during his consular stay at Campeche, Yucatan, Mexico, lost his life. He managed to hide his wife and three children under a trap door in their three-story house, which extended out over the water. They crouched in a pool of water while the Indians beat Perrine to death and set fire to the house. Then they escaped in a small boat and were later picked up by a passing vessel.

A survivor of the Indian attack that day was Henry Bateman Goodyear, brother of the inventor of rubber vulcanizing. With Dr. Perrine's help he had planned to investigate the rubber possibilities at Cape Sable.

Naturally, reports of these massacres did nothing to attract visitors to Biscayne Bay. The development of the country was at a standstill. Settlers moved out.

Three years later, Fitzpatrick signed over his holdings to his nephew, whose mother and Fitzpatrick's sister, Harriet English, had been holding mortgages on it all along.

The gold rush to California was on when William English was constructing his buildings on the land known as Fort Dallas. As the South Carolinian sat looking out over the gleaming blue-green waters of Biscayne Bay, it came to him he would like to create a shining city on his land. It would be a tropical paradise where people could come to live on plantations with slaves to watch over their comfort. There is indication that he actually platted the land on the south bank of the narrow Miami.

It was a lively dream, but it required more capital than he had. Why not go to the gold rush, get the millions he needed, and come back and build the city?

English went by boat, chartering the steamer *Commodore Stockton* in Philadelphia with funds advanced by his sympathetic mother and accompanied by his ebullient uncle. The pair appeared to be of the opinion that they could combine adventure and business by running a boat line to

California. Potential prospectors with means had evinced a preference for traveling by water, the popular route being across the Isthmus of Panama. It is presumed this is the one English and Fitzpatrick took.

Bad luck dogged them. They lost their vessel on some sort of technicality after being forced into a Mexican port by storm. They did not find gold. English, in dismounting from his horse, accidentally shot himself and died in Grass Valley, California. The dream for creating a city on the south bank of the Miami died with him.

One wonders if William Brickell, who two decades later purchased that same land from Harriet English, had met her son in California. Brickell had gone to the gold rush on horseback from his home in Steubenville, Ohio, and achieved a broken nose from the sting of an Indian arrow en route. He had liked prospecting so well he took off for the Australian gold rush which followed. Before coming back to establish a home in Cleveland with the bride he met in Sydney, New South Wales, he toured the Orient and became, he said later, "a friend of the Mikado's."

After the impulsive departure of English for California, tropical growth encircled Fort Dallas, and in 1855 when the army returned to reoccupy the spot, the troop commander succinctly reported accommodations "meager."

"A two-story stone building without roof, the first-story wall of a long structure and a small frame building," the report itemized.

There were one hundred and seventy-one men to house, and the army got busy, first leasing the land from Harriet English for two hundred and fifty dollars a year, then adding a roof, a piazza, a bake house, and a hospital kitchen. The small frame building was used as the hospital. The troops built "one stable to accommodate seven mules, one forage house, one blacksmith shop, one carpenter shop."

This, then, was Fort Dallas in its full flower, in which condition it remained until 1858, when the army moved out and the land reverted once more to the English family. The military may have improved the building situation at Fort Dallas, but the English heirs later recovered from the government twelve thousand dollars for damage done to plants and trees during the army's occupation. At the same time the troops attempted to raise vegetables for their table, records show.

During the War Between the States, abandoned Fort Dallas became the

19

refuge of a company of dubious characters, including deserters from both the Confederate and Union troops, Union spies, and blockade runners. They have been described as dangerous, ill-assorted, and double-dealing.

The end of the war brought Reconstructionists to Florida and a carpetbagger named William H. Gleason to Biscayne Bay. He always insisted he was no carpetbagger but a Virginian with funds eager to invest in the Southern wilderness, but he kept company with members of the radical Reconstruction regime and immediately assumed the high position of lieutenant governor. This was an honor heretofore unknown for a resident of remote Dade County, which claimed only seventy-five registered voters, in an area then nearly as large as the state of Massachusetts.

In order to assume his duties at Tallahassee under Governor Harrison Reed, Gleason sailed to Key West and caught a steamer for New York. Then he took the train going south. Immediately on his arrival in Tallahassee he became a controversial figure. He and the governor began to feud openly, and Gleason made bold attempts to have Reed impeached. The story was that Gleason had cooked up a shady land deal in which the governor was to be cut in, but Reed refused to go along. In the end, Reed ousted Gleason, who took himself off to Europe until the unpleasantness blew over.

The Tallahassee *Floridian* brought to light some singularly questionable deals in which Gleason had operated as the main figure in Eau Claire, Wisconsin, and again in Meadville, Pennsylvania. He was not, it pointed out, a Virginian.

After his European sojourn, Gleason returned to Biscayne Bay. This time he made the trip with Mitchell Oxar, the barefoot mailman who had run away from Germany to escape military service and got caught in the draft of Confederacy troops. Now, he was out of the army and settled on the bay for good.

Gleason and two others who made up the walking party were unable to keep up with the agile-footed Oxar and were left trailing behind with the promise that the barefoot mailman would send Gleason's partner, W. H. Hunt, to the headwaters of Biscayne Bay to meet them with a boat.

Carrying his shoes in his hand and with his clothes soaking wet from a trip in a leaky boat across New River, the deposed lieutenant governor was not a dapper sight when picked up. The party had been living largely on coconut milk.

Gleason, who came within an inch of establishing the Florida Agricultural College at Eau Gallie as a land-promotion stunt, next presented himself at Tallahassee and was accepted as a delegate, being the only Dade Countian present.

His claim to the land on which Fort Dallas stood, the entire six hundred and forty acres north of the river, originally named the James Eagan donation when granted by Spain in 1808 and later purchased by Fitzpatrick, was an interesting piece of skullduggery. When James Eagan secured the allowance of his claim as an act of Congress after Florida became United States territory, the name Eagan, pronounced Hagan by the Conchs, was written with an H. This fact clouded title to the land, particularly when Gleason produced quitclaim deeds from a man legitimately named James Hagan!

It took a while to straighten things out, but eventually the courts ruled that Hagan be stricken from the records and the entire land donation be renamed Egan for all time.

Mr. Gleason also turned to drainage as a get-rich-quick scheme. He set up a company named the Southern Inland Navigation and Improvement Company, but was having trouble selling stock. Even before the Great Swamp Lands Act of 1850, which created the Board of Internal Improvement and brought five hundred thousand acres of swampland under the state's control, men had been eying the watery expanse of the Everglades with the idea of developing it for their profit. Gleason, keen and glib, followed in their wake.

The land on the north bank of the Miami now passed into the hands of the Biscayne Bay Company, a Georgian organization which had high plans for developing the territory. They established J. C. Lovelace as superintendent, ran a company store, and reactivated the Miami post office. In spite of all their efforts, the venture failed.

One of the heavy investors in the company was Joseph H. Day of Augusta, Georgia, who sent his nephew J. W. Ewan of Charleston down to survey the scene. Ewan moved into Fort Dallas with the Lovelace family for a winter, admitted the business had failed, became won over to the bay life, and stayed.

He became known as "the Duke of Dade." People said he earned the title by reason of his punctilious manners, his wit and charm, but actually it was given him in the state legislature.

The Duke of Dade tried his hand at everything from serving in the legislature to running the mail boat. He was county treasurer, county surveyor, notary public, and inspector of customs. He entered a homestead and shipped the first vegetables north, getting sixteen dollars a barrel for eggplant and seven dollars and fifty cents a crate for beans.

He brought his mother down from Charleston to stay with him in the old officers' quarters after the Lovelace family departed, and she assisted the women of the bay in their Sunday school work.

The Duke himself was fascinated by bay history. He often said that in point of fact Miami was older than St. Augustine and that Ponce de León had visited the bay first in 1513 when he sailed along on his mission of discovery, calling the coral reefs off the Florida Keys *Los Martires* on the grounds they looked like men in agony and naming the last of the keys *Las Tortugas* because there his men caught innumerable tortoises without effort.

But the Duke of Dade knew that old Ponce had not been in search of any Fountain of Youth, as mythology would have it, but was rather in search of a double will-o-the-wisp: gold and prestige. A vigorous fifty-three, Juan Ponce de León was not in the least occupied with old age.

The discoverer, who was quite sensibly mystified by the Gulf Stream, which remained uncharted until Ben Franklin came along, also found the Bahama Channel, destined to become the main artery for treasure galleons.

Following the discoverers came the missionaries.

In 1567 the first white settlement in Dade County was established at the mouth of the Miami, the Jesuit Mission of Tequesta. It consisted of a blockhouse for thirty Spanish soldiers and a Jesuit lay brother named Brother Villareal, who must have had a frustrating time of it. The Tequesta Indians were rugged. The mission was abandoned, and little is known of it beyond the fact that it was once there.

The land had seen English rule, and the name of Governor Patrick Tonyn, appointed governor of East Florida by King George III, who divided the state into East and West Florida, appears on an early land grant in the region.

Once, long before Columbus discovered the New World, there had been a city of Tequesta Indians at the mouth of the Miami. The women had moved about lightly in skirts made of Spanish moss, while the men covered themselves with breechcloths of braided palmetto with a raffish tailfeather of moss that was purely for comfort when sitting down. Sometimes raccoon tails were substituted, but they were more for show.

Here at this quiet spot, the Tequesta Indians held their feasts, at first burying their dead in refuse piles called middens, later burying them apart in mounds. They used the conch shell to good advantage as every kind of implement, smeared themselves with fish oils against mosquitoes and sand flies, and built their houses platform fashion away from snakes and prowling animals. Some were constructed on pilings out in the water. The Tequesta Indians learned to make pottery and decorated the utensils with sharp and dramatic scratches of design.

The people of the bay, fishing and hunting and buying their sugar and salt at Old Man Brickell's, were glad to listen to the Duke of Dade. He talked interestingly. But they were more interested in what the next wreck would wash in than in what happened in the faraway yesterdays.

The low stone building known as the barracks but which had begun life as slave quarters was now the Dade County Courthouse, but not much legal business was transacted there.

In 1876 the men of the bay took a real interest in politics. They aimed to run carpetbaggers, with their slick ways, right out of the bay country, and they brooked no interference. All over the state, the Democratic party was taking on new life and in the bay country it was the same.

William Gleason's opponent for the state legislature was John J. (Pig) Brown, a gentleman who, as might be suspected, kept pigs.

Dade County had three precincts: one at Michael Zahr's house on the bay, the second at Hypoluxo, and the third at Jupiter Lighthouse. Of the seventy-five registered voters, fifty-one cast votes and forty came from the bay precinct, so Mr. Gleason's adopted homeland was an important spot.

The returns gave twenty-seven votes to "Pig" Brown and only twenty-four to Mr. Gleason, who thereupon lost his political hold as well as his temper. Fighting mad, he brought charges of gross irregularity against the Zahr precinct, charging "one vote was cast after sundown and by lamplight. Two persons of foreign birth were allowed to vote . . . After all ballots were removed from the box the Democrat ballots and split tickets were returned to the box but the Republican ballots, left lying on a table, fell, or were knocked, to the floor and were gathered up by many persons including bystanders and false ballots substituted."

Despite the suit, "Pig" Brown was seated when the legislature convened in Tallahassee.

It was the end of the Reconstruction regime and the Democrats were back in the political saddle.

A later election that caused excitement was that of 1888 in which Juno got the county seat away from Miami, the bay, and old Fort Dallas. There was much gun-toting and suggested threats, and in the end, when Miami lost the election, the men of the bay refused to give up the records. With much secrecy and in the dead of night with the help of a Seminole Indian the men of Juno stole the records, which were properly theirs, and made their getaway.

By law, Miami was required to wait ten years until an election could be held to regain the county seat, so the men of the bay country would eventually get it back.

From the beginning, the land on which Fort Dallas stood had a destiny.

Peacock Inn

Brickell had been saying since his arrival in 1870 at the mouth of the Miami that the railroad would one day cut through to the bay country.

When he made this declaration to homesteaders from the pineland, they made, behind his back, circular motions with their fingers laid aside their heads. No doubt about it, they whispered, Old Man Brickell was touched.

The Crackers had a name, too, for the first winter visitors who began to sail in. Behind their hands they referred to them as "the swells."

The swells were the first tourists, although nobody thought to call them by that name. They were an articulate, well-educated, world-traveled bunch who exclaimed in flowery language over the colors of the bay, the sky, the colored fish, and the sea gardens. They lived on boats and in tents and, finally, they crowded The Bay View House, later named Peacock Inn, which evolved because of their coming as the area's first hostelry, barring the Tropical Hotel back on Indian Key.

This forerunner of hotel hospitality in a region which would eventually bow to tourism as its number-one industry was built by a man named Charles Peacock on the shores of Coconut Grove.

Peacock had been operating a "ham and beef warehouse" in London when his brother Jack first discovered the magic of the bay. As the glowing reports of the tropical life began to seep back, Charles could no longer endure London and sold out, turning his back on fog and rain and setting sail for Key West with his wife and three small sons.

"Jolly Jack" Peacock kept the House of Refuge established by the government for shipwrecked sailors over in the wilds of Miami Beach and with his wife, Martha, became noted as a warm host to all who appeared at his door. He was a colorful figure who often sat up all night reading tales of adventure. He must have permitted his vocabulary full sway in writing his brother back in London.

It is said that his first sight of Coconut Grove in 1875 sent Charles Peacock's stout heart to the bottom of his English boots. His wife, Isabella, bore up at the sight of the islandlike wilderness. Perhaps she could hear prophetic voices from the future calling her the "mother of Coconut Grove."

For the moment, however, she agreed it would be better to move up to the mouth of the Miami River where the Brickells were already ensconced and where the Lovelace family and the Duke of Dade were living.

The Peacocks lived the bay life for seven years before building Peacock Inn, which followed the driftwood pattern of all the early houses, but boasted a porch, unscreened in the beginning, where you could sit and look out toward Cape Florida Lighthouse, now disappointingly dark because it had been replaced by the steel light on Fowey Rock. The shingles of the inn had been made by hand with an old-fashioned froe from the white pine foremast of a wrecked brig.

The food, gourmets from everywhere agreed, was surpassing and cost, along with the room, ten dollars a week. Sailboats were available for rent for two dollars a day any place on the bay. Seagoing sloops manned by a crew of two were available for fifty dollars a month.

This vacation spot was in the hands of a few winter visitors daring enough to board the mail schooner *Flora* at Key West for a trip that might be a day's run in a good wind, but could stretch into a week's sail if the wind failed. Good fishing and hunting lay at the end of the sail. Could a sportsman ask for more?

A young boy named Charles Harrison Thompson, the son of the Fowey Lighthouse keeper, was born on a blowy night at the Cape Florida Lighthouse and grew up on the water. He learned fishing and hunting lore from the Seminoles and began to be known as an excellent guide despite his youth.

From the beginning, Peacock Inn flourished, calling for a two-story annex, then another. Twin dressing rooms stood down at the bay's edge, one for gentlemen, one for ladies. Here they left their towels and other impedimenta before testing the blue-green waters of the bay, the ladies completely covered as to limbs and arms.

Confederate General Jubal A. Early sailed in on one of the first yachts that began to find their way to the bay. A Confederate doctor, Horace Porter, planted coconuts and mangoes and limes and avocados and named his plantation Cocoanut Grove in the period following the War Between the States. When a hurricane wiped out his young trees, he abandoned the plantation, and in the years following it was no longer remembered that he had, through government connections, established a post office in 1873 during his stay. (He used the "a" in Cocoanut Grove, but it was later dropped.)

Ralph Middleton Munroe, number-one tourist, rediscovered this fact and managed to reactivate the post office, so no longer was it necessary to sail up the bay on the odd chance Miss Alice Brickell would be in a mood for handing out mail.

The skipper of the mail schooner, which now came weekly instead of bimonthly, was vociferous in his damning of the Coconut Grove post office and muttered about coming clear off his course for a parcel of fellows who never would get a worthwhile letter anyway.

That was not quite a fair statement.

Count James L. Nugent, a tall and striking black-bearded Frenchman whose Irish grandfather had been one of Napoleon's generals, got some very interesting mail. So did his close friend, Count Jean d'Hedouville. Count Nugent, who wore loud plaid shirts, was an excellent man on a picnic to Arch Creek or a shell-hunting expedition to the ocean beach, a trip that usually took in the large crocodile hole.

The ladies were fairly loaded down with wearing apparel up to and including hats, and there was small danger of sunburn setting in. They never hesitated at a boating expedition, but some wore veils to protect their complexions. You might not be able to see them, but they were *there*.

Tea every afternoon was a pleasant ritual at Peacock Inn, and dinner was ceremonious and unhurried. Isabella Peacock, who became known as Aunt Bella, frequently wore a crinkling taffeta gown for dress-up occasions, and the women all donned fresh garments and took special pains with their hair for the evening meal.

27

Following dinner, the ladies sat demurely rocking on the porch—they called it the veranda—while the men repaired to the rustic rockers in the small smoking room off the newly screened dining porch and lit their pipes and Cuban cigars as a prelude to discussing the affairs of the world.

Kirk Munroe, a writer of adventure stories for boys, might hold forth on the new bicycle craze which had hit New York. The slender enthusiastic Kirk, no relation to Ralph, had imported the third bicycle seen in New York City and was commander of the League of American Wheelmen.

The writer had encountered Lillian Russell on one of his rides in New York's Central Park and was courteous enough to share this adventure with the men.

One spring evening over coffee, the two Munroes decided that what was missing was a meeting place for yachtsmen. On the spot the Biscayne Bay Yacht Club was born. Kirk appointed Ralph first commodore and the latter accepted. Then the Commodore appointed Kirk secretary.

From then on Ralph Munroe was never anything but "The Commodore." He designed the club flag bearing the emblem of a large N interlaced with the figures 25, signifying twenty-five degrees north latitude to point up the fact that the club was the most southern yacht club in the country.

E. A. Hine of Newark, New Jersey, who with his brother Thomas had just purchased Long Key, obligingly became vice-commodore, and Count d'Hedouville became the first treasurer.

The count was noted for his dignity and for the fact that he brought the first player piano to the bay. In the house he later built along the water he used the piano in his cooking. Each dish was timed to a particular piece of music, and as the tune died away, he knew it was time to turn the fish or remove the turtle steak.

D'Hedouville had a well-kept secret. He kept maps, old maps of buried treasure, under the cloth on his dining-room table. Later, he really found his treasure in South Florida. The land he purchased kept all branches of the family in funds.

Nugent, who first brought d'Hedouville to the bay, immortalized himself by appearing at a bay wedding in full dress attire, but barefoot. He confided to the count that at the last moment it seemed ostentatious to wear shoes.

Count Nugent later married Miss Florence Baldwin, head of the Baldwin School at Bryn Mawr, and on later trips to the bay in company with his wife he was never without shoes.

While the men were enjoying their cigars the ladies were not precisely inactive. Mrs. Kirk Munroe, Mary Barr, whose mother's book, *Remember the Alamo*, had created a stir, was a woman of spirit whose voice was often raised in forceful conversation. Rocking back and forth on the veranda, the ladies plotted a literary society called the Pine Needle Club, which resulted in the Coconut Grove Library when Mrs. Andrew Carnegie stepped from her yacht to look over Coconut Grove one afternoon and stumbled into a meeting. On her return north, the wife of the steel king sent bundles of books, enough to begin the library.

One evening on the porch at Peacock Inn, Miss Flora McFarlane of Rock Hill, New Jersey, who was homesteading with Charles Peacock's assistance, proposed the first women's club, to be known as "The Housekeeper's Club." When the gentlemen, after their session in the smoking room, joined the ladies, Commodore Munroe grandly presented the land for both library and club.

In the clubhouse Mary Barr Munroe would get into rip-roaring argument and one day would be asked to resign, but would be reinstated.

She was a woman of firm opinion, and perhaps this is the place to record that it was she who insisted on dropping the "a" in Coconut Grove, although the library had book plates all ready for use with an "a." Mary Barr Munroe was born in Glasgow, Scotland, and when she was two, her parents took her and her three brothers to Galveston, Texas, to live. Yellow fever claimed the father and three sons so that Mary and her mother were left alone. The mother was Amelia Barr, and she solved the problem of making a livelihood by removing herself and daughter to New York where she secured tutoring work. In her spare time she wrote novels. Her first book established her as a popular writer, and eighty-eight novels in all flowed from her pen.

Those who loved Mary Barr Munroe felt her determination to be heard sprang from the fact that she had lived in her mother's shadow for some time.

A church was started. Known as the Union Chapel, it had for its first preacher a winter visitor named Charles E. Stowe. *His* mother had also written a stirring book. Her name was Harriet Beecher Stowe, and the book of course, was *Uncle Tom's Cabin*. His mother, Mr. Stowe informed the guests at Peacock Inn, always said that "God had written it."

Commodore Munroe gave land for the church, too.

Like many a tourist to come, he began plotting ways and means of making a living while staying on in the land of perpetual sunshine. Frankly eager to give up his northern business affiliations he dreamed of making his year-round home in the Grove.

Ralph's family had come originally from Concord, and paternal Grandpa manufactured the first lead pencil in America (with Thoreau in his employ and also a boarder in the home). Ralph had been wrapped up in the sea ever since Susan Emerson, sister-in-law of the Sage of Concord, had presented him with a copy of *Masterman Ready* shortly after he learned to read. Perhaps there was some inherited seafaring blood as well from his maternal grandfather, whose father as lord mayor of York did not quite cure his son's interest in the sea by shipping him out on a Newcastle collier. Although he went into the manufacturing of chain cables, he awaited the first opportunity to go sailing, an opportunity which presented itself during the Crimean War when one of his vessels got into difficulty near Sevastopol. He hurried to the scene and took command and from then on sailed his entire family all over the world in a square-rigged vessel turned yacht.

Commodore Munroe actually fell in love with Biscayne Bay before he saw it from tales told him by that old yarn-spinner William Brickell when Brickell visited Staten Island for supplies for his trading post at the mouth of the Miami. A meeting with Old Ned Pent, north on a trip for a wrecking company, had fanned his desire to see the bay. Now he was determined to spend his life along its blue waters.

He tried growing sponges to make an income, turned to canning pineapples, which at the time were grown extensively in the area, and started the production of rope from sisal. He went into the business of making guava jelly, and this venture failed largely because hiring help proved impossible. The independents who made up the early Grove had no time for standing over a hot stove when the bay was calling.

Over on the long peninsula dangling between the ocean and the bay there was a stirring of activity with the arrival of the Field and Osborn expedition to plant coconuts, but the Commodore viewed those proceedings with an unenthusiastic eye.

Henry R. Lum had bought land at thirty-five cents an acre from the government and proposed making a fortune out of coconut production. Through him, Ezra Osborn and Elnathan T. Field, who hailed from Middleton, New Jersey, got the bug and their expedition set sail for Key West on a Mallory steamer. Aboard were twenty-five stalwarts from northern life-saving stations who were assigned the roles of clearing mangrove and catching coconuts as they were tossed ashore.

The expedition had its bizarre aspects. Mules, tents, one portable house, wagons, food were all stowed aboard a schooner and carried from Key West and then sent ashore at Miami Beach. The mules were unceremoniously shoved over the side to swim, and the workers came ashore in lifeboats, towing the portable house sections in over the waves.

After unloading, the schooner took off for Trinidad and Cuba and Nicaragua to load up on coconuts.

The workers, among them Richard Carney, who stayed on to become the Commodore's crony and sheriff of the county, knew the water, but they didn't know much about clearing mangrove. Despite the resistances of the snakes and mosquitoes, bears and rats, they persisted in the attempt to plant eighty miles of coconuts from Cape Florida to Jupiter.

The coconut expedition, which looked so foolproof on paper, failed to yield its golden promise for many reasons. Some of the nuts failed to germinate; others were eaten by rats and rabbits; still others were smothered by strangler figs or mangrove.

The campfires of the men lit up the coast for many months, and some of the coconuts planted lived to beautify the future playground of America.

The portable house was floated down to Coconut Grove by Dick Carney where it was used as a tool shed until the 1960s.

Carney was an addition to Coconut Grove. Merry and full of youthful spirits, he was addicted to playing practical jokes and once painted stripes on a mule so that for nearly a week its owner kept driving it off, meanwhile searching diligently for his mule.

His "best" joke was played one night at the Housekeeper's Club when he went into the small room where the babies were all sleeping peacefully, and methodically shifted them about, mixing up blankets and outer clothing. Not one of the mothers observed this fact when, in the flickering lantern light, they gathered up the babies. There was considerable confusion, some

31

weeping, and much cursing late that night after the long sail home when the trick was discovered.

Kirk Munroe passed the incident along to Owen Wister who used it in *The Virginian*. The women always forgave Captain Dickie. He was so good about auctioning off leftovers at the club fairs.

Commodore Munroe introduced the sharpie-type boat to the bay and then he sat down and designed the Presto, a development of the bug-eye canoe used on the Chesapeake, with almost a flat bottom and a hard turn to the bilge. It proved to be the perfect craft for getting about the shoal waters of the region. Contented, he settled down to a lifetime of designing and building yachts.

He took photographs and wrote pressing pamphlets directed to the government. One was called *The Green Turtle and the Possibilities of Its Protection and Consequent Increase on the Florida Coast*.

Nobody in Washington got too interested. Certainly, the idea of conservation had never hit any of the bay people.

An old settler out hog-hunting reported that he had seen a grove of towering palm trees out near Little River and could not understand why a botanist named Charles Sprague Sargent and the Commodore got so excited nor why they spent days plunging through swamp to locate the trees. Royal palms they were, and the *Scientific American* printed photographs of them as proof that the palm grew in the United States of America.

The Commodore built his home, The Barnacle, overlooking the bay, and Kirk Munroe built his, Scrububs, close by. The Commodore reported on plant life to the Department of Agriculture, kept the Bureau of Fisheries informed on local fishing conditions as well as reporting generally to the New York Museum of Natural History.

Kirk settled down to writing *The Coral Ship*, a story of buried treasure and piracy on the Florida Keys.

To beat the silver fish, a fleet, gray insect which eats up books and woolens of innocent first-timers in South Florida, the Kirk Munroes hit on a happy solution. They kept a snake indoors, fed it bread and milk from a bowl, and reported that it disposed of all marauding insects.

These were the pre-penicillin days when "sea voyages" were prescribed for gentlemen of means in order to recoup failing health, so a good portion of the early bay visitors were individuals sent south for weak lungs or other disability.

Such a man was Paul Ransom, a graduate of Williams College, who now with the help of Kirk Munroe proceeded to establish a private boys' school, a migratory school which would move with the weather—summers in the Adirondacks and winters on Biscayne Bay. He called it the Adirondack-Florida School, and to it began to come young men of some affluence. Later, one of them, a boy from Long Island named Hugh Matheson, would be so captured by the place he would write his parents back on Long Island, "You *have* to come. I've chartered a boat for you."

Because of their coming and staying, today people swim at a public bay-front beach reaching back into protected, beautiful woods at Matheson Hammock Park south of the Grove, while others dip in the Atlantic at Crandon Park on Key Biscayne on land donated by the Mathesons to make the most beautiful bathing strip in the world, many feel.

Visitors to Peacock Inn were not cut off from medical help as the bay people had been in earlier days. A lady doctor named Eleanor Galt Simmons now practiced her profession by sailboat and pony, and the Seminoles camped outside her door to try out her medicines.

A product of Bryn Mawr and the Woman's Medical College of Philadelphia, the doctor left her New York practice to accompany her husband, a New York lawyer, south for his health. He joined the Florida bar, but since neither medicine nor law was a lucrative field in the remote region, they hit on making wines and jelly for northern markets. Their mango jam and pineapple wine had been sampled locally and declared excellent.

Out in the lonely palmetto near where the University of Miami would one day stand, a Scotsman moved with his family. His wife went crazy one spring night when the chuck-will's-widow had begun its lonely cry, and Dr. Simmons saddled her pony and rode out, following one of the small sons who came, round-eyed, to fetch her.

Day and night she answered the calls of the bay people no matter how distant their homes, and in one instance went to treat a dangerous criminal barricaded in a cabin with ample artillery. After treating his wounds she persuaded him to give himself up.

It is odd that she should be best remembered for the fact that she

33

requested that her body be cremated when she died. To the bay people this seemed like a strange procedure. Her husband, Captain Simmons, who told marvelous stories, would have enjoyed the one about his own burial.

His request was that his remains be tossed into the Gulf Stream, and he entrusted this wish to Kirk Munroe.

In life the captain had a peculiarly uneven gait, and when the body was tossed over the side it refused to sink but bobbed along on the water in a most distracting fashion. It took the ship's anchor to make the captain's remains disappear in the ink-blue waters of the stream. Nobody aboard ever forgot the sweat-provoking moment.

In 1890 there was a mild land boom along the bay, and wreckers shook their heads and muttered at each new arrival. It was hard enough pickings for those already here.

A mule stage line between Lantana on Lake Worth and Lemon City on the bay was opened, making it possible for the first time for men to reach the isolated region by land. Uncle John Clemenson was the first driver and he sauntered ahead of the mule team playing his fiddle. The stage went over uncomfortably rough roads at the rate of three miles an hour, the journey of sixty-six miles took two days, and the fare was ten dollars. The stagecoach was a threat to the seaman's paradise that Biscayne Bay had been until now.

Homesteaders had exhausted the Indian River lands after the Indian River steamboat service began operating, and now people were crowding into the bay region. A good many settled at Lemon City, which now had a school, the Grace Methodist Church, a post office, and a saw mill as well as several boardinghouses. On certain evenings "very enjoyable hops" were held at Spivey's hall.

On Sunday afternoons, the men would gather on the dock and swap stories of the sea, tales of wrecking, and stories of Black Caesar, the legendary African prince who paid back in vicious cruelty as a pirate the fact that he was removed from Africa by force and for whom Caesar's Creek was said to be named. The boy children, nodding after a Sabbath meal of venison steak, topped off with comptie pudding and guava jelly, listened intently when the talk got around to piracy.

There was a loosely organized woman's club, referred to by the men as "The Red Shawl Gang" for reasons lost in the noisy, go-getting years in

34

between. William A. Filer was postmaster and a few miles south at Buena Vista, Captain Samuel Filer pointed with pride to flourishing orange groves as proof that limestone soil was a good home for citrus, an idea not commonly shared by the rest of Florida, which made its livelihood from growing and shipping citrus and vegetables.

There was talk of steamer lines being established out of Jacksonville and Key West to the bay, and as the sun went down, stirring up the sky into a flowing mass of color, violet and gray, coral and blue and pale yellow, the people wondered if such a thing would come to pass.

Julia Tuttle

J ULIA DE FOREST STURTEVANT TUTTLE was a pretty and persuasive woman who was thrown into business by the illness of her husband. If after his death she had been content to go on operating his iron works business, H. B. Tuttle and Son, in Cleveland, Ohio, meanwhile living a pleasant social life with her two grown children, things would not have happened so suddenly and spectacularly at the mouth of the Miami River.

Julia, who was married on her eighteenth birthday to Frederick Leonard Tuttle, had a face too square to rate her a true beauty, but a camellialike skin, striking hazel eyes, and a warm smile made her seem one. On their New York honeymoon, Julia and the handsome son of Calvin Rutter Tuttle cut dashing figures: she, tiny in voluminous taffeta with a fetching lace-trimmed bonnet; he, lean and Byronesque with broad forehead and brooding dark eyes. His bonnet was some shakes as well. He wore the gray top hat of the era and, of course, carried a stick.

His father had assisted in the launching of the knitting machine and the double-dasher churn and was one of the first to use iron-bar chains in modern suspension bridges. His income was pleasantly ample, and the young couple had no financial worries.

Julia and her bridegroom moved into an elegant four-story home which they called Gaydene and proceeded to raise orchids. Both sang in the choir and Julia taught in the Sunday school.

Julia was nineteen when her daughter, Frances Emeline, was born. A dark-eyed, spirited child, Fanny, as she was called, had a way of fighting her mother's wishes always. Perhaps the fact that when she was only two a son, Henry Ethelbert, was born to the Tuttles had much to do with it. In babyhood Harry suffered a serious illness which left him with a withered arm. Julia devoted herself to Harry unstintingly, and trips to hospitals in Philadelphia over a five-year period were only some of the things that separated Julia from her daughter.

In the family circle it was agreed that "Julia spoiled Harry." Finally, she sent him away to the Curtiss School for Boys at Brookfield Center, Connecticut.

Then Fred Tuttle developed the popular disease of the day, tuberculosis. Unable to devote himself to business, he took up the painting of china and the study of shells and ferns. For other diversion, there was always his library stocked with Shakespeare, Dickens, and the complete Waverley Novels.

Julia's first visits to the ironworks were experimental but she took to business at once, enjoyed it, and managed her husband's affairs astutely. She learned the satisfactions connected with a business deal, but remained the finishing-school young lady who had majored in music, languages, and botany, soft-voiced, full of arts and graces.

Julia Tuttle was a woman men liked. They admired her intelligence and were disarmed by her femininity. Julia could say no with a smile.

When Julia was a little girl, her mother, who had been a teacher at the Indian School at Tallahassee, told her bedtime stories about Seminoles. Who can say whether these images later were instrumental in pulling the widowed Julia back to the bay country where she had wintered earlier.

Julia's father, Ephraim T. Sturtevant, first came to the bay in the company of William Brickell, who was searching for a freer life than Cleveland afforded and had about decided that the unopened Florida peninsula was the place to find it.

It is said that back in Cleveland in 1870 people laughed heartily at the intrepid pair, claiming "the old fools" were on a search for the fountain of youth. Sturtevant took the precaution of making his will, "being about to leave home on a long journey by land and sea and aware of the liabilities to accident and danger in such cases."

Both men lost their hearts to the peninsula wilderness, and Brickell

38

pointed to a spot on the south bank of the Miami across from Fort Dallas and indicated he would build his home there. It was the spot known later as Brickell Point, a prize location with an unsurpassed water view.

Sturtevant agreed to remain and supervise the unloading of building material which Brickell would send from the North. Brickell left for Cleveland to settle his business—it was wholesale grocery with markets all over the world.

Sturtevant fit right into the bay life and two years later became a state senator, serving for four years at Tallahassee while also serving as county judge.

The Brickells arrived in time for a tropical Christmas, carrying aboard their vessel a grand piano and a governess for their children.

Somewhere along the line argument broke out between Sturtevant and Brickell. Sturtevant, who had been living south of the river, picked up and moved ten miles north on the bay to Biscayne, now known as Miami Shores. There were threats of "shooting on sight" but nobody believed either man would take such action and neither did.

Julia Tuttle brought her children on a trip south as early as 1875. She and the Duke of Dade explored the region by sailboat during his first visit. When Fred Tuttle became ill with tuberculosis, Julia brought her ailing husband south in the hope the climate would assist in his recovery. When he died, she came south again for a winter visit with her father and stepmother. Actually, she had in mind moving her family to a milder climate and was considering either California or Italy.

After her father's death, when the land he had acquired reverted to Julia, she began to exhibit a business interest in the area. Soon she was back, bent on purchasing land of her own. Her eye was on the land on the north bank, which the Biscayne Bay Company was glad to unload.

It appears that in addition to knowing a deal when she saw one, the smiling Julia had fallen upon a dream, the kind that involved true vision.

Like English, when she looked at the wilderness along the mangrove-lined Miami River she saw a thriving city, and when she turned her eyes to the wild beauty of the mouth of the river where it poured into the broad shining bay she did not see the full-grown coconuts planted in the twenties by James Egan; she saw instead a hotel.

She wrote to a friend in these words: "It may seem strange to you, but it is the dream of my life to see this wilderness turned into a prosperous country and where this tangled mass of vine brush, trees and rocks now are to see homes with modern improvements surrounded by beautiful grassy lawns, flowers, shrubs and shade trees."

It never occurred to her that this was the kind of change Commodore Munroe and Count d'Hedouville and the others would consider disastrous.

Julia Tuttle was not operating entirely on hunches and visions. It is established that she had invited James E. Ingraham to dinner at her Cleveland home before closing the deal with the Biscayne Bay Company.

Ingraham was then employed by Henry B. Plant, who was then busily building railroads on the west coast of Florida but at a not too distant date would be a key man in the Henry Morrison Flagler organization. Flagler was buying up railroads and pushing south on the east coast of the peninsula.

It is more than likely that Ingraham and Julia Tuttle discussed the future of the bay country, but whether Ingraham bent a receptive ear to her dream that evening is not known. As a handsome gentleman he must have enjoyed the company of his charming hostess, and it is a fact that later, as head of Flagler's land and agricultural departments, he was definitely in favor of extending the railroad to Miami.

However it went, Julia decided to move permanently to the bay, and she brought with her all the treasures that had made Gaydene attractive: the books and paintings, the statuary, her Italian fish set, the chair with the inverted cane bottom that had been her husband's favorite. Neither did she leave behind the silver goblet he had received for "the best white Dorkings" at the county fair, nor her grown children's baptismal robes.

In the fall of 1891, Julia Tuttle came floating in on a barge, complete with all these things and accompanied by Miss Fanny, then twenty-three, her son, Harry, a housekeeper named Maggie Carney, and two Jersey cows. The land on which these pioneer cows stumbled had seen many comings and goings. The practical Julia proposed to house them in the Fort Dallas barracks while she and her family moved into the quarters built by William English.

There was a delay in disembarking when it was discovered the date was November 13. With a gambler's superstition, Julia refused to budge until the next morning. The whole caboodle, Miss Fanny protesting noisily, stayed aboard the barge until the dawn of the fourteenth.

On landing Julia remarked that the first thing she would do after hanging her china plates on the wall was see about clearing the tangle of vines and bushes and making a neat lawn.

During the remodeling period a ship en route from Barcelona was wrecked off the Florida Reef, furnishing the Tuttles with exquisite Spanish tile that Julia used for flooring.

Fort Dallas and the rest of the Egan tract on the north bank passed into Julia's hands, and the Duke of Dade obligingly moved out of the old fort and took himself down to Peacock Inn, where he charmed young and old alike.

Eunice Peacock, granddaugher of Charles and Aunt Bella Peacock, asked one day to examine the ring he wore, a golden snake with a diamond for an eye. They were seated on an upper porch at one of the annexes, and the ring slipped through the child's fingers and fell below.

It was never found despite extensive beating of the bushes, and through it all the Duke insisted it was a matter of small moment, drying the little girl's tears with a clean white pocket handkerchief. She never forgot the incident nor the Duke, not even when she grew up to marry a boy named George Merrick who dreamed up a city called Coral Gables and joined the gallery of Miami dreamers, first-class.

Some said the Duke of Dade dreamed of marrying Julia Tuttle. There was little doubt that he admired her and found her company delightful, but he never succeeded in charming her into matrimony.

A Seminole admirer of Julia's sacrificed the lobe of an ear and was put on a lonely key for three moons as punishment for answering her request to search for the overdue Ingraham Mission attempting to cross the Everglades. Tribal law forbade Seminoles to guide white men in Indian country. This trip across the Everglades was instigated by Henry Plant, who had his business eye on draining the watery saw grass country and wanted to find out if the job could be done. Ingraham reported that it could. Later, in 1904 he wrote of his findings in the magazine *Success*.

"We ascertained that the Everglades along the whole one hundred and sixty miles of the eastern side are rimmed by a rock ledge," he wrote. "We furthermore learned that all of the lakes are several feet above sea level and decided there was nothing to prevent the water of the lakes from flowing into the ocean and leaving the land drained if vents could be made in this long ledge of rock."

The trip had been tougher than the men had anticipated. The saw grass cut their feet, and as they pushed heavy boats through mud and water they knew they had brought the wrong supplies. They ran out of food and slept in mud with one eye open for rattlesnakes. Sick and lost in a timeless nothingness, they actually were rescued by Julia Tuttle's Indian admirer. The Seminole forced them to pause at the headwaters of the Miami while he changed his shirt and greased his hair. They had no idea how near they were to civilization until they shot the rapids over the rock rim and saw Fort Dallas.

Julia was waiting for them. She ran up the American flag and there were tears in the eyes of the explorers, all of whom were then put to bed at the Tuttles' and the Brickells'.

Her Indian admirer invited Julia to be his squaw and presented her with a gift: a club fashioned of ironwood, a handy weapon of solid proportions covered with the primitive pinprick design. Julia thanked him and placed the gift on a taboret under her painting of a Seminole Indian chief. Her mind was not on romance but on bringing the railroad to the mouth of the Miami River. Just as well for the lovelorn Seminole. White-Indian mergers were also forbidden by tribal law.

Julia wrote to Henry Flagler offering him half of her six hundred and forty acres in exchange for his railroad. His reply was polite but noncommittal. She paid him a visit, making the long, arduous journey by launch with young Charlie Thompson as captain. She had taken the seventeen-year-old Charlie into her home, put him in charge of her boat, and spoke of sending him away to school, she had grown so fond of the lad. The visit may have flattered Flagler, but it did not bring the railroad. Flagler, who was then considering extending his line to West Palm Beach, wrote Julia in April, 1893, suggesting that the completion of the inland waterway might serve the same purpose as the railroad. A month later he began building the Royal Poinciana Hotel at Palm Beach and prepared to extend the line.

Flagler had first come to Florida in the winter of 1883, and his immediate impression of St. Augustine was that it could be built into an

"American Riviera." At once he planned the Ponce de León Hotel and before the building was up started another, the Alcazar, across the street. It was apparent that transportation on the little Jacksonville, St. Augustine, and Halifax River Railway left much to be desired. Being a man of action as well as means, Flagler promptly bought it. It was the beginning of his Florida East Coast Railway.

Flagler went on buying small railroads, but it was not until 1892 that he became a railroad builder with the organization known as the Florida Coast and Gulf Railway, later changed to the Jacksonville, St. Augustine, and Indian River Railway. This was the railway that began pushing south—to Daytona, New Smyrna, Cocoa, Eau Gallie. Within less than a year eighty miles of railroad were constructed and put into operation.

All this was pretty far away from the bay, but when he pushed farther south and created West Palm Beach, people stopped thinking Julia Tuttle was a candidate for an asylum. It remained stationary for more than a year, and it must have seemed as though he had come to the end of the line.

Julia never gave up hope. She consulted with William and Mary Brickell, who also agreed to offer land donations to Flagler if he would continue his railroad to the bay country.

When the curtains were about to part on the city-building drama Brickell was already seventy years old. He would sit on his veranda and point to a spot over which oleander cast its shadowed fragrance and say, "When I die, bury me there." He often added, "Heaven can be no lovelier than this spot."

It is doubtful if William Brickell, despite his belief in the country, had any inkling that before the year was out great changes would take place.

The story of the Brickells has never been told nor can it be fully. The last of the Brickells, Miss Maude and George, retired into deep silences before their deaths. The family records were in Miss Maude's hands and she allowed certain little peeps and then retreated.

The early gossip was that Mary Bulmer Brickell had been a ladies' maid and that her husband was a "ticket-of-leave man." This talk seems spiced with illusion. It appears that what happened to the Brickells was that some time after their arrival they suffered serious business reverses. Brickell had counted on running his wholesale grocery business at long distance with a partner in charge, but it didn't work, so that not long after they took up residence at Brickell Point, the family fortunes nose-dived and the Brickells were in the same financial boat as the rest of the bay people.

While living in the wilderness world of Biscayne Bay may have had its advantages, it may also have made the Brickell daughters appear queer to city people. Miss Alice was already educated when they arrived and for her it seems evident the life was frustrating and unrewarding. The same pattern followed for the rest of the girls, Edith, Belle, and Maude, none of whom married. Two of the boys, Charles and Will, were sent away to the Eastman Business College and that and later marriage changed their personalities and their lives.

Mary Brickell was, no matter how you put the pieces together, quite a woman. She was well equipped to handle the avalanche of business that the coming of the railroad brought to the family. As a young woman she was dainty, with an eighteen-inch waist. A satin gown carefully tucked away on the schooner which brought the Brickells to Biscayne Bay testified to that. It was reported that she had last worn it at a party at the Fifth Avenue Hotel. She was also imperious and as she grew older and assumed the role of business head of the family, men would refer to her as "steely-eyed," while others would counteract the impression by telling of her kindness. There were men living in the 1950s who would tell you, and with some emotion, that "Mary Brickell never foreclosed on a mortgage." All agree that she looked like Queen Victoria, "only prettier."

Mrs. Brickell was rabid against women coddling themselves, and between the Seminole women and herself there was a great respect. She was kind to blacks provided they did not drink and was known to make clothes for their children. For years on Sunday mornings, as the town grew, blacks stood in line to pay back loans to Mary Brickell.

Some say her smile faded the day her daughter Emma was stricken with what a passing physician diagnosed as spinal meningitis and died suddenly in the black tropic night. The Brickells buried her in their fragrant garden overlooking the bay but not before considerable delay after Mary Brickell refused to permit the burial until her husband returned from Key West. Concern mounted as the need to bury the child increased. The day William Brickell's sailboat appeared in sight, his wife was delivering another daughter prematurely. They named her Maude. They buried Emma the next day.

The Brickells were clannish. Perhaps living alone at Brickell Point made them that way. They did not spend their money nor did they join clubs. This seemed later to irritate people. Their townsmen were united in reporting that the Brickells, every one of them, were scrupulously honest.

They call Julia Tuttle "the mother of Miami" and it is an earned title, but in the very beginning there were two mothers—Mary Brickell the other, one on each side of the river. It is historically accepted that the word Miami means Big Water and reached the city via Lake Okeechobee and then the river, but there are other suggestions among them that the river was once known as "the river of the mothers." It is certain that two women held in their hands the valuable land that would make up the new city. New settlers attempting to buy land from either of them protested bitterly at the high prices they demanded before sailing down to Coconut Grove or up to Lemon City, which had, after all, so much more to offer.

Ned Pent was inflamed because he was forced to carry a heavy-as-lead parcel-post package for Julia Tuttle along the wild beaches. It was so heavy he yearned to throw it in any one of the convenient swamps—but the mail, he kept telling himself, had to go through.

On his arrival when he found he had been carrying five bricks his disgust was unbounded. A big man with a high squeaky voice, he nearly cried as he asked those assembled at Brickell's trading post, "What could that woman be plannin' to do with them bricks?"

"Ain't you heard, Ned?" drawled a wag. "The lady's aimin' to build a railroad."

It was a joke that brought down the house.

The Word Is Railroad

THE APPEARANCE OF SANTA CLAUS in central and northern Florida in the year 1894 was quickly followed by an unwelcome visit from Jack Frost, who brought financial ruin to fruit and vegetable growers in his cold, cold hands. For years in Florida, there were people who dated events by saying "before the freeze" or "after the freeze," much as other Southerners were known to date family history by the periods before and after the War Between the States.

The temperature started going down on the night of December 28, and as the cold front closed in, whole families joined forces at keeping smudge pots burning, working through the night, shivering, drinking the hot coffee the women kept boiling. The thermometer fell to fourteen degrees in Jacksonville, eighteen degrees at Titusville, and twenty-four as far south as Jupiter. Not in sixty years, certainly beyond the memory of most growers, had there been such a freeze in Florida.

A good many families went broke.

Then, as a double disaster, a second freeze hit in February, striking at the trees which were coming back, a death-dealing blow to the trees themselves. This tied up the situation neatly with diminishing dollar signs. The big freeze of 1894–95 is what the twin cold waves were called and together they brought financial losses estimated at one hundred million dollars.

To get an idea of the extent of the damage, the year before the freeze Florida groves had an estimated yield of five million five hundred and fifty thousand, three hundred and sixty-seven boxes. The year after the big freeze only one hundred and fifty thousand boxes were shipped.

The Florida East Coast Railroad, its welfare tied up with the growers, moved into instant action. It distributed free seed to begin immediate

47

replanting, distributed crates, and, for men too knocked out to pick up and go on, Flagler made personal loans. Fertilizer was hauled free, and everything was done to stabilize and reactivate the fallen industry. Ingraham, at Flagler's command, set out on an inspection trip to view the damage at first-hand. It was complete and his heart sank as he made the tour—until he reached the bay region. At Lemon City he found fruit trees untouched by the killing frost. He stopped by to see Julia Tuttle, and she was ready for him.

After repeating her offer of land donations, she handed him a box to take back to Flagler. In it she had packed on dampened cotton fragrant orange blossoms to prove the point: South Florida was frost-free.

Climate had handed Julia Tuttle a trump card.

Flagler, who had made his fortune along with John D. Rockefeller in Standard Oil, was not a fellow to miss the point. He held the sprig of orange blossom in his hand for a moment. Then he asked Ingraham, "How soon can you arrange for me to go to Fort Dallas?"

It took three days to get the word through to Julia Tuttle, and then a launch carried the Great Man from West Palm Beach to Fort Lauderdale, where a slicked-up carriage awaited his presence. The party transferred again to a boat at Little River and sailed down Biscayne Bay. Flagler clearly intended business, for with him were the men who had built the hotels at each new terminus created by the railroad.

Rumors and guffaws flew about like leaves in a hurricane. Three quarters of the people had never seen a railroad car, barring the one washed ashore at Cutler. Some said it couldn't be done. The wreckers growled.

Down the bay sailed the man who was changing the whole face of the east coast of Florida. At Fort Dallas he sent his compliments to Mrs. Tuttle, who arranged to take him to dinner at Peacock Inn. There, he praised the food and later visited with the people of the Grove. At The Barnacle he admired Commodore Munroe's royal palms and offered to buy them.

"I will name my hotel the Royal Palm," he said graciously.

The Commodore refused to sell his trees and asked Flagler if he had considered the Miami River as a more likely terminus for his railroad.

Flagler sent for William Brickell and Old Man Brickell said, "Tell Flagler he knows where to find me. Same distance from my place to his."

The financier sent back the message that he was interested in buying

Brickell Point, the story goes. Brickell, who loved his home, was speechless. Then he said, "Mother, go get the suitcase of diamonds down and show them to the gentleman."

No suitcase of diamonds at Brickell Point, but soon there would be trunks and suitcases of greenbacks. As time went on and the railroad brought lots of cash money to the bay, the Brickells would gain a reputation for keeping theirs at home in just such containers. New settlers would whisper that Old Man Brickell made his musty hundred-dollar bills as a pirate.

Flagler sat down to discuss terms with Julia Tuttle, and after the amenities Julia asked point-blank how much railroad stock he owned.

The impressive white-haired financier flicked an ash from the cigar he was smoking before answering. "Mrs. Tuttle, I own that railroad as completely as I own this cigar or my umbrella. You have no cause to worry. The railroad will come to this spot."

Before Flagler returned to St. Augustine he had decided where the townsite should be, where he would build the Royal Palm Hotel, and where he would put the railroad terminal. The deal he made was to take each alternate lot in Julia Tuttle's five hundred and twenty-five acres on the north bank of the river while the Brickells gave every alternate lot in four hundred acres south of the river. When Flagler still hesitated Julia threw in a hundred acres of land along the bay and river for his hotel, but reserved Fort Dallas and thirteen acres for her own home. She was careful to insist that nothing be built to interrupt her view of the bay.

Then Flagler declared himself willing to build the hotel, clear the streets, finance water works, an electric light plant, and other improvements.

The march to Miami had begun.

They marched in while the land titles were still being examined. On foot and by boat they came to look the situation over and get in on the ground floor. Men who had bought and sold land at a profit in the West Palm Beach area now shoved south, pitching tents along the river, building rude shacks along the bay, riding horseback to view the terrain to the south of Miami. They swatted horseflies, getting down from their horses to shake off the buzzing insects that covered the beasts like blankets, leading the horses, cursing the giant flies as they swatted. The sound of the hammer began to echo and re-echo as every available piece of lumber was called into play. They ordered two-by-fours and nails from Key West and cheered when the surveyors began their measuring and laying out of streets, narrow streets despite the pleadings of Julia Tuttle and the Brickells.

"The town will never be more than a fishing village for my hotel guests," Flagler told them.

There would be other arguments and property disputes between Flagler and the Brickells concerning land they owned in Fort Lauderdale along the path the railroad traveled.

The early birds worked on what would be Twelfth Street and in the twenties renamed Flagler Street, claiming a dollar a day from sunup to sundown for chopping down the pines. When the sun hid behind a cloud or when a sudden shower came up, the men howled and said they only contracted to work when the sun was shining, and sat down and cooled off.

Talk, talk, talk all through a hot summer about what the place would be, how rich everybody would be, while men burned piles of rags to keep away mosquitoes, marveling at the way the bay people appeared to ignore the pests.

Julia Tuttle, still busy with her dream of a shining city, saw to it that a clause prohibiting the sale of alcoholic beverages was inserted into the land deeds, but realistically bowed to Flagler's demand that for three months of the year guests at his Royal Palm Hotel, now being planned on paper, would be free to have their little nips.

In September, under the brilliant sunsets, a cheer went up. The actual laying of the tracks had begun. Slowly the railroad beat a path of steel to the unlocked doors of the bay people. On one fifty-mile stretch the railroad workers encountered but one house. Now businessmen from Titusville and Bronson, Kissimmee and South Georgia, paid visits to see about getting up buildings to be ready for the business the railroad would bring. They found it hard to get lumber. Julia Tuttle was sending a boat out to Cape Florida to intercept the lumber as it came up from Key West.

Harry Tuttle was supervising for his mother the building of a barnlike structure to house workmen. The night the floors were laid, Harry, who dearly loved a party, gave a dance there to celebrate. Within a month, it was being called the Miami Hotel and men were sleeping in it as it grew around their ears. Stairways were not yet constructed and ladders were being used temporarily to get to upstairs rooms. Rooms were bare, cots being the only furnishings. Food was bare too: turtle steak, bacon, and grits and served with a nice social distinction in two dining rooms, one for "mechanics," the other for "guests."

J. E. Lummus of Bronson, eager to be ready with his general store when the railroad chugged in, went to Julia Tuttle. "Mrs. Tuttle," he said, "you got me hamstrung by catchin' the lumber at Cape Florida. I want to give you the money and have you build me a house and store attached."

Julia promised to consider the matter overnight and in the morning told him she would start a two-story building for him at once. Others followed J. E.'s example, and Julia rented her stores for twenty-five dollars a month. Brown, unpainted, no-account-looking structures they were, all of them.

Some people left in disgust before the railroad ever completed the tracks. Food was scarce, they complained. Brickell's shelves were swept bare by the demand. In the land of plenty, with fish jumping in the bay and the hammocks stocked by nature with turkey, they hungered.

The men went swimming in the clear water of the Miami River. One evening a fellow named John Olmstead ran into a crocodile. While spectators gasped, the creature opened its jaws and got a firm grasp on Olmstead's chest. Olmstead rammed his fingers into the creature's eyes, breaking the hold. Then he managed to swim to shore. Not content with his miraculous escape, Olmstead swore to get vengeance and sat, night after night, with bandaged chest, a shotgun handy, waiting for the crocodile to reappear. It did and he shot it dead, then proudly exhibited it. It was fourteen feet long.

Another incident of the time had to do with two carpenters who built a better-than-usual shack to live in. It had a shingle roof with a ridgepole down the center and a luxurious glass window on each side. The men quarreled and one of them sawed the house clean down the middle and moved his half away.

In March a boat pulled in with John Sewell and a crew of black workmen, sent by Flagler to clear the streets in earnest. The railroad would follow in a month, Sewell said. As luck would have it he was able to find accommodations for himself at Captain Vail's Floating Hotel, which had docked that very morning.

For years the captain of a vessel plying between New York and New Orleans, Captain E. E. Vail had retired and built the St. Augustine Hotel, which brought him a handsome income. Some months before, it had been destroyed by fire and the captain had displayed his manhood by calmly smoking a cigar while his investment of sixty thousand dollars went up in smoke. Admiration for Captian Vail increased when it was learned that his insurance policy had lapsed the day before the fire. Now he had purchased the steamer *Rockledge*, one of the first steamboats on the Indian River, and turned her into a floating hotel, hoping to recoup his losses in the new city. The men flocked to its barbershop in such droves it became necessary to make an appointment. The Floating Hotel was filled up in a week.

The stake-pounding and the sawing and the sweating increased, and now there were stores, Lummus and Sewell Brothers shoe store in the rear of the Miami Hotel and Budge's hardware store. Thomas Townley sent away for an order of Shoo-Fly and marked it urgent for the opening of his drugstore.

Young Dr. James Mary Jackson, the son of a Bronson doctor and grove owner, was sent for to act as house physician for the unbuilt hotel and to begin a practice in the town-to-be. A graduate of Emory and the Bellevue Medical School in New York, young Dr. Jackson needed the practice. His family had been wealthy—until the freeze. He had decided to accept the medical opening, but when he arrived two weeks before the railroad and caught a glimpse of the pile of tents and primitive buildings he turned abruptly away.

"When does the next boat leave?" he asked.

By the time the next boat docked a week later he was converted. He wrote his wife: "There is a spirit about this place. The people are young and active and ambitious and hopeful. You feel it is a land of promise."

Mrs. Tuttle agreed to build Dr. Jackson an office. Until it was done he would make his office in the back of Sewell's shoe store or Townley's drugstore.

The day scheduled for the arrival of the first railroad train was April 15, 1896, and it is safe to say nobody went fishing that day. Early in the morning the sailboats rounded Brickell Point and families came ashore to view the promised spectacle of a rolling, puffing, honest-to-Heaven railroad train. When the first little wood-burning locomotive chugged in with a load of building material a shout went up from some throats. Others were silent.

52

After coming to a halt, it coughed and backed up and a Conch yelled, "Look out, she's comin' about!"

Only then did a roar go up from the three hundred people gathered to welcome the vehicle that now connected the bay people with the rest of the U.S.A.

City in the Sun

Now the ancient hammock land along the bay was being uprooted to make way for the Royal Palm Hotel, still in the blueprint stage but with future guests selecting rooms from the architect's sketches. One hundred black laborers, led by John Sewell, advanced into the jungle to make a smooth green lawn for the Rockefellers and the Goulds, the Vanderbilts and the Duke of Manchester. Black men marching in a V formation, black men from the Bahamas and from Georgia and Alabama, the first bunch carrying bush hooks, the next axes, and the next grubbing hoes. The jungle fought back. Fumes from the poisonous manchineel tree sent men falling on their knees, heads reeling, faces swelling in the hot sun. They learned to destroy the manchineel with fire. Next, the ironwood tree broke ax after ax until the dynamite was brought in. Then the boom-boom rang out steadily, a new accompaniment to the staccato hammering and the laughing and the bargaining.

At the sound of the explosions, Julia Tuttle came out of her house to watch. She was still excited about the new city, determined that it grow up as she had dreamed it. She complimented Sewell on the dispatch with which he was clearing the land.

Sewell thanked her and went on dynamiting.

Near the southeast corner of the proposed site of the hotel, he ran into the historic Indian mound where the Tequesta Indians had buried their dead in the long-ago era of moss skirts and treetop houses. To make space for the hotel veranda, Sewell and his men dug into the mound, taking out between fifty and sixty skulls. These were tossed into barrels, and later some were given away as souvenirs.

The Fort Dallas Land Company, Flagler's subsidiary, offered a free railroad excursion from Jacksonville to Miami, but it was not an unqualified success. It was summertime, and the mosquitoes were uncommonly active. The excursionists looked at the plank-board streets, at the city of tents and shacks, and seemed uneasy. They looked over their shoulders, beyond the string of keys where the flashing ocean lay, and they said that some day that ocean would sweep in and carry the new city away.

They complained of mosquitoes and reached for sand flies they could not see, examined Edwin Nelson's combined undertaking and furniture establishment where palmetto-fiber mattresses were on sale for two dollars and fifty cents; they peered in at Captain Ed Chase's billiard parlor and visited the racket store, forerunner of the five-and-tens where they purchased souvenirs—conch hats for fifteen cents. They were appalled at the temporary jail in an old box car, unimpressed by the new Bank of Bay Biscayne, and finally begged to be taken back to "civilization."

Before that happened they bought out every mosquito bar in town.

The railroad had opened the gates and new men were coming in every day. Bakers and bricklayers, lawyers and butchers, preachers and printer's devils, retired sea dogs and escaped convicts, they all poured in. Now there were fifty businesses operating.

On May 15, 1896, the first newspaper, hopefully named the Miami *Metropolis*, was full of enthusiasm in its debut issue: "This is the first paper ever published on beautiful Bay Biscayne, the most southern newspaper on the mainland of the United States, published at the most southern telegraph terminal and express office on the mainland at Marvelous Miami, the town with one thousand souls and the survey of the place not yet completed. The coming metropolis of South Florida."

Immediately it began campaigning for a city charter and street paving, taking time out to predict that the railroad would never extend to Key West, adding that the paper had it "straight from Flagler's lips." When will the first bridge be laid across the Miami River and what is to be done about the post office? asked the *Metropolis*. Already people were complaining about having to row across the narrow stream to get their mail at Brickell's trading post. The *Metropolis* briskly pointed out that the post office should be moved. It soon was. The *Metropolis* began to bellow editorially for streets, complaining that the footpath down toward the bay "played havoc with patent-leather shoes and the bottoms of Sunday pants."

It was discovered that crushed rock would make a good base for a road, and now a new sound was added as the oölitic limestone was ground to make the streets on which men walked, blinding white streets, blazing headache-producers by day, like snow on a moonlit night.

Twelfth Street, blinding or not, was a good spot for a bicycle race or a game of mumbly-peg or migs. Business began to turn in that direction and the men and boys gathered there daily. There was always something doing. When George A. Worley, a mammoth, flamboyant lawyer whom everybody called "Judge," needed a tooth pulled, Frank Budge obliged with a new pair of mechanical pliers while a crowd gathered in front of the latter's hardware store to encourage the operation.

People, earnest people, were worrying about the best way to lay out streets (about which they never had anything to say), start a school, build a church. They met in a community tent to discuss matters. Even before the scheduled election to incorporate as a city the cry of "special interests" had gone up.

It would seem that Henry Morrison Flagler was never to receive fitting thanks for the railroad from any but his own workers. On July 28, 1896, when the City of Miami was incorporated with five hundred and two voters, the name of the new city was voted to be Miami after the river—not Flagler, as the railroad men had urged. One wonders if it would have spelled glamour to the nation if it had been called Flagler—or Dade or Dallas, which were names considered at the meeting.

There was some sharp politicking before the election, and John Sewell, who was blunt but got things done, boasted that his "Black Artillery" of one hundred registered black voters brought in as a surprise move had swung the election to a mayor sympathetic to railroad interests. They swung the election but their names were removed from the citizen roster shortly thereafter.

The new Miami had been much too busy with politics to notice Independence Day when it crossed the calendar, but down in Coconut Grove it was celebrated with a regatta, the library pole raising, a basket dinner, and an oration. The Grove went calmly on its way, unmarked by the madness along the Miami.

In every issue the *Metropolis* ran a standing head reminding its readers that "filth, the contents of cesspools, offal, garbage, foul water, urine, stable manure, decay of animal or vegetable matter thrown or placed or allowed to remain in or upon any private premises, street, avenue, alley, sidewalk, gutter or private reservation" was punishable by a fine of from five to twenty-five dollars. A sewer pipe was laid and filth began to run into the sweet water of the Miami River. Some people complained by letter to J. Y. Porter, the health officer at Key West, and so the sewer was extended out into the channel.

"This," the *Metropolis* pointed out, "will do away with the grounds for complaints."

Out of sight, out of mind would be Miami's treatment of sewage through the years until the day would come when she had fouled up her clear, sweet river and her blue shining bay to such an extent that it was no longer out of sight and fish would die and sea gardens would disappear and the beautiful, broad Biscayne Bay would lie, a pollution before man and God.

A gentleman from Atlanta observed the hammock being burned and pointed out that the wood would make fine furniture. To prove his point, he made himself a cane and polished it. Captain F. W. Hahn carved a fine inlaid workbox of crabwood, Madeira, and red stopper and agreed that this was so. But they went on burning the hammocks or sawing fine woods into stacks of firewood to be burned later.

Julia Tuttle took a part in everything concerning the city. When a man applied for a permit to operate the first icehouse, Julia was on hand to air her views. She did not like the site he had selected in the center of town and along the river.

"You are a smoky fellow," she told him with a smile. "We don't want you puffing in our faces at close range."

He agreed to move back from the river.

In her efforts to create a city free of "malt, vinous, or intoxicating liquor" she was not so successful. It was true that Julia Tuttle's liquor clause prevented men from "buying, selling, or manufacturing" alcoholic drinks on her land at the risk of having it revert back to her, but it was a simple matter to open up outside the city limits. Twenty feet over the city line the saloons opened up. Men called it North Miami and smiled. North Miami flourished, and Miami's first marshall, a bandy-legged Texan named J. Y. Gray, who wore a ten-gallon hat, spent a good deal of time there one way or another. He was known to imbibe too freely, but he never failed in his duty. He might be drunk enough to require help in mounting his bicycle, but he would ride right into the thick of the fray, brandishing his pistol, shouting, "Stop in the name of the law!"

A group of men got together and decided to break Julia Tuttle's liquor restriction by stocking a saloon within the city limits. They opened, and Juilia had the sheriff close them up. The fight was being carried to the courts, and during the litigation the stocked liquor establishment remained padlocked.

Flagler began building houses for his employees, plain little two-story houses that could belong in Kansas or Vermont, and the ladies who were arriving in number to join their men moved inside them joyfully.

But some people were never satisfied. Now they were complaining about the drinking water, said it was too hard and made them sick. The *Metropolis* took a hand in the discussion. "The water is too hard for laundry purposes," the paper agreed, "but only one out of ten people get sick from it, not nine out of ten as claimed."

Harry Tuttle put down the first big well, about fifty or sixty feet with a four-inch pipe and attached a steam pump to it to tap in on water for the Miami Hotel. Then the construction crew for the Royal Palm put a similar well down to furnish water there. Admittedly, the water was hard. Julia Tuttle appealed to Mr. Flagler to construct a pump near the rapids of the river four miles outside town where a spring existed and a powerhouse with gasoline engine was established at that point. The gasoline was carried up the Miami River on lighters, then put on a small push car and carried two hundred yards north of the pump station over a tiny narrow-gauge railroad constructed especially for the task. Later this system was abolished and the pumping station was installed in the city and the water carried there by pipeline.

The Miami River began to present a lively scene, with boats docking regularly from Jacksonville and Tampa, Key West and Pensacola and other Gulf ports as well as schooners from the Bahamas. Flagler spent twenty thousand dollars dredging a channel into the river and the slogan was "Watch the Port of Miami." Harry Tuttle purchased a bright new captain's uniform to run a passenger boat from Miami to Key West and had his picture taken in it, smiling and smoothing down his mustache, the first time the vessel docked at

Key West. When the steamer *City of Key West* began a regular run, he stopped his boat service.

There was great excitement when the first steamer was due from Key West, with dances and entertainment planned for the passengers, and acute was the disappointment when the *City of Key West* was forced to anchor a mile or two down the bay because the water was not deep enough. The *Metropolis* asked why a railroad dock could not be built out to the water.

Meanwhile, the government of Nassau, eager to cash in on the excitement of the coming Royal Palm Hotel, raised funds to run the *Monticello*, a side-wheel vessel with elaborate staterooms, between the two spots during the coming tourist season. Not to be outdone, Peacock Inn announced it would run a launch, the *Daimier*, into Miami daily to pick up guests. The *Daimier* left Coconut Grove at eight A.M. and docked in Miami at nine. The trip cost twenty-five cents each way and left the river at ten-thirty.

Hundreds of men worked at building the Royal Palm Hotel, which was said to be "modern Colonial." Thirty men worked every day just on the grounds alone. The dining room would seat five hundred, the people learned. Moreover, there would be still another dining room for maids and children, a billiard room, a ballroom forty-five by fifty feet long, and a swimming pool with a casino equipped with one hundred dressing rooms.

All this was music to the ears of the merchants, who rubbed their hands in anticipation of the money it would bring to their coffers. They played poker and pinochle and baseball and counted their chickens before they were hatched. It seemed a pretty safe thing to do.

Isidor Cohen, who had opened a drygoods store, wrote in his diary: "This is going to be a wonderful city. Things happen in rapid succession and everybody is happy. Various associations are being formed. I am joining most of them excepting the Tuxedo Club. I am disqualified for membership from that because of lack of a tuxedo suit."

Brickell's trading post was no longer the center of life along the bay. In fact, cut off by lack of a bridge from the town growing up across the river, the Brickells were somewhat out in the cold. This was a temporary situation since a road to Coconut Grove was in the offing and Mary Brickell had registered herself as a real estate broker to handle the sales of their hammock land to the south, which would be opened up directly. The big question in William

Brickell's mind was where the first bridge would go to join the north and south banks of the Miami. Naturally he wanted it at Brickell Point, but Flagler had other plans and settled on Avenue D for the first bridge. This angered Brickell, and the story is that he vowed never to cross the river again—and that he never did.

It must have been a period of constant irritation for William Brickell. In dredging the mouth of the river for its steamers, the Flagler men had left a thirty-foot pile of broken marl and shell on Brickell Point, cutting off the family's view of both river and bay. Brickell insisted that this was to have been moved to some low land by the railroad men, but they merely shrugged and went about their business. Although Brickell finally sold the fill to the road-makers, his bitterness was real.

Meanwhile, Brickell had dedicated land for roads going south to Coconut Grove and he planned them as wide, double-lane avenues, and a doff of the cap to Old Man Brickell who gave Miami two of its loveliest streets.

Sailors from Coconut Grove, Commodore Munroe particularly, took a dim view of Flagler's deepening of the channel from the river across the bay to Cape Florida since the spoil banks created reduced the sailing area in the upper bay. The sharpest sting came when the engineers put in a row of heavy pilings as guides for the steamer pilots. Like a row of telephone poles they stood, a constant menace to boats at night because they were unlighted. These obstructions were illegal, the Commodore pointed out, and a threat to all craft on the bay. The final insult was that the line of the river channel cut across the upper half of the long-established Biscayne Bay Yacht Club race course and forced its abandonment.

The city of Miami, the long summer behind it, was looking forward to its first Christmas. For weeks Watson's hardware store had been a delight to the eye, filled with holiday gifts of every description, and those who were going home to Titusville or Kissimmee or Georgia to spend the holiday with their families regretted having to leave.

A display of fireworks was scheduled for Christmas Eve, and the women planned a big community party Christmas Day for the one hundred and fifty-five white children of school age in the casino of the Miami Hotel with a tree and carols and presents for all. The Miami Hotel was now an impressive three-story structure and boasted "eight hundred feet of broad piazza" and an order in for carpets to cover the entire building. Christmas visitors had arrived from far-off Monterey, California, and Butte, Montana, and all in all a feeling of well-being and accomplishment possessed the people. The black population had planned a parade for their own children Christmas morning.

The *Metropolis* in its pre-Christmas message said: "May no sickness or distress or adversity darken your doors this Christmas. May you be happy and gay . . ."

At four A.M. Christmas morning fire broke out in Brady's grocery store, spread instantly to the Bank of Bay Biscayne, next hit the poolroom of Captain Chase. Nine-year-old Henry Chase, grandson of the captain, roused from his bed by the licking flames, never forgot the prevailing feeling of helplessness that early Christmas day as a stiff east wind whipped the fire into a fury that reduced the buildings, twenty-eight of them finally, into smoldering ruins. Henry Chase would grow up to be Miami's all-time, number-one fire fighter. In the 1950s, as Chief Chase, looking back over the years, he would say somberly, "Nothing to do but throw stones at that fire. We had no equipment."

Watson's gayly decked hardware store was saved. Willing hands carried buckets of water, and a hose from the Miami Hotel was used to play against the scorched building.

Julia Tuttle, jumping into her clothes and hurrying to the scene, manned a pump and worked along with the men.

Three blocks of business houses were wiped out by the fire, and in all that lot there was only seventy-five hundred dollars' worth of insurance.

One man was injured in the leg from the head of an ax and another died as the result of an explosion at Zapf's bottling works. His name was Julius M. Frank, and he left a wife and six children.

During the fire's height, the men, showing a latent spirit of conservation, broke down the door of the padlocked saloon. Along about six A.M., the fire having spent itself, they enjoyed a morning tipple, right there in the center of Julia Tuttle's dry town.

Julia sat down on top of an upturned bucket and viewed her ruined city. She complained of a headache, and Harry took her home. Part of Julia's headache was financial. Increasingly, she was disappointed in the amount of help Henry Flagler was willing to give her dream city. Just before Christmas she had written him and the answer had been clear enough.

"I cannot accept the responsibility of your suffering," he had written. "I have advised against your becoming so deeply involved in debt."

Later, men said that the fire was a blessing. It did away with the crude brown board barns that made up the early business section. Everybody was glad that the Miami Hotel, the Biscayne Hotel, and the Connolly House, which had been moved down from Lemon City on a lighter, as well as the River View House had survived the fire. Everyone rejoiced, too, that the new jail was untouched. Just opened next to the ice factory, it had four cells and the second floor was given over to the Common Council chamber and mayor's court. But other men walked the streets, everything gone, looking for work.

The Royal Palm Hotel was not ready for a January 1 opening, but Harry Tuttle and Tom Decker gave a party to usher in the new year. Despite a heavy rain, one hundred guests attended the event, which was given at the Miami Hotel. They stayed until three A.M.

The people boasted that the mile of rock road along the bayfront was the most perfect in the state. Adam Correll ordered nineteen blooded horses for his livery business in anticipation of a big season. A gentleman from the London *Daily Times* arrived to do a series of articles for this paper, and H. W. Merrill, the manager of the Royal Palm, announced that the hotel would open on January 16. Everything would be in order, he added, down to the pale green ladies' stationery which boasted an embossed cut of a royal palm with a wreath around it and the inscription: Hotel Royal Palm, Miami, Biscayne Bay, Fla.

Everyone who had the money and the right clothes attended the opening dinner. From the beginning the people of Miami had a feeling about the Royal Palm. They were proud of it. The wealth it represented gave them a feeling of security. They wanted to be and were impressed by it. Julia was there, of course, escorted by her son. Her daughter, Miss Fanny, was not present. Fanny was about to marry Conrad Saunders and live in Nassau. It was a marriage of which Julia disapproved.

For a time Fanny had been wooed by Will Brickell and there was talk of marriage, but at a large party at Palm Beach she had flirted with a telegrapher. Will, livid with anger, had called the whole thing off. Now Saunders had opened a store in Nassau and was charging his supplies to Julia. Grimly, she was paying for them.

Professor P. J. Oehl played music, and the dinner was excellent—from the green turtle soup clear to escallop of pompano à la Normandie, filet of beef larded à la Cavaur, sweetbread glacée with asparagus tips, quail sur canapé, and ribs of beef, ending with claret jelly and tutti-frutti ice cream.

But Julia's heart was not entirely in the proceedings that evening.

Phil Armour, the big Chicago meat man, took the train ride down from Palm Beach in order to sail to Nassau on the *Monticello*, but before leaving Miami he wired his wife and daughter at Palm Beach to "come at once to the Royal Palm." Mark Hanna, who had dreamed up the McKinley winning presidential slogan "a full dinner pail," arrived from Cleveland and pronounced the cuisine to his liking. A Chicago yachtsman, Commodore Laurie B. Heyworth of the Calumet Club, came for his honeymoon. His bride, it was gleefully reported in the *Metropolis*, was "worth ten million." W. C. Price, retired managing editor of the New York *Journal of Commerce*, arrived to study the flora and fauna. His valet assisted him in his natural history explorations. From the beginning Miamians preferred titled visitors. That winter they contented themselves with Baron E. de Rovile and Baron von Koenig.

These first visitors took boat trips to the deserted Cape Florida Light, climbing the rusty iron stairway where in July of 1836 the Seminoles had attacked the lighthouse keeper and burned the lighthouse. It was a pleasant, two-hour, morning boat trip. They considered the crocodile hole at Miami Beach a great attraction, and experts said it was one of the largest breeding spots discovered. A trip to the rapids of the Miami River was another point of interest and so was a carriage ride to Sam Filer's orange grove. Then there was always the rotunda of the huge, rambling, many-porched Royal Palm. Six stories high, the rotunda offered a view of bay and ocean, keys and hammocks and pineland. For the more adventurous, there was an observation platform rising above the rotunda, and a golf course on the Royal Palm grounds was a constant attraction.

The most exciting pastime was deep-sea fishing with Cap'n Charlie Thompson. Charlie, who had gone to college to please Julia Tuttle and remained less than twenty-four hours, now came into his own with millionaire senators and manufacturers. Catches that had to be photographed to be believed were daily occurrences, and proud parties lined up on the dock to exhibit themselves standing over tarpon and whip ray and herring hog. The ladies, with shining pompadours, large hats, and golden mesh bags, came down to the dock to greet the returning conquerors and graciously pose with the monsters of the deep.

Bicycling became a popular sport, and when Alfred A. Pope of Boston declared the bicycle path to Coconut Grove a "delightful passageway" everyone was pleased. Mr. Pope manufactured bicycles and in addition was president of the American Good Roads Association. He confided to T. C. Van Petts of Brooklyn one morning that it seemed likely that the unicycle would soon replace the bicycle since obviously one wheel would run with less friction than two.

The first tourist season ran its course, and toward the end, Miamians were permitted to swim in the Royal Palm pool for fifteen cents during restricted hours. All in all, it had been a quiet season, not nearly what the merchants had anticipated. When the hotel manager, Mr. Merrill, left in the middle of March for the Crawford House in the White Mountains, everyone agreed that things hadn't really gotten started. But just watch us next year, they said.

Why, this place is going to be the Naples of America.

Shadows on the Sun

MIAMI TOOK THE SPANISH-AMERICAN WAR HARD. No need to whip up public opinion with slogans like "Remember the Maine" and the military music of John Philip Sousa. Miami *was* aroused. A near-panic existed when the cream of the military potential marched off to train in Tampa. Miamians fully expected Spanish warships to fire on their city. A military company of "males from sixteen to eighty" was organized and given the name of the Miami Minute Men. The federal government obliged with a consignment of hand-me-down guns, and the solemn band began drilling under the Miami moon and the waving palms. Few of the volunteers had ever had military training.

One evening, the editor of the *Metropolis*, a gentleman named W. M. Featherly, who had exchanged his .3856 rifle for a sailboat by means of an advertisement soon after arriving in Miami, suddenly crumpled while marching. John Sewell caught him, throwing down his gun to execute the maneuver. The gun went off and the marching men, convinced a Spanish warship had fired the first shot and hit their comrade-at-arms, turned, pointing their guns to the water. Mr. Featherly, picking himself up, confessed he was subject to dizzy spells.

People were frightened enough to leave town, and when Admiral Cervera's fleet was reported heading westward from the Cape Verde Islands a demand went up for coastal defense guns. Commodore Munroe scornfully pointed out the hysteria of such notions but nobody listened. Strict orders were sent to Coconut Grove to Dick Carney and the Commodore to pilot no more boats into the bay. With the Commodore's spyglass, the pair could see approaching ships in time to meet them before they even signaled for a pilot. They went on meeting them, ignoring the order.

Water from Kirk Munroe's spring was being pumped into barges by the navy and taken to Key West to supply the ships. Coconut Grove considered itself a vital contributor to the war.

The government began to build Fort Brickell in the hammock south of the city and coastal guns were rushed to the city by rail. The shipment was given pre-eminence over all other freight and arrived safely, but before they could be mounted, word arrived that Admiral Cervera was headed for Apalachicola, and the tracks were cleared to whiz the guns northward again. Tempers and blood pressures rose and fell until the army announced it was sending troops.

Miami, which was becoming a respectable-looking city with rambling houses boasting cupolas, became once more a city of tents. Miami now had fifteen hundred civilians and seven thousand soldiers.

Soldiers began to clear downtown pineland for their encampment, griping as they cleared that they were "working for Flagler." One way or another Henry Flagler caught it. The saloon keepers in North Miami spoke out in self-righteous voices against the man who made Miami. They said he was a monopoly-seeker and that the liquor clause was proof of that.

In off hours, soldiers from Texas and Louisiana and Mississippi and Alabama, many of them released convicts, played havoc with the city. They swam naked in the bay, and houseboats took up anchor and moved away. Business was good, but no woman was safe on the streets after dark.

Stella Budge, daughter of the hardware man, rode in the dray beside her father's black servant Sam Walker to protect him from the soldiers as he made deliveries. One stalwart shot and killed a black man whom he accused of "brushing against a white lady" while leaving a store. Another chased a black man down the street and when he caught him twisted his neck until he broke it. It was small comfort that the fellow eventually went to prison for attacking a fellow soldier with a knife.

A company of New Orleans men visited The Barnacle and tried to shoot the coconuts off Commodore Munroe's trees. One soldier attempting to climb a tree to bring down a clump of nuts was knocked unconscious when hit on the head by several. The Commodore called it "an act of God."

68

One Miami man shot and killed a soldier for "molesting his wife." Another shot and killed one for trying to break into his home. One night a rumor started that a black man had killed a soldier. That night, a mob of soldiers advanced on the colored section of town and ran frightened blacks out of their shacks and out of town.

Men wore pistols as a matter of course, and there was hardly a night that somebody wasn't murdered. The path in front of Dr. Jackson's house, then situated on Flagler Street, diagonally across from what is now known as Gusman Center auditorium, often looked in the morning as though animals had been butchered there. Black and white, victims of knife slashings and bullet wounds, they all came to Doc Jackson's to be sewed up.

If there was any pleasure in connection with the war (aside from increased business, which was always a pleasure) it had to do with the docking of the first prize ship captured from Spain. Miamians pleaded with the Spanish prisoners to sell the buttons from their uniforms as souvenirs and bidding proceeded at a fast clip.

During all this agitation the Royal Palm Hotel remained open through the summer for the first time. It was used as headquarters for officers and newspaper correspondents, who played an important part in the war which historians would later call "newspaper-inspired."

One evening a soldier strayed into Julia Tuttle's place and in the old stone barracks shot and killed himself. This unnerving event was followed by the army placing a guard over Fort Dallas and the Tuttle home.

Julia had not been in good health and more and more sought seclusion in Fort Dallas. There had been some small unpleasantness in having to prove by survey the distance between her place and the Royal Palm in order to prevent further hotel building between her residence and the bay. Now, increasingly, she appeared willing to extricate herself from the city and rest behind a high wall of shrubbery. Like everyone else she expressed relief when the war ended and the troops were withdrawn. She had begun to make plans for "the biggest tourist season yet" in her city in the sun when in September she fell ill and took to her bed.

She had invited a girlhood friend, Fannie Comstock, to come to live as a companion at Fort Dallas and to her one afternoon Julia complained of a violent headache. Mrs. Comstock brought her a headache powder, which she took. Within an hour Julia Tuttle was dead. Nobody could believe it. Her daughter, Fanny, who arrived from Nassau for the funeral, and her half-brother, Wheeler Sturtevant, were bitter in their belief that if she had had proper medical attention she would have lived.

This did nothing to strengthen the bonds of affection between Fannie and Harry, who was keeping company with pretty Corrie Fowler, both of whose parents were homeopathic doctors and who had advised in Julia's illness. Dr. S. Mills Fowler, who had trained in Chicago, and his wife were considered excellent in their field, and Harry was not tolerating any hint of aspersion cast upon their reputations.

Fanny called in a dressmaker to alter some of her mother's gowns and wore one when she left for New York after the funeral. Harry pointed to this as a mark of irreverence to their mother's memory.

Julia Tuttle, at forty-nine, was dead and men said, "She drove herself too hard."

The dream she had begun would go right on.

Some envisioned changes. The Miami Hotel announced immediately upon Julia Tuttle's death that it would install a bar.

On the heels of Julia's death, yellow fever broke out. Harry Tuttle, honeymooning with Corrie Fowler in the north, escaped the period of quarantine when for three long months the city of Miami was shut off from the rest of the world, the only time in her history when the population was not marching.

Dr. Simmons diagnosed the first case in Coconut Grove, a sailor from a ship. As the disease spread, the Dade County Health Unit was organized to meet the emergency. Armed guards stationed about the city discouraged any fleeing. People were frightened by the epidemic and responded according to their own natures. Some paid guards in order to slip by them and get away. Others made their wills and prepared to die.

All the Brickells caught the fever and resorted to the uncomfortably hot baths prescibed by Dr. Jackson for the disease commonly referred to as "the Black Vomit."

Yellow flags were tacked on the doors of those who succumbed to the disease and a list of the dead was placed on a blackboard each day in front of

Townley's drugstore by J. K. Dorn who drove along in the carriage with Dr. Jackson on his calls. Fortunately, other doctors had arrived by now. Dr. P. T. Skaggs, Dr. Edwin Pugh, and others worked through this emergency.

"Judge" Worley got a couple of barges and hitched them up along the river out from town. One barge, he said, handing his six children hammers and nails, was for play. The other was for living. Every morning before departing for the office, "Judge" Worley, who had faith in the therapeutic value of good whiskey, gave his children a dose along with a quinine pill, and the Worleys escaped the fever.

The dead were removed in a wagon and buried. Their clothes and effects were burned in the middle of the streets. John Frohock, who helped bury the dead, remembered, "You'd talk to a man today, tomorrow he'd be dead. They turned as yellow as gold in death."

The surprising thing was that the Royal Palm Hotel enjoyed a good season after the quarantine was lifted in mid-winter.

For years to come Miami would have her alarms about "the tourists." Would they come or stay away? Everything must be slicked up and pretty for the tourists. When, during the height of a later season, smallpox broke out among the help at the Royal Palm Hotel, local authorities spirited the affected workers away into the woods where they set up a secret hospital to nurse them back to health. When they were well they were put on trains going north. What the millionaires at the Royal Palm didn't know wouldn't hurt them. Besides, wasn't Florida billed by the Flagler land companies as the place where "the gates of death are farther removed . . . than from any other state"?

Visitors to Florida were not necessarily all millionaires, and the bulk of Flagler's income came from the combination of his tourist hotels and the lands he sold to future farmers and grove owners. As for tourists, in 1898 a five-week return trip to Florida from New York with stops at any of the Flagler hotels cost a mere three hundred and fifty dollars or ten dollars a day.

The millionaires did come, of course, and young Pat Railey, who was clerking in Sewell's store, sold one dozen of the new soft collars to John D. Rockefeller, who cautiously asked to try one on before buying. Rockefeller wouldn't leave the soft collar on, however, after he decided to purchase it for two thin dimes.

"I just put this stiff one on clean this morning," he said, showing a nice frugality.

Forever after, Railey, who had helped Rockefeller button the newfangled collar, boasted that he had "put his arms around John D."

Harry Tuttle leased his mother's old home to a high-class gambler who opened it as the Seminole Club, with the understanding that gambling would be "for tourists only." The painting of the Seminole Chief looked down on dark green gaming tables on which pools of yellow light were centered, while men and women titillated over a game of *chemin de fer* or roulette. Now gambling had its paw inside the city gates.

The People vs. The Railroad

T HE FOOT OF FLAGLER STREET IN THE EARLY 1900s presented a scene of small-town respectability. The yellow Fair Building extended out over the bay, and here the young in heart tapped their feet to "C-h-i-c-k Spells Chicken" or "Under the Bamboo Tree," while on other evenings decorous church suppers or home-talent shows attracted the citizenry.

Looking north on the boulevard (it was then known as Biscayne Drive) you observed the neat rock sea wall which had replaced the wandering sea grape along the bayfront, the large and turreted home of the James C. Hunters of Pittsburgh, the identical little short-eaved houses of Charles D. Leffler and Mrs. Elvira Romfh and her brood. A wooden band shell stood where the Southeast Bank Building is today. A bit to the rear of the present site of the Everglades Hotel stood a tiny white building with a businesslike sign: Smith's Private School. Farther north was the dock built by "Judge" Worley and used generally by people tying up rowboats or going swimming. Close to the foot of Flagler Street was a large rock pit, the source of the rock sea wall no doubt, and Seminoles began to use it as a dressing room, stepping down to change their clothes after coming in from the Everglades in their dugout canoes, dressing up in pants, white man's fashion, before going down to shop in white men's stores.

In the summertime Dr. Jackson's cow grazed on the Royal Palm lawns, and in the hot afternoons, while the caretaker napped, the young fry rode their bicycles 'round and 'round the hotel's protected veranda, the more daring riding their wheels down the porch steps without once slowing down. Not one of Flagler's hotels, which were advertised throughout the nation as Halls of Joy, was ever put to more wholehearted use.

Signs of progress rose to the blue sky in the form of telephone poles and electric wires, but not everybody had iceboxes and it was common summertime practice to burn smudge pots under the dining-room table against mosquitoes. The Tatem brothers, who had opened up the city's first real estate subdivision, Riverside, wore newspaper vests as protectors when out riding in their carriage at the height of a mosquito invasion.

Black baptisms in the bay on Sundays attracted young boys who kept a discreet distance as was the custom. One day two prostitutes from North Miami drew up in a carriage and stared openly at the ceremonies. This did not disturb the blacks, only the boys hiding in the bushes who never forgot the scene.

For the children who lived near the bay there were regular swimming hours off Worley's dock. One morning the railroad sent in a crew to construct a barbed-wire fence along the bayfront. No signs were necessary. The inference was plain: the railroad owned the bayfront.

"Judge" Worley, who now wore Prince Albert coats and wide-brimmed hats, hollered to Heaven, quoted the Bible and law with more Bible than law, then deliberately went out and clipped the barbed-wire fence so that the children could get through without scratching their legs.

Charles Leffler and George Worley shared a two-story building and agreed on nothing, so that loud argument between the two was always good for entertainment for the Flagler Street loungers. Once Leffler brought suit against Worley for an unpaid grocery bill. Thundering into court, Worley produced canceled checks that said he had paid the bill. Leffler's voice insisting that those checks were merely evidence of his accommodating Worley by exchanging cash for checks was lost in Worley's oratory.

On the matter involving the bayfront they were agreed: down with the barbed-wire fence. A crew of railroad workers came and repaired the fence. That night it was cut again, and each time the railroad repaired it someone snipped the wire.

A watchman, one Peanut Johnson, was installed to patrol the bayfront by night to guard the "railroad's property." Most nights Peanut slept on the Lefflers' front porch. When the patrolling failed to stop the cutting, the Florida

East Coast had Worley cited for contempt and put him under an injunction restraining him from any further cutting.

In disgust Worley took his large family and moved up to Buena Vista to "the country" where they could swim in peace. This was a blow to the younger set who would now be deprived of the music available at all times at the Worley home, music in the form of the violin, horn, mandolin, guitar, organ, piano, and phonograph. Most of all, they would miss the grandfather clock, which instead of striking the hour played music. It played four classical numbers and four ragtime pieces. The general favorites were "Goo-goo Eyes" and "Ta-ra-ra Boom-de-ay."

Worley, a criminal lawyer who prided himself on defending "the underdog" (and who frequently brought seedy characters home for board and lodging only to tire of them within twenty-four hours), went on fighting the railroad. (It is not irrelevant to add that Mrs. Worley was considered "a saint" by all who knew her.)

He declared on street corners that Flagler was "bottling up the town." He referred to a map which clearly showed the word "park" designating that land for the people. Finally, the FEC railroad brought suit for "injunction and relief" against *George A. Worley et al.* Out-of-town landowners like the Hunters of Pittsburgh and Bostonian Luther T. Townsend shared the suit.

The railroad was not merely objecting to bathers when it put up the fence. Far more serious matters were involved: the railroad was fighting for its right to the bayfront which Harry Tuttle had sold to Flagler. The fence was put up mainly to prevent schooners from docking and unloading merchandise because an odd thing had happened. The merchants had begun shipping by water again, by-passing the railroad.

While FEC checkers sat yawning in the sun, a brisk trade by schooner had sprung up. Some say Charlie Leffler began the move in the interest of economy. When it was discovered that a great saving in money was involved, the idea spread like rays from the rising sun. Flagler's railroad had to make it clear who was boss in Miami and in a hurry.

Everybody in town was called to testify at the trial and an interesting sidelight was the discovery that half the city council were legal residents of Titusville or some other place and were still voting back home.

The same city council had met hurriedly in extraordinary and secret session to pass a resolution rejecting any "dedication implied by the word park on the recorded plat of Miami."

The railroad attempted to prove at the trial that the word "park" had been written to denote an area which Flagler, Julia Tuttle, and Joseph Day had considered turning into a "private park for their own income." The FEC, now sole owner of the land, assured all present that the area in question was never intended for, nor would it ever be, a park. J. S. Frederick, the engineer who had written the important word "park" on the plat (and who was a member of the city council voting to reject the idea of a claim) said he had no recollection of what was in his mind when he wrote it on the original map.

Worley was the star performer. He carried his three watches and wore a large amethyst ring which he declared had once belonged to "the Pope." At every opportunity in testifying to the circumstances surrounding his controversial dock he hammered home the idea that "nobody had any right to give permission and none was asked."

In the end, the state supreme court ruled that the land marked "park" belonged to the people. That was the beginning of Miami's Bayfront Park. In the twenties the city purchased additional bayfront from the FEC to extend it.

Flagler's brushes with the people of Miami were a nuisance to him. Now he decided to extend his railroad south to Homestead, opening up the rich Redland agricultural district. He began seriously to consider a route to Key West, which had a deep-water harbor and was only ninety miles from Cuba, strategically located for West Indian and South American trade.

Flagler decided to go ahead. Nobody thought he would ever complete that railroad to Key West. It was an undertaking both daring and involved. Surrounded by water on all sides, Key West lay more than one hundred miles away from the mainland and it would be necessary to fill in sections of shallow water between keys, build bridges spanning deep-water channels, and transport men and material and food as well as equipment from great distances. Even drinking water would have to be carried to the workmen.

Engineers refused to take on the job so Flagler called in Joseph F. Parrott, his FEC vice-president, and assigned it to him. With an able engineer named Joseph Meredith the staggering job began. Towers had to be erected to make it possible for surveyors to sight their instruments, all manner of deterrents presented themselves, even to labor turning a cold shoulder to the job. Finally, the FEC recruited men from all over the nation, offering high pay and free transportation, and the "extension workers" as they were called answered with a bellow from the Bowery to California. Deep-sea divers in Greece heard the call and came; so did Cubans and Bahamians and New York's immigrant laborers, Irish, Italian, Swedish. They brought in thousands of men for the march toward Key West, but hundreds deserted when they caught their first sight of the tropical wilderness.

Commodore Munroe, watching the plans go forward, wrote to Flagler advising against the use of solid fill the full length of the Homestead to Key Largo run, especially at Jewfish Creek. Solid embankments, he pointed out, would interfere with the free flow of water back and forth between the Bay of Florida and lower Biscayne Bay in the event of a hurricane.

This suggestion was perfunctorily received and blandly ignored. The Commodore wrote again, this time suggesting that the island below Jewfish Creek be spanned by means of an arch rather than solid fill, pointing out once more the need for an escape valve. Neither of these suggestions was adopted.

On the keys there were murmurs among the Conchs who could see with their own eyes the dangers involved in case of storm. The FEC began laying its tracks from the center of Miami.

The influx of the extension workers helped fill North Miami honky-tonks, and in Coconut Grove when the tracks began creeping in that direction people began to lock their doors. Mrs. Jack Peacock offered Mrs. Stephen Van Rensselaer Carpenter, the president of the Housekeeper's Club, a large dinner bell to ring if she needed help. Mrs. Carpenter was alone with her five grown daughters while her son, Del, was off working on the railroad supply boat.

Now for the emergency of the influx of extension workers Miss Hattie, the schoolteacher daughter, armed herself with a pistol. One morning as she pedaled through the Punch Bowl district on her way to school, a row of tough-looking workmen blocked her way. Miss Hattie, soon to be the principal of Miami's first high school, opened the basket on her bicycle and lifted out the gun. She held it loosely in one hand and continued pedaling toward the unbroken line.

"Good morning, boys," Miss Hattie said.

The line opened and she went on to school.

Later Del Carpenter, whose biggest headache as boss of the supply launch for the army of extension workers had been to prevent the Japanese cooks from drinking up all the vanilla, would have the unhappy task of burying some of these men.

Derelicts from the Bowery and immigrants from the Old World—men good, bad, and indifferent—lost their lives in 1906 when a hurricane destroyed whole sections of the completed embankments. Conch survivors of that storm tell the tale of lashing themselves to palm trees and, during the lull when the men began to move about freely, shouting, "Go back, go back." It was no use. Nobody knew what a hurricane was in that mob of men. They were blown into the sea and for weeks survivors kept turning up in ports as far away as Liverpool after having been picked up at sea. The figures are not exactly known but run to nearly two hundred dead. Human toll for progress.

It would take more than seven years and much sweat and more loss of life but the FEC would lay that railroad.

The *Metropolis* had grown to be an eight-page daily and was receiving competition from first the Miami *Record*, an evening daily begun by Judge Frank B. Stoneman and A. L. La Salle, and then the Miami *News*. The two papers merged and later became the Miami *Herald*, with a lawyer named Frank B. Shutts buying in.

The *Metropolis*, which had been highly criticized as being "a railroad organ" at its origin (it was named by Henry Flagler), came under the editorship of S. Bobo Dean in 1905 and took on new life as a railroad-fighting, crusading newspaper. Dean, an able newspaperman, never compromised and it was always a fight to the finish. He got himself into some narrow places as a result. As editor of the Lake Worth *News* Dean had supported Flagler even unto the famous divorce law which the magnate had pushed through the Florida legislature as a means of freeing himself from his second wife, who was incurably insane. Flagler changed his residence from New York to Florida, and the bill permitting divorce by one marriage partner if the other were proven insane went through the Senate and the House in little more than two weeks. The Flagler divorce was also rushed through in record-breaking time: forty-eight hours. A week later, the magnate announced his engagement to Mary Lily Kenan, with whom he had been associated for a decade.

All this was aired and commented on unfavorably in many Florida newspapers. Dean stuck with Flagler through that, but from the moment he took over the *Metropolis* he fought the railroad tooth and nail.

First on the agenda and in the people's minds was the matter of freight rates. As early as 1901 Lemon City growers protested that they paid fifty thousand dollars for freight and didn't even have a station agent. Deliveries were thrown from the freight cars at the owner's risk and claims for damages went unrecognized. It was not until 1908 that a group of livid growers formed the East Coast Fruit and Vegetable Growers Association to protect themselves. T. V. Moore of Miami, known as "The Pineapple King," took a leading role in the fight. Miami pineapples, then a leading industry, reached the market weeks after the Cuban pineapples, which was a natural drawback. On top of that, the railroad was giving preferred rates to Cuba in connection with a rate war which broke out between the FEC and the steamship lines plying between Mobile and Havana. To prove that Cuban rates were cheaper Moore shipped a consignment of pineapples to Cuba and then had them shipped out.

The farmers of Dade County demanded that the railroad adjust its rate and give them "an equal rate with Cuba over the same railroad line through the same territory to the same destination." When the burning question reached the Interstate Commerce Commission in 1910 it became part of a statewide investigation which had been under way and resulted in the lowering of the rates.

This success was taken by the pro-railroad faction that had always been in the ascendancy in Miami as a slap against their benefactor, Henry Flagler. A letter was drafted to Flagler expressing regret and disapproval of the stand taken by the *Metropolis*. Perhaps as a threat, or merely in the hope he would discontinue his fight against the railroad, they took the letter to Dean (whom they privately called the "Bobonic Plague") before mailing it. Dean managed to lock it in his safe and the next morning *Metropolis* readers were treated to a front-page disclosure of ". . . a highhanded effort to muzzle a metropolis by appealing to the businessmen of the community . . . There will be no change in the policy of the paper in any manner whatsoever."

The merchants, furious at being exposed down to their middle initials, withdrew their advertising. The farmers and the people living in outlying districts responded by threatening to boycott every merchant who had signed the petition. Meanwhile, the advertising columns consisted mostly of invitations to buy Everglades land. In the end, Dean won the fight.

Miss Hattie Carpenter, who was having a fight of her own with the school board, which was making changes that threatened the accreditation she had won for her high school, up and quit as principal and joined the fighting *Metropolis* as editorial writer.

The fight went on between the *Herald* and the *Metropolis* and when other steamy controversy was absent Frank Shutts objected to Dean keeping a cow. The Deans had moved into the land on the south bank of the river when the Brickells opened it up. Then it had been country, but now, no doubt about it, the town was growing up. There were such things as city restrictions. Sorrowfully, Dean led Daisy, the cow, draped in black crepe to the horns, slowly by the *Herald* office.

The Last of the
Frontier Sheriffs

CARRIE NATION CAME TO THE WICKED CITY OF MIAMI to expose the ungodliness. Despite the gentle family life, the parades, the rocking on the porches, the trips to Seybold's ice cream parlor—the ungodliness was there, a few blocks away, ready to spring. In a dramatic denunciation from the platform in a big tent set up by the W.C.T.U., Carrie lifted a bottle of whiskey from the folds of her dress. Miami, she thundered, was not the dry city it professed to be. Carrie was right.

The sailors who docked in Miami said that Hell's Kitchen could not compare with North Miami. Saloons were open around the clock. Roulette wheels ran in the middle of Miami Avenue. Opium dens flourished. Chinese, blacks, and whites lived together in an atmosphere in which violence bubbled always beneath the surface. Three reported killings a night were about average. Ministers, churchmen, citizens, kept saying that something must be done.

A young man named Dan Hardie stepped into the arena to announce himself as candidate for sheriff of Dade County. A man whose zest for life was equal to his love of danger, he first came to Miami before the town stirred. Where the Everglades Hotel now stands he built a palmetto hut and over the door he printed a sign, "Waldorf Astoria." He fished and sailed and reveled in the loneliness and serenity. It was, he often said later, a good place to dream. He was exactly seventeen and his dreams involved finding out everything there was to find out about life and to prove how tough he was. He had adopted the motto: "Never Quit."

At home in St. Louis, his family had been patient when he found grade school too tame and enrolled him in a business school. There he developed such speed at the Pittman method of shorthand and became so adept at handling typewriters, he could take them apart and put them together again. The leading newspaper devoted half a column to this remarkable boy.

Dan told his mother life was too tame and he couldn't breathe. He said he had to go out and see the world. When he left home at fourteen his mother made him promise that he would never drink. He was glad to make the promise and to keep it. Out of a generous heart he threw in another promise. He said he wouldn't smoke either. He never did.

He traveled in Indian country, wandered about Mexico, and was on his way to Africa when a man told him the toughest people in the world lived at Fort Pierce, Florida. He headed there without hesitation, later drifting to Miami. He helped cut down the pines on Flagler Street, helped paint the Royal Palm Hotel, and lost no time in joining up for the Spanish-American War. In Cuba serving with the First Texas Volunteers, he encountered a Zouave company and was completely bowled over by their maneuvers and brilliant Oriental uniforms. By the end of the war he had mastered their bag of tricks and worked out fifty variations of his own.

Little boys always followed broad-shouldered Dan Hardie around, and he began to drill a small group. Ultimately, he organized a full-fledged company of Zouaves made up of boys from six to fourteen. The boys would have done anything to get into the Zouaves and all unwaveringly accepted the restrictions. You had to look Dan Hardie straight in the eye at all times and you had to promise that you wouldn't smoke until you were twenty-one. This Roddey Burdine and the others were more than glad to do.

On Thursday nights Hardie spread Japanese mats down the middle of Flagler Street and drilled his company. The drills brought out the town. Little girls who were sent to bed cried to go sit on the steps of the First National Bank and watch. Families came riding in carriages to cheer. The Zouaves became so efficient that Dan sent away and ordered Turkish costumes for them. In costume they became so outstanding that B. F. Keith, who wintered in a bayfront house, enthusiastically offered them a spot on his vaudeville circuit, an offer regretfully refused by all hands.

Dan Hardie organized the Fire Department band (although he couldn't play a note of anything). He added a new wrinkle to his Thursday night shows—a dash by the horse-drawn fire department down Flagler Street bent each week on breaking its previous record for speed. These "fire drills" were discontinued after more timorous citizens petitioned against them. They said "somebody was surely going to get killed some Thursday night."

The men asked Dan Hardie to be their first fire chief. He agreed, providing "not one drop of liquor was ever touched by a man in uniform." This was a hard go because traditionally every fire called for a barrel of beer. There was even a committee of citizens known as the First Aid Committee whose sole function was to see that the barrel arrived soon after the fire horses. Grumbling, the men agreed.

Dan accepted the post, and the first thing he did after becoming chief was send away for uniforms, spanking, all-white uniforms. Next, he saw that the first steam pumper was purchased, a second-size American La France, and the men named it the "Dan Hardie."

When improvements were being made in the fire department, members of the City Council posed questions that sent the fire fighters into guffaws. One member asked what they would do with the hose wagon now that they had a pump. Another wanted to know why they wanted hot water instead of cold. He assumed that the "boiler" was used to warm the water before putting out the fire.

Hardie was a natural-born showman and his best show was about to come. In 1908 he ran for sheriff and won. That was his real role, sheriff of Dade County—the last of the frontier sheriffs, a man who was tough but who never failed to help a down-and-outer and who always offered a prostitute "a ticket home to Mother if she'd go." Often he took the law into his own hands, but he did what he campaigned for: he cleaned out North Miami.

The campaign established him as a spellbinder and he did not hesitate to point into the crowd and name names. At a blistering Flagler Street rally, a leading churchman, who had been actively campaigning for "a clean-up," was exposed in this forthright fashion as the hidden owner of a house of prostitution.

Dan Hardie carried a .38 special weekdays and a .32 on Sundays, and he let it be known that "in six weeks time I am going to raid North Miami and clean out the whole rats' nest." One by one the gamblers and honky-tonk owners began slipping in to see Hardie to say they were "settling their affairs and leaving town." Hardie kept his promise. He cleaned out North Miami and the people gave it a name: Hardieville.

With his pump gun he sloshed through saw grass in the Everglades to find a criminal in hiding. He had always had a reputation as a fighter. Now he earned one as a hero. He played the role to the hilt. One thing the people could be sure of—Dan Hardie was scrupulously honest and he meant war against the criminal.

When Hardie became sheriff, the Rice gang was ransacking the countryside, robbing, killing, and spreading terror. If the Rice gang settled in a town, the good people had to move out. The ringleaders were Leland and Frank Rice, Hugh Alderman, and a man named Jim Tucker.

Tucker was a large man, dreaded as a fighter and quick to use his shotgun. One night Hardie got word that Tucker was eating in a North Miami restaurant and went there to arrest him. The dingy restaurant, the crafty-eyed Tucker sitting at a table with his eye on the door, were strictly cinematic. Hardie walked up to Tucker and told him he was wanted for robbing a bank.

"Who be you?" drawled Tucker.

"I am the sheriff of Dade County," Dan told him, coming closer.

"Wal, I don't reckon I'll go to jail today," said Tucker.

Hardie reached forward with the handcuffs and Tucker rose slowly. Dan used his fists first, next his gun, and paraded Tucker to the jailhouse. He admitted to a New York *Times* reporter that he didn't relax his watch until authorities removed Tucker to a North Florida jail. The Rice gang thought nothing of coming in and taking members from behind bars.

Hardie cleaned up the Rice gang, but in their stead came the Ashleys, who as youngsters had been followers of the Rice men. Like Jesse James, who robbed at will and then retired into the Western wilderness, the Ashley mob roamed wild, withdrawing into the Everglades where they hunted and shot plume birds and grew vegetables if they had a mind to. "Meet me in the 'Glades," was their insolent reply to officers of the law.

The time hadn't come yet, but Dan Hardie would dog the Ashleys through the saw grass, living off the Everglades country for twenty-one days and nights. His deputy would be killed but he would return with John Ashley. Bob Ashley, attempting to liberate John from the Miami jail, would be killed.

John would later escape from a North Florida jail. It would be some time before the Ashley gang was wiped out.

One Sabbath at noon Sheriff Hardie raided the Spanish Club, which was going strong at that hour. After turning over drunks and toughs to the city police, Hardie went up the back stairs and uncovered a nice little gambling setup, shades drawn, electric fans whirring away, and a shaded electric light installed over a roulette table. The pity of it was a number of young men of "good family" were trying their hand at the wheel and the *Metropolis* announced it was withholding their names to "spare their friends the humiliation of the publicity." The sheriff brought a dray to cart away the gambling equipment and churchgoers received a bit of excitement that morning. Traditionally, the city police department always acted surprised when Hardie uncovered lawlessness.

For eight years, the phone at the Hardie house rang day and night. Mrs. Hardie would hand Dan his gun before answering the phone.

"That will be 'Self-defense' calling," she would tell him.

"Judge" Worley, who had a reputation for beating murder raps, would throw his hands to the ceiling and cry, "Tear down this temple of justice on my head," with the old vigor. Dan Hardie would bring in the criminals.

Progress, Duly Noted

M IAMI WAS FIFTEEN YEARS OLD and celebrated with a burst of oratory and back-slapping. The Duke of Dade, a moody spectator, was asked to say a few words.

"As Virgil said, 'Events which I myself saw, and in which I was myself a chief participator,' and as Tennyson makes Ulysses say, 'Myself, not least, but honored of them all.'"

Not all in the crowd that responded with uneasy laughter had heard the words before. Mr. Ewan was noted for his eccentricities, and half of what he said was intended to be funny.

When he said, "I would like to see the cupola on the court house sold to the highest bidder for thirty cents," they laughed. When he added, "It is a great detriment; it is of no earthly use," they weren't sure he meant it to be funny. (*He was a queer duck, lived in these parts before there was even a town.*)

The people were proud of their courthouse: cupola, pillars, and all. Flagler had donated the land for it and the edifice was a far cry from the two pool tables shoved together to constitute office furniture, "the one page of a jail register," and the wooden jail moved down from Juno on a lighter when Miami won back the county seat in 1899. (There had been a lone prisoner staring out through bars as the jail floated in.)

John Frohock "shook the fringed top off his surrey" before he reached Cutler, getting signatures of out-of-the-way settlers in an effort to bring about that election. The roads were still no more than cart paths in those days. John Sewell registered his Black Artillery and Miami was also accused of voting "Bahamians and dead men."

It was all laughable now, twelve years later, but there had been nothing funny about it at the time. Interest had run at fever pitch, and J. E. Lummus had to be restrained from taking a swing at the unsmiling sheriff who came down from Palm Beach to take his post at the voting place and who was charged with "trying to intimidate the voters."

Miami rewon the county seat. She had a right to it as time had since illustrated. On her fifteenth birthday Miami had seven hundred and eighty-two white children in her schools and two hundred and eighty-two black, more than half the enrollment of the county. Furthermore, she had the promise of the new Central School of steel and cement construction which architect Walter C. De Garmo had designed, with kindergarten and first-grade classrooms on the ground floor "to relieve the little ones of any tiresome climbing."

The city fire department was as good as "any in the South" with fifty-five thousand dollars' worth of equipment, including a fifteen-thousand-dollar central station, seven "full-paid men at the station," and twenty volunteers. Henry Chase was the fire chief, "the youngest chief in the U.S.A." Once he had watched the raw new city of Miami burn to the ground on Christmas morning for lack of equipment.

Dan Hardie and Chase ran the first "trackless trolley" as far north as Buena Vista and south to Fifteenth Road and were successful until the Tatem brothers came along to ask the people for a franchise for an electric system. The Tatems got it.

The first horseless carriages appeared on the streets, and Mayor Lummus made a test run in one to see what rate of speed should be adopted. He decided on eight miles an hour on curves, ten on a straight road. Count d'Hedouville bought an automobile but spent all his time underneath tinkering with repairs.

When Howard Gill arrived to fly his Wright byplane in the skies of the celebrating city, the Miami *Herald* said in awe: "In 1896 there was not even a sewing machine in Miami." They were wrong. Old Man Brickell had sold sewing machines to the Seminole women. In Miami everything began with the railroad, and now it was assumed there was no history before its coming.

Miami had survived the financial panic of 1907, due, in part, to the help the Brickells gave their townsmen in this crisis. Miss Edith, who took care of much of the family business, went about carrying a large satchel-like purse, lending money and paying off obligations in bills as high as one thousand dollars. Miamians had reason to be grateful for the Brickells' eccentric distrust of banks during that period.

A year later, William Brickell was dead from injuries received in a fall from the broad white steps of the veranda he loved so well. He had hoped to live until ninety, but had not made it. Another of his wishes was carried out. He was buried in the garden near the oleanders.

Brickell did not live to see the dynamiting of the rapids of the Miami River as part of the drainage canal program. It made the passage smooth for boats market-bound, but the clear waters of the river were turning muddy as the rock ledges which held back the salt of the sea were shattered. It was no longer possible to dip a tin cup in the Miami and drink, but men were getting from five to seven hundred crates of tomatoes an acre and were boasting that the January crop of Dade County beans "went to every state in the Union." The drainage of the Everglades was bringing people from all over, people bent on getting in on a good thing, "The Everglades: Empire of the Sun."

In a spirit of recklessness, draining went on. All over the country, people in the same mood bought Everglades land sight unseen. Defending itself against criticism in a fifteenth anniversary issue in the Miami *Herald*, the Everglades Land Sales Company declared: "Since October 1, 1909, when the Miami office opened, one thousand people have come to the Magic City to investigate their proposition. Out of all these hundreds only two per cent were displeased with their purchase." In the light of cold fact this was a conservative estimate, but it hit the note Miami liked to hear.

During all this real estate excitement, Mrs. Kirk Munroe made news in the interest of conservation of this vast and little-understood water-land. One day on Flagler Street, while bystanders gasped, she snatched an egret from a lady's hat.

Mary Barr Munroe was aroused to the point of fury over the death of Guy Bradley, the young violin-playing Audubon warden who gave his life while protecting Cuthbert rookery from plume hunters. Her husband, who was vice-president of the Florida Audubon Society, had recommended young Bradley for the job.

The egret plumes, which back in the era of the bay had brought a dollar

89

and a quarter at Brickell's trading post, were worth much more than that in New York when Bradley, now called "a martyr to millinery," was killed. Egrets had been shot nearly to extinction and other Everglades birds were in danger of this mass murdering to provide feathers for women's hats from Maine to California.

The little coterie of conservationists in Coconut Grove banded into their own Audubon society to push their message, and pretty Mrs. E. A. Waddell, whose husband built the first concrete house in Miami, was invited to the organizational meeting. No one had informed her of the nature of the meeting but luckily she heard soon enough to remove her own feathered hat and hide it in the folds of her skirt.

In a birthday declaration, the city's first mayor, John B. Reilly, said boldly, "There is perhaps nothing in the way of municipal improvements that Miami needs except the extension of paving sidewalks and sewers to the suburban areas."

Certainly much had been accomplished, not the least being the creation of Government Cut, which for six years now had connected the Atlantic Ocean and the bay, forming a navigable channel into Miami. By an appropriation ordered by the Rivers and Harbors Committee of the United States Congress, giant dredges had cut a slice through the Miami Beach peninsula, and Mayor John Sewell had proclaimed a holiday the day the dredge was due to complete the work.

It was odd how often the unorthodox occurred in Miami. That day the dredge broke down within a few feet of completion. While the entire citizenry of thirty-five hundred lined the channel banks waiting for the historic moment, Sewell tore off his coat and necktie, picked up a shovel, and made the dirt fly. In thirty minutes, while the people cheered, Sewell saw the first trickle of water from the Atlantic mingle with the waters of Biscayne Bay.

By the next morning there was a free flow between the ocean and the channel and the cry was, "Watch the port of Miami."

Too bad Julia Tuttle couldn't see her city now. The rambling and beautiful Halcyon Hotel designed by Stanford White brought men like Henry Watterson and James Whitcomb Riley to Miami, men whose presence at a dinner party assured good conversation.

Substantial homes, sidewalks, well-tended lawns, lent a prosperous air to the city, and the tax assessor's property value for 1911 backed this impression to the pleasant round reality of one million six hundred fifty-six thousand nine hundred seventy-five dollars. Miami in 1911 was the city Julia Tuttle dreamed back in the era of the bay.

It was a city of churches, with a functioning women's club that began life at the turn of the century as the Married Woman's Afternoon Club and that established the town's first library. On land given by Flagler, members were now calmly preparing to raise ten thousand dollars to erect a clubhouse.

William K. Vanderbilt was a regular winter visitor, Gifford Pinchot declared a trip to Miami was "a new lease on life," and Philander C. Knox was quick to call the Magic City "the peer of any winter resort in the world." All this was music to the ears of Miamians.

When the Duke of Manchester was sued by a Palm Beach photographer for nonpayment of a bill, Sheriff Hardie handled the entire affair with such diplomacy, dexterity, and delicacy that not a word of it reached the outside world. The sheriff advised the duke to "pay the bill and avoid publicity." The duke said he would and offered the sheriff a cigar which the sheriff couldn't use, not being a smoking man. He took it anyway.

Percy Caville taught the Australian crawl at the Royal Palm swimming pool, and lawn tennis was an interesting diversion at the Biscayne Hotel. The town had the Gertie Reynolds Theater for live plays and no longer needed to depend on "Budge's Opera House" for home-talent shows. The Alcazar motion picture theater possessed a home-grown version of air-conditioning consisting of cakes of ice placed under the floor and played upon by electric fans. Henry Chase opened a movie house and called it The Elite. (It was generally pronounced E-light.)

Under layers of small-town respectability the independent spirit still burned in the breasts of the bay people. The captain of the *Lady Lou* refused to leave the Miami docks bound for Miami Beach and Smith's Casino until he had at least six passengers. A visitor to the Halcyon made the trip daily with his daughter, who had been sent south by her physician for "ocean baths." Weary of waiting one day, the gentleman offered to pay the six fares.

The captain was outraged. "No sir," he said. "It's not the *money* I want. It's the *people*."

2 | Dream On!
1911–1926

The Birth of Miami Beach

CHARLES H. LUM, who was a fifteen-year-old lad when he first visited the dangling peninsula that would be Miami Beach, came back in his early thirties, bringing his bride to live in the lonely spot between the sea and the bay. That first trip with his father, Henry, who had then caught the coconut-planting notion and passed it along to Osborn and Field, had been something Charles never forgot, and in 1886 he built a home overlooking the sweeping Atlantic. Except for the House of Refuge and a few fisherman's shacks, there was no other building on the stretch of mangrove and sand. Dick Carney had unbolted the portable house left by the unsuccessful coconut planters and removed it to Coconut Grove.

Charles Lum built a two-story house with a porch while his bride learned to make omelets of turtle eggs and stews of the oysters that filled Indian Creek. The Lums gardened, raising Lima beans, tomatoes, beets, and celery, and made good use of the wild fruits.

When the railroad excitement hit Miami, Lum and his bride sailed across the bay to share in it. For weeks they stayed at the rooming house run by Mrs. Ed Chase. When the bill had run up to eighty dollars, Lum asked Mrs. Chase if she would consider taking ten acres of Miami Beach land instead of cash.

"Land sakes," Mrs. Chase said crossly. "What in the world would I do with all that swampland?"

Others were not so disparaging of the land, although that was distinctly the prevailing opinion. But a man named John S. Collins had invested five thousand dollars in the Field and Osborn expedition and when the venture failed paid a visit to see the kind of land he'd bought. He arrived just before the railroad and he liked what he saw. He bought out Osborn and made Field a partner in the business of raising avocados, known in those days as alligator pears. Field showed a preference for raising grapefruit, and in the end, Collins bought him out, becoming the sole owner of one thousand, six hundred and seventy acres of ocean front, comprising nearly five miles on the Atlantic and another mile along Biscayne Bay.

Collins has been depicted as a "gentle Quaker." His family unanimously hooted down this idea. John Collins, they recalled after his death, was a small man, but a he-man, full of energy and will and impatience. He was past seventy when he decided to build a wooden bridge across Biscayne Bay to connect the beach land with Miami.

There was plenty of opposition to the idea. First the owners of the *Lady Lou* and the *Sally* rebelled vociferously against the preposterous idea, which would "strip them of their business." Collins was refused a franchise by the Dade County commission.

Collins took an automobile down to the Miami dock of the *Lady Lou* one bright morning and demanded to be taken across the water to his land. He knew full well neither the *Lady Lou* nor the *Sally* were built to carry cars. He made his point and the permit to start bridge-building was reluctantly granted.

Collins' three sons and two daughters back in New Jersey had no little bit to say about the bridge-building. Their father had made and lost several fortunes and they had no intention of permitting him to dissipate any remaining money in his last declining days. Collins had established a nursery in Moorestown and acquired a farm in Merchantville where he raised Wilson blackberries with huge success, and he then went on to founding a farm-machinery business which his son Irving was running in New Jersey. When John Collins began building a canal (without the assistance of an engineer) and talked of building a bridge, a family council was held. His daughter Katherine and her husband, Thomas J. Pancoast, were tapped to go down to check on father's activites under the coconuts.

Contrary to the prevailing belief, Collins—and later Pancoast—had real estate, not avocados, on their minds when they started to build that bridge. John Collins did build a windbreak of Australian pines that would later give the name to one of the finest of Miami Beach streets, Pine Tree Drive, and planted Red Bliss potatoes and Cavendish bananas along with the avocados in his grove near where Forty-first Street is now. Miami was beginning to grow. The bridge, both Collins and Pancoast agreed, would open up their real estate to tourists.

One hundred thousand dollars from the Collins coffers went to the bottom of Biscayne Bay in the form of pilings, yet the bridge was still unfinished. This was the situation when Carl Graham Fisher, aged forty and possessor of a solid fortune gleaned in Prestolite, the trade name for carbide gas headlights for automobiles, arrived on the scene.

The coming of Carl Fisher was comparable to a cataclysm of nature. He has been called the Aladdin who rubbed the lamp. The late Will Rogers dubbed him "the midwife of Florida." It is certain that his coming changed the face of that dangling peninsula forevermore. He lent Collins the money he needed to complete the bridge and then became so imbued with the idea of building a city that he drove himself to perform miracles. His insistent need to "get it done now, not tomorrow," coupled with a genius for publicizing his ideas and backed by his own millions and the millions of his friends, drew a new map for South Florida.

Carl Fisher began his business life at thirteen hawking magazines and candy on trains, advanced into bicycle racing with Barney Oldfield, started a bicycle shop, pioneered with automobiles both as racer and salesman, and "retired" at forty with the Prestolite fortune. All this he had accomplished with the handicap of faulty vision.

By mail he purchased a house on Brickell Avenue which he and his young wife called The Shadows. It was inconceivable to his friends that the dynamic, restless Fisher would be long content with a quiet life, but he insisted that aside from his pet Indianapolis Speedway, which he had promoted and built and now owned, he was through with promotions. Before he was finished with this latest promotion his best friends were worriedly telling each other that "the Skipper should be put away for his own good."

Fisher's first sight of John Collins delighted him. He said later, "That man is like a bantam rooster, cocky and unafraid." In his speedboat, Fisher tore up the Collins Canal to pay a visit. John Levi, who accompanied him, waited on the way back while Fisher strode about in the sand at about where Twenty-third Street is now.

Perhaps that is the moment Fisher began to have visions. He stood on the spot where he would later build his popular Roman Pools and remarked that the view from that point was unsurpassed. He strolled over to where the Roney Plaza Hotel would one day stand and appeared lost in thought.

For many years a sign erected by Fisher would occoupy that spot, saying: "If anyone will build on this site a modern tourist hotel costing two hundred thousand dollars we will give them this entire block of land." It was a big joke to Miamians who thought up a new saying: "The climate is balmy and so is Fisher."

Collins offered the City of Miami acreage for a public ocean-front park provided Miami would fill it in. The city turned it down. Today that land, which constitutes Collins Park, is worth millions of dollars and in the center of it stands the Miami Beach Public Library, a branch of the Miami-Dade Public Library which encompasses twenty-nine libraries in its system.

There were a few Miamians who saw a future in Miami Beach, among them the Lummus brothers, J. E. and J. N.

J. E., as president of the Bank of Bay Biscayne, had lent Collins fifteen thousand dollars for his bridge. J. N., as president of the Southern Bank and Trust Company, had advanced ten thousand. The pair decided to buy up the south end of the beach and begin a developing program. They called it Ocean Beach and it consisted of six hundred and five acres of swamp land from Lincoln Road south. They paid from one hundred and fifty dollars to as high as twelve thousand, five hundred for one acre which they needed in order to lay out streets.

Workmen in the process of clearing Ocean Beach killed seventeen rattlesnakes, hundreds of raccoons, "rats by the thousands." J. N. advertised for cats and got them in bags. They cleaned out the rats. With his son Tom and their dog Black Joe, he hunted 'coons. Of the land J. N., said, "When I use the word swamp I mean swamp and mangrove trees so thick a man could not get through without an ax to cut his way."

Fisher, who had taken two hundred acres of land as part of the loan of fifty thousand dollars to Collins for completion of the bridge, met the Lummus brothers and asked them why they didn't move forward more rapidly with their development. When they said "lack of money" he lent them one hundred and fifty thousand dollars which they agreed to pay back at eight per cent interest. They also gave him one hundred and five acres of swamp land from Lincoln Road south to Fifteenth Street "as a bonus." J. N. says, "We had paid one hundred and fifty dollars an acre for that land. That and that alone is what started Miami Beach in a big way."

Fisher called his development Alton Beach and Collins gave the name Miami Beach Improvement Company to his. With the Lummus development known as Ocean Beach, there were three developments in the beginning, all of which were later thrown together under the name Miami Beach.

The Collins Bridge was opened on June 12, 1913, and a parade of automobiles, horse-drawn carriages, bicycles, and baby carts moved over the rattling boards, many of which had not yet been nailed down. Nobody stayed at home. It was an event comparable to the puffing in of the first railroad train seventeen years earlier. When the parade got as far as Bull Island (Fisher had not yet changed the name to Belle) it turned around and came back since the bridge ended at that point. Nevertheless it was quite a ceremony and Mayor J. W. Watson of Miami solemnly declared, "No more novel ride can be offered anywhere than this auto trip over the sea, no less interesting than the trip by rail over the FEC extension to Key West." These were powerfully enthusiastic words, since the completion of Flagler's railroad to Key West on January 22, 1912, had been hailed throughout the nation as the achievement of mammoth proportions that it was.

A three-day celebration was held at Key West with a full-scale circus brought over from Havana for the event, the staging of a Spanish opera, and an elaborate ball with five bands supplying constant music. Flagler, who arrived on a private train with dignitaries from the committees on both Naval and Military Affairs of the United States Congress as well as the Rivers and Harbors group in tow, heard the toots of boat whistles, received a gold-medallion likeness of himself, was escorted to the presentation by the Cuban National Band, United States soldiers and sailors, and a troop of shining-faced Boy Scouts. As a final fillip, one thousand school children strewed American Beauty roses in his path. It must have been a rewarding day for the multimillionaire. It was the day Flagler got his innings, pleasant innings for an accomplishment men said was impossible.

He was absent from the ceremonies in connection with the opening of the Collins Bridge. Flagler died one month before the bridge opened, aged eighty-two. A special funeral train carried his body to St. Augustine where it was laid to rest, and during the funeral service "every wheel of the Florida East Coast Railway remained motionless for a period of ten minutes in silent tribute to its great builder."

Carl Fisher was also absent from the bridge-opening ceremonies, making ready at that moment to leave on the first cross-continent automobile tour with the Trial Blazers, a trek that would result in the creation of the Lincoln Highway, another of his brain babies and named by him for the man he most admired: Abraham Lincoln. It is said that when Fisher first observed the Collins Bridge in the process of being erected he asked, "Where does it *go?*"

His active mind soon gave him the answer and now even as he was drumming up the tying of East and West with the Lincoln Highway, he was planning the Dixie Highway to connect North and South. He would bring the Dixie Highway to the Collins Bridge.

While he was out West trail-blazing, John Levi, who was responsible for Fisher's coming to Miami in the first place, began to supervise the clearing of the land for him. Once more, black men picked up machetes and slashed out at palmetto, replacing the machete with the ax in dense mangrove. It was summertime, the time of mosquitoes and sand flies and killing sun. Mules were brought in to tug at stubborn palmetto and mangrove roots.

Fisher and the Lummuses signed a contract with a Baltimore dredging company "to move six million cubic yards of material out of the bay side of the beach and make a motor boat race course at the same time." The Lummus brothers put up three hundred and fifteen thousand dollars while Fisher's share of the expenses was two hundred and eighty-five thousand dollars.

Now dredges began their slow parade across the bay and began their day-long and eventually night-long work of sand-sucking, pumping up the sand from the bay bottom to spread it out over the jungle which was gradually being entirely denuded of growth. In the heat of August, Fisher was back to supervise the work. The man who liked to see things accomplished "now" found dredges breaking down and even the mules suffering from insects. He studied the movement of sand flies under a microscope; he got right down with the men, talked to them, tugged in an agony of frustration at the roots of palmettos with his bare hands.

A warm man, Fisher had the ability to gain wholehearted support from the people who worked for him. He was stocky, with a barrel-like figure, but hard and muscular, and his hands were strong and large. He liked expensive clothes and floppy felt hats but seldom wore evening dress. He had his shoes made to order. (Without laces, they were actually the forerunner of the loafer-type shoe which one day would walk all over Miami Beach.) To read, he would push back his horn-rimmed glasses on his forehead and bring his eyes close down to the print before him. He was never known by any of his associates to deal in anything approximating dishonesty.

Fisher licked the palmetto roots by importing a powerful machete plow, made to order for the job and shipped south from Indianapolis. It accomplished what human hands could not. The dredges pumped away for more than a year and before their work was finished Fisher found that instead of spending the sum earmarked for the work, he had spent millions—just in creating the land. There was a period when this sand-sucking operation cost more than fifty thousand dollars a day.

When the work was done and they spread the sand, shining white under the sun, over his land, there was no vegetation visible but the coconuts planted by the Field and Osborn expedition at the rim of the ocean. It was time to think about immediate planting. Otherwise, the hard-bought grains from the bay bottom might blow away. No expense was spared as brilliant red hibiscus and pink and white oleander were ordered brought in, to rest on earth from the Everglades which had been carted across the bay on barges. Black men, women, and children, crouching in lines, planted the grass by hand, sprig by sprig. Bougainvillaea in shades of cerise and purple were planted even before the grass took root. In a matter of months, the jungle had become a cultivated garden spot.

There was something shocking to the people of Miami in the creation of this ocean-front paradise. The shocking aspect lay in the illogic of making more land in country with undeveloped land lying all about. The smooth green grass, the yellow allamanda vines, the brilliant hibiscus were pleasing to the eye—but were they real? The whole eye-blinking paradise was nothing but a mirage to the people of Miami. They did not see what Carl Fisher saw when he looked at the land. He saw an American Riviera.

All the machinery with which man builds a modern city was marched across the wooden Collins Bridge as Fisher declared himself ready to lay out streets and construct hotels and homes for his city. To distribute building material he constructed a narrow-gauge, mile-long miniature railroad and sent passes to all the important railroad presidents in the U.S.A. to come ride on it. This caused a flurry of amusement in leading newspapers and publicized Miami Beach. To assist in the clearing and building, he engaged the services of two elephants, named Carl and Rosie, who became colorful fixtures in early Miami Beach Life.

Rosie particularly was adored by the children. Fisher had a gayly painted cart designed for her to haul the young about the beach. A black man named Yarnell was the proud keeper of the elephant, and any child who was having a birthday had merely to whisper this happy fact into Yarnell's ear and he would be on hand to provide transportation and entertainment for birthday child and guests.

Fisher built his home, a glass-enclosed tennis court, an office building, and began work on the Lincoln Hotel before the land was completely cleared. Next, he constructed cottages for his staff, the head painter, engineer, gardener, and so on, all of whom came with him from Indianapolis.

In 1915 when Miami Beach was incorporated, the Beach had three hundred residents, but only thirty-three registered voters. Fisher offered free lots to anyone who would build a home and settle on his land. There was no rush to accept this offer. The people stared at Fisher's creation, but refused to accept what their eyes told them.

They understood better the big casino Sheriff Hardie built on the Lummus land. It was a two-deck affair flying the flags of all nations, with Old Glory in the central place of honor. Upstairs there was dancing in the windswept ballroom. Downstairs were locker rooms where you could rent bathing suits for a quarter. Families liked to spend all day Sunday at Hardie's Casino, bringing elaborate picnic lunches that they spread out on the long benches overlooking the ocean. Clergymen and their families were on the cuff always. It was one of Hardie's inflexible rules in the operation of his casino.

Sometimes during those days when he was struggling to establish his dream city, Carl Fisher rolled his white Packard over the Collins Bridge and paid the sheriff a visit. They had much in common, these two. Both were men of integrity, intensely human and driven by a need to perform.

Fisher, persisting in his dream of creating a resort city in the face of what seemed like failure, told Hardie one day, "When you've got a bull by the tail, you can't let go."

One afternoon the sheriff asked Fisher if he would put up five hundred dollars to bring a carnival to the beach.

Fisher said mildly, "Dan, I'll give you five hundred to keep it away."

Both Collins and the Lummuses resorted to the talents of Edward E. (Doc) Dammers to sell their land, and, in fact, Doc had sold land for Collins even before the bridge went in. He had a spiel that admittedly would "sell ice skates to a South Sea Islander." When that failed or the attention of the audience strayed, he reached back into a wagon and brought out fascinating pieces of crockery, silver plate, and whatnots and gave them away by drawing numbers. The people flocked to "get something for nothing," and in flocking purchased a number of lots.

Fisher, spending millions on developing his part of the beach, refused to use these "cheap" methods. He guaranteed sidewalks, sewers, and schools with his land. There were still no takers.

He decided to reverse himself. Instead of offering free land he would raise his prices. He would make it fashionable to flock to the land of trade winds and sunshine. He started a streetcar system to Miami. Rosie, the elephant, stuck her head inside a trolley one day, so terrifying a passenger that he jumped through a window and broke a leg. He promptly sued the wealthy Mr. Fisher for fifty thousand dollars.

One evening, Fisher was walking about the beach when he came upon an old Conch tugging at a bathtub in an attempt to lift it into his wagon. It was a piece of equipment for the Lincoln Hotel. Fisher asked what the fellow was up to and the latter explained in no uncertain terms he was spreading the wealth of the world a bit more evenly. "No one's got a right to be as rich as that danged Fisher," he said.

Fisher gave him a hand with the bathtub and watched him cart it away.

It was Fisher who built a monument to Henry Flagler. An illuminated square white shaft, it lies on Bay Island and is visible to travelers who cross the central causeways connecting Miami and Miami Beach. At the corners of the base are symbolic figures which represent Pioneering, Engineering, Industrialism, and Prosperity.

City on Paper

DREAMING UP CITIES WAS CATCHING. Young George Edgar Merrick, who had first come to the bay country as a boy of twelve along with his clergyman-father, Solomon, began to put his plans for a city on paper. Out at the family orange grove "in the sticks" he sat up nights sketching the elaborate city hall and walled entrances of his dream city. No ordinary city this, it was to be a "City Beautiful" as well as "a place where castles in Spain are made real."

George Merrick had docked at Peacock Inn in 1899 with his father when they were seeking to establish a family. Had it not been for the raging blizzard that hit New England in the winter of 1895, it appears unlikely that the Reverend Merrick, who had trained at the Yale Divinity School and was well-launched in his ministry in the Congregational Church in Duxbury, Massachusetts, would ever have made such a leap into the wilderness world of south Florida.

The flu epidemic accompanying that bitter blizzard claimed many lives and among them was the Merrick daughter, Ruth, Helen's twin and George's baby sister. The Reverend Mr. Merrick turned his sights toward a milder climate in which to raise his family.

George wrote later: ". . . my father definitely embarked on an undertaking, which in connection with all his circumstances, traditions, previous living and environment, called for the same courage, steadfastness of purpose and will power as fired Columbus on his adventure from Palos into the Great Unknown."

Solomon had the full cooperation of his wife, the former Althea Fink, a painter who before her marriage had headed the Fine Arts Department of

Lebanon Valley College, in Annville, Pennsylvania, which is where she and Solomon met as fellow students.

With the help of the Reverend James Bolton of Union Chapel in Coconut Grove (later the Plymouth Congregational Church) the Merricks found one hundred and sixty acres of pineland which they purchased sight unseen, paying out the sum of one thousand, one hundred dollars, virtually the entire family fortune.

Lesser souls might have been dashed when, following their arrival after the long trip, father and son were turned away from Miami because of the yellow fever quarantine. They turned to a clergyman friend who took them in up near Jupiter until the quarantine was lifted.

Two decades after claiming their land, the Merricks would build a native rock house with a gables roof and call it Coral Gables.

George was in New York studying law when his father died in 1911 and he hurried home to look after the grove. Solomon had often expressed the desire to divide his land into individual groves for retired clergymen and professors and in fact had built a few houses as the start of a winter colony. Now George took his father's dream and elaborated on it.

In Miami they said George Merrick was a fine boy. Ever since he had appeared in knee pants, delivering fresh vegetables and fruit to the back door of the Royal Palm Hotel or the Lummus grocery store, he had been well liked. Nevertheless, bankers turned him down cold when he tried to borrow money on his ideas. By now it was apparent that the trend was toward Miami Beach. Who would want to buy out in the pineland?

George's trouble, the bankers said, was that he read too much poetry. Even wrote some himself. No businessman. In spite of the fact he had studied law he was just a dreamy poet. When the bankers turned him down, Merrick subdivided part of his inherited eleven hundred acres and hired Doc Dammers to help sell some lots. When people failed to come, he rented a bus and offered free transportation and lunches to anybody willing to ride out and "look things over." He managed to sell some lots. Original plans for the city of Coral Gables called for homes of coral rock like the family home, and Merrick imported Cuban masons to build the first houses.

Contrary to the bankers' theory, George Merrick *was* a businessman, a master organizer. He established a manager on his fruit grove and entered the real estate business in Miami. From that point he worked methodically toward the goal of establishing his "Master Suburb," buying up land, making his plans, biding his time. The main disadvantage as set forth by the bankers had been the distance of the pineland from the water. What tourist in his right mind would enjoy a vacation away from the bay or the ocean? Later Merrick began to accumulate land nearer and nearer the water until finally he had pushed through to Biscayne Bay at a spot just south of Coconut Grove.

His marriage to Eunice Peacock, who had been a toddler the day he docked at Peacock Inn, spurred him on to the completion of his goal. He would call his city Coral Gables for the family home, he told his bride. The granddaughter of Charles and Isabella Peacock, who had stouteartedly left London for the unknown country of Biscayne Bay with their young sons, never doubted for an instant that her husband would be successful.

A large man, he dreamed large dreams, sitting up nights reading A. E. Housman or sketching in plans or writing his verses *Songs of the Wind on a Southern Shore*. There is a sadness to "When the Groves Begin to Bear" in which, after the beginning of his success, he felt pangs of regret that his father, who had struggled hard in the rocky soil, was not alive to share in the realization of the dreams.

Everybody Dream!

S HARING MERRICK'S FONDNESS for the grandiose in building was a man with the means to indulge his fancies, one James Deering, whose millions came from the International Harvester Company. Warned by his doctors that overwork had brought him to a dangerous state of health, he turned to play as the antidote. For a thread on which to string the play hours he elected to build a Venetian palace in the Brickell hammock two miles south of Miami. He made a production of the operation. The *palazzo*, which took five years and cost eight million dollars to build, was reason for touring Europe for two years, searching for furnishings and art objects to fill it.

The one-hundred-and-sixty-acre estate, which Deering named Vizcaya, and which Miamians called Villa Vizcaya so persistently that eventually it became that in the public mind, became second only to the Royal Palm Hotel as symbol of plenty in the minds of the people. They spoke familiarly of tapestries from France, massive furniture from Italy, and the Deering's paintings of John Sargent and John Singleton Copley as though they had seen them with their own eyes. Any other detail of Deering's life that leaked out was digested as thoroughly.

James Deering never married and speculation as to his romances became more pleasurable than an evening game of euchre. It was whispered that conveniently close to Vizcaya lived a lady who had captured Deering's heart.

A slight man, he presented an impeccable figure in imported white linen as he drove his Fiat up to Buena Vista to inspect the plants growing for his estate on his brother Charles' land. He employed an Italian mechanic to baby his Fiat and drive his Rolls-Royce when he entertained guests.

109

Charles Deering, who already owned two castles in the Mediterranean, contented himself with a bayfront house in Cutler, where the post office was now housed in a neat building instead of a wreck of a railroad car. To the house he acquired, Charles Deering added a wing to hold his gallery of Spanish paintings and his collection of rare books.

The bachelor brother remained the romantic figure in the minds of Miamians. None of the splender of the fortresslike Vizcaya, with its magnificent formal gardens, was visible from the road, where mellow pink walls and arches of bougainvillaea enclosed the surrounding hammock, but sailors reported an excellent view from Biscayne Bay.

Farther south, in Coconut Grove, Arthur Curtis James, once rated the second-richest man in the world and one of the twentieth century's leading railroad men, purchased a hunting lodge from William J. Matheson and called it Four-way Lodge. James, whose grandfather, Daniel James, had made a vast fortune in copper, silver, and gold mining as an associate of Anson Phelps and William E. Dodge, managed to triple what was left to him. An enthusiastic yachtsman, he had been commodore of the New York Yacht Club and brought his yacht *Aloha* south with him. The square-rigged vessel was also converted to steam and had its own laundry and refrigeration plants. It was considered one of the finest yachts afloat.

Commodore James fitted into the Grove picture without a pinch. He had a gruff manner, but he gave tea to the boys from the Adirondack-Florida School, the forerunner of Miami's co-educational Ransom-Everglades private school, and became in time a kind of public benefactor, supplying educational funds and other assistance to deserving natives, although his charities were always dealt out secretly.

It was largely through his wife's efforts that Plymouth Congregational Church (the original Union Chapel, renamed) was built with its great Spanish door that for three centuries had swung in an ancient Basque building in the Pyrenees. Phillipi, a Spanish mason, was shipped to the U.S.A. with the door and for a full year he laid with loving care the beautiful rock used in the twin-belfry church.

During this period, the population was steadily on the increase. All over the country people were beginning to dream about the new tropical land, not earth-shaking dreams like those of Carl Fisher or as complete in design as

Merrick's but man- and woman-sized dreams. Up in Minneapolis, a soft-voiced young woman named Julia Fillmore Harris, a teacher of Latin in the high school, began to dream of establishing an out-of-door school where children could learn what they had to learn under healthful conditions. Taking her winter walks in the Minnesota wind and entering the airless classrooms, she found herself more and more occupied with this idea. Because it was warm in the new city of Miami, she decided to investigate the situation there. On her arrival, she was assured by the Chamber of Commerce that nobody in Miami was "rich enough to send children to private schools." She was about ready to give up when a group of women from Coconut Grove offered their support. It was not until she had formed her school that she learned the advice given by one of them constituted the voice of experience and that Countess Nugent was the founder of the Baldwin School. Thus Miss Harris' Florida School was born, a unique institution that attracted boarders from both North and South America until it closed.

Up in Chicago, Harold Dorn dreamed of giving up his bank job and raising tropical fruit in some of that Everglades land the bank was selling. Cautiously, he arranged to visit Florida before buying. He made a trip to a place called Progresso that was making great claims in advertisements but which he passed by in favor of Miami. Two years later, he returned with his brother and elderly parents. They cast in their lot with the new city.

The following year, he returned to Chicago to bring back a bride. Mabel Frances White's study of medieval history at the University of Chicago was of small assistance in helping her acclimate to the ten acres of scarified land on which they built their home in South Miami. While her husband was planting the new Haden Mangoes, Mabel tried her luck with sweet peas and asters. When they died, she looked out over the pines and palmetto and the "white roads going no place" and cried. She planted a mango tree by her kitchen door to get some shade. Every time she felt like crying she went out and fertilized it. She killed it with her constant fertilizing. But she became bit by bit, a leading authority on the plants of the region and started the first garden club for lonesome Northern women like herself living on land they did not understand. Her husband became a leading fruit producer.

A plant introduction center started by the United States Department of Agriculture proved a godsend to the new settlers. In the Brickell hammock, plants from all over the tropical world were being put out. A leader in this movement was David Fairchild, who followed the path trod by Henry Perrine and Charles Torrey Simpson and John C. Gifford, all of whom were drawn to Miami for reasons that had to do with horticulture.

Fairchild, who wandered the world as a protégé of Barbour Lathrop, married Marian, the daughter of Alexander Graham Bell, and the pair bought the old Simmons house in the Grove which they renamed The Kampong. In the little shed where Dr. and Captain Simmons had made their jellies and wines, Fairchild's illustrious father-in-law slept when he came for a visit.

The visit put the officials of the Miami Telephone Company into a tizzy and they made a visitation in order to install a courtesy telephone for the father of their industry. The white-bearded Mr. Bell explained with some embarrassment that while he had invented the telephone he could not abide using the instrument, and refused the offer. Solitude and privacy were his twin delights and the light burned sometimes all night in the erstwhile jelly factory while Bell worked out some puzzling or tempting line of thought—or merely dreamed.

It seems apparent that while Fisher was constructing his golden city and Merrick was feeding free lunches to prospective buyers in the pineland that would soon be known as the city of Coral Gables, some fairly fascinating souls had already gathered in the spot that would become the heart of the region soon to be known as the Florida Gold Coast.

A slight interruption in the flowering of this American Dreamland thrust itself forward at this moment in history in the shape of World War I.

Prelude to Action

THE FIGHTING IN EUROPE held up the construction of a new causeway which had been carried to the people as a six-hundred-thousand-dollar county bond issue—and passed two to one. It also slowed down Carl Fisher, who went to work for the government for a dollar a year and applied his hustling energies to the field of aviation. Congress had appropriated six hundred and ninety-two million dollars for "flying machines" and a new American engine known as the "Liberty Motor" was announced with fanfare. At Miami Beach, Glenn Curtiss began training aviators on a stretch of land near the bay. This constituted a novelty of the first water.

A few boys from the Adirondack-Florida School were permitted to drive over in the school Buick for flying lessons, which cost, they reminded each other gloatingly, one dollar a minute. The boys always stopped first for luncheon at the Royal Palm where their favorite menu of *crawfish à la chafing dish* did nothing to dim their enthusiasm for flying. They usually polished off the day with a trip to the cinema in Miami, where the showing of the latest installment of *The Iron Claw* happily coincided with their flying day. Among these boys was Lloyd Fales and despite the rich combination of the day's events he managed to become, at sixteen, the youngest licensed pilot in the U.S.A.

The army began sending down boys from Harvard to train with Curtiss, among them Herbert Pulitzer, and these worldly-wise gentlemen reported that "Pershing considers an airman worth a cavalry division." Curtiss was forced to move his school out near what is now Hialeah because the few hundred

113

residents of Miami Beach objected to the noise of the whirring planes even before Phil Rader tied the note to a grapefruit and sent it sailing in the direction of a lovely damsel's home. He said later he had no idea it would go clear through the roof.

The marines landed and took over the Curtiss air-training facilities. Thus was the Marine Air Corps born in the U.S.A. Three OX-Jennys and later an abundance of twenty Jennys with Hispaño-Suiza engines constituted the equipment. It was the only field given the Corps during World War I.

Trainees from New York, Louisiana, and New Jersey turned up in uniform at Elser's Pier, the new gathering place for the young in heart. Here, for a penny, you could turn the crank that brought before your amazed eyes Helen, the Hula dancer. There was a shooting gallery, pink cotton candy, and cherry pop, a stuffed alligator and a stuffed tarpon. And there was dancing.

Dinner Key at Coconut Grove was established as a naval aviation base and while construction was in progress recruits crowded the Fair Building. The navy also opened an aerial bombing training station across from the Royal Palm Hotel, but this so disturbed hotel guests that activities were moved farther south.

With the influx of servicemen, Miami matrons turned themselves inside out to provide a sample of Southern hospitality. Home entertaining reached a new high, romances flourished, and among the marriages that followed World War I meetings "down among the sheltering palms" were Dr. Thomas W. Hutson and Dr. Jackson's popular daughter Ethel, as well as Bess Burdine and Albert Cushing Read, not yet an admiral.

Gasoline-less Sundays were strictly adhered to, but Saturday nights saw transportation available for dancing parties at Green Tree Inn or over at Hardie's Casino.

Bobo Dean fought America's participation in the war until feeling against him ran red-hot. Slogan-loving Miamians had adopted the idea of a "war to end all wars" and wanted to get on with it. People stopped their regular subscriptions to the *Metropolis* although Dean observed to a friend that "the street sales jumped." Miss Hattie Carpenter wrote some of the antiwar editorials calling the conflict "a money-making scheme" and shared in the abuse showered on Dean. By now, Miss Hattie was used to being in the thick of the newspaper fight and enjoyed it.

When America declared war on Germany, however, Dean went all-out for war. It was not generally known, but members of his staff who joined the armed forces remained on the payroll.

Miami citizens went off to training camps and families put stars in their front windows. A group of marching mothers, dressed in all-white, dramatized the fact that Miami Boys were fighting for their country, and as they paraded down Flagler Street, white women followed by a delegation of black mothers, there was a choked silence instead of cheers.

A. C. Goggins, who was born a slave and whose proudest claim was that he had been Wade Hampton's orderly in the War Between the States, volunteered for service and was accepted. A stalwart of seventy-nine, he had served with distinction as a spy for the Confederacy. The army knew a good man when it saw one. Goggins was put to work training black troops on Long Island for "the war to end all wars."

Marjory Stoneman Douglas, the writing daughter of Judge Stoneman of the *Herald*, left her job on the paper amid handshaking and partying for service in France as a member of the Red Cross after first serving a year in the navy.

Flaming patriotism, which caused people to break into spontaneous song when "Over There" was played at band concerts down by the bay, descended as body temperatures rose in the fearful influenza epidemic. All the Coast Guard stations in the country were knocked out at one point when the men fell ill with the disease that claimed a million lives in North America. One of the worst recorded plagues in history, it took its toll of lives in Miami. It claimed Miss Edith Brickell, who had played an important role in the panic of 1907 when she went about with her satchel of money.

In churches and at home, Miamians prayed for the end of the war without fully realizing what changes it would bring. The end of that conflict would see an automobile-happy group of Americans, their pockets jingling with war profits, all bent on riding about, seeing the world, spending as well as making a quick dollar. Between them Carl Fisher and George Merrick would point the way in a Niagara of ecstatic prose to the tropical worlds they were creating in the southeast corner of the U.S.A.

Some of the people who love Miami best say that "the sweet smell disappeared in the twenties."

Biggest Fish, Biggest Thirst

VISCOUNT WILLIAM WALDORF ASTOR spent a Christmas vacation hunting big game fish with Captain Charlie Thompson and before returning to London sent the native son of Biscayne Bay "a slight memento" in the form of an exquisite watch from Tiffany's. Astor had served as minister to Italy and was defeated for Congress before turning his back on the vulgarities of his native land in favor of life abroad and a title conferred for a consideration. But when he went fishing he was not recognizable as the arrogant gentleman who shook off the sand of Newport after engaging in a feud with his uncle, William Astor, on the bitter question of whose lady should be arbiter of important social events. In fact, wearing the denim overalls which had been the Bay uniform when Brickell's trading post was the only supply line with the world, his head covered by an old Nassau straw hat, Astor was just another fisherman, affable, eager, content.

As a fishing guide, Cap'n Charlie left nothing to be desired. His eyes, which were the color of bluebells, could spot the fin of a fish a quarter of a mile distant and identify it. He told fish stories with a straight face, such absurd tales that the bay people shook their heads and said Charlie was "an out-and-out liar." Charlie went on telling his merry fish stories. He and Will Rogers planned a company known as Ocean Dairy Products in which Sea Cow Milk would be canned for popular consumption.

A manatee, or sea cow, an herbivorous, fishlike mammal, does not give the kind of milk liable to be popular with humans—but they were having their little joke. This humor left some of the natives slack-jawed and incredulous.

Charlie's biggest catch, like his usual run of fish stories, was preposterous. There was not the slightest doubt it was "the biggest fish in the world." The Smithsonian Institution said so. It centered attention on Biscayne Bay in a way to make Miami proud. It happened prior to World War I.

Charlie was guiding a party of tourists when The Thing caught his line and began dragging the boat out to sea. When they regained their voices, members of the fishing party shrieked to Cap'n Charlie to cut the line. Curtly, he refused. One passenger, a gentleman recuperating from an attack of typhoid fever, piteously offered a thousand dollars if Charlie would oblige with this small service. It was necessary, finally, for Charlie to hold a pistol on his fearful crew of paid passengers, who were destined to spend thirty-six hours at sea, being whisked hither and yon by the monster of the deep, which occasionally rose, lifting the boat with it.

The creature resisted five harpoon thrusts and one hundred and fifty large-caliber rifle bullets. Charlie lost sixteen pounds in the battle. The Thing weighed an estimated thirty thousand pounds and was forty-five feet long. Its liver alone weighed seventeen hundred pounds and it had swallowed a black fish which weighed fifteen hundred pounds. A Miami minister gleefully pronounced from his pulpit that the story of Jonah and the whale was now substantiated since not one but four men could easily slip down the throat of The Thing.

The Smithsonian gave it the name of *Rhinodon Typicus,* at the same time offering the eerie explanation that the creature must have been blown up by some subterranean or volcanic upheaval which injured its diving apparatus so it was unable to return to its native depths.

Indeed, it was such an unusual fish and made so much money for Cap'n Charlie that the captive passengers who had witnessed the catch eventually sued to gain ownership of it. They were not successful. For a time, The Thing rested at Elser's Pier where William Jennings Bryan, perennial Democratic candidate for president, then secretary of state under Woodrow Wilson, visited it. After an impressive silence, the Great Commoner dubbed it The Smell. It was moved eventually and mounted, whereupon Cap'n Charlie left on a grand tour with it aboard the yacht *Tamiami.*

He had, on tour, his usual difficulty. Nobody believed his fish story. In New York and Atlantic City, city slickers insisted Charlie must have made this fish himself. It was necessary to procure written testimonials from both Mayor

Watson and Secretary of State Bryan before these doubting Thomases would accept the carcass as authentic.

The most devoted and loyal of Cap'n Charlie's followers was quiet, likable William K. Vanderbilt. The two met in 1900 when Vanderbilt sailed in on his yacht *Tarantula* and for thirty years, they sailed the seas of the world as fishing companions. Cap'n Charlie made two trips around the world with Vanderbilt, one on the yacht *Ara*, another on the *Alva*, and for fishing under scientifically luxurious conditions these trips could not be matched. Vanderbilt carried as crew an artist and a taxidermist, and when Charlie landed a colorful specimen of the deep, it was plunged instantly into a tank so that the artist could paint an on-the-spot, living likeness. Then the taxidermist stepped in and mounted it. Vanderbilt was so taken with tropical fish that he built a museum at his home in Huntington, Long Island, and Charlie Thompson helped him stock it.

Cap'n Charlie held the esteem and affection of a good many celebrated souls as he went his carefree way, but in the beginning there were those who would have changed him. Julia Tuttle wanted him to go to college. Senator Johnson Newlon Camden of Parkersburg, West Virginia, one of the earliest and most habitual of Royal Palm guests, wanted to educate Charlie, too. He urged the boy "to make something of himself." Finally, he gave up, disappointed, chiding Charlie about the ambitionless life he led.

Carl Fisher liked Charlie as he was and gave him a black sapphire ring set in platinum which to the uninitiated passed for silver and onyx. It cost ten thousand dollars. Charlie wore it cutting up bait and towing in devilfish and one day a harpoon chain chipped a corner of it.

Charlie fished with four presidents of the U.S.A.: Grover Cleveland, the professional outdoorsman Teddy Roosevelt, scholarly Woodrow Wilson, and Warren Harding.

Of President Cleveland, Cap'n Charlie said, "He was essentially a trout and bass fisherman, but he had the avoirdupois to handle the big babies. The longest tarpon was never able to push him from his cushions."

Harding, who once landed three sailfish, one right after the other, made many trips with Cap'n Charlie during his "Back to Normalcy" reign. To show his appreciation for good sport, President Harding presented the angler with a sterling silver monogramed flask.

That flask was a symbol of Prohibition days in the Miamis when rum-

119

running ruffled the waters of Biscayne Bay and the Florida coast and the Bahamas became intimately reunited in the interest of pressing the illicit liquor trade. Boats of every size once more plunged across the blue-black Gulf Stream. Hijacking was inevitable. The Ashley gang took to the water, and after five successful years of running rum two of the brothers disappeared, conceivably murdered by hijackers.

Some of Miami's "best citizens" were engaged in rum-running. After all, people reasoned, importing it was no worse than drinking it, and federal judges and the president of the U.S.A. himself were getting yacht deliveries in the middle of the bay of scotch and champagne, brandy and gin. Downtown Miami saloons operated on an open-door policy and tourists accepted this freedom as part of the June-in-January setting. In Miami it was not so much that people did not observe Prohibition—they blatantly ignored its existence. It was almost as though Miami, which had once considered itself part of the Bahamas, became so again.

Liquor was shipped north under cover of darkness and labeled fish or oranges or avocados. Bankers, merchants, law enforcers, were all fully aware of what was going on. The attitude was to leave the problem with the federal men. Those gentlemen got no cooperation whatever from Miamians or the government of the Bahamas. That British colonial arm was raking in gold at such a fast clip that all connected with the colony were more than willing to turn away if not positively assist in defeating "America's fool law."

Frustrated Prohibition officers made a dramatic arrest when they trailed Charles Vincenti, head of a Baltimore distillery, to Bimini, where he was about to set up "a second Monte Carlo," being prepared to spend several million dollars to bring it about. Posing as liquor dealers, the federal men met Vincenti, who assured them he could supply them with any amount of liquor and that he, himself, anticipated making a million dollars a year at the game. They invited Vincenti on board their boat to discuss the deal, then whisked him away to the mainland, where he was placed under arrest. All they got for their inventive methods was dismissal when the courts ruled that an American citizen was entitled to a more conventional arrest. (Today, this is common police practice, known as a drug "sting.")

Prohibition brought a shocking oddity in the form of the state of Florida bringing murder charges against four United States Coast Guardsmen who had in the line of duty shot and killed one of the popular bootleggers of the era, D. W. (Red) Shannon.

Shannon was considered "a high-class bootlegger" and he delivered booze to all the VIPs on their yachts. One night as he went about his appointed tasks, the Coast Guard gave chase and when Red playfully eluded them they spattered the bay with bullets. It was the height of the tourist season, and people crowded the Fleetwood Hotel dock squealing their excitement at the beginning, then gradually going still as Red Shannon's red blood ran out on the moon-washed waters of Biscayne Bay.

Feeling against the Coast Guard ran high. The Miami *Herald* pointed out that "an offense condoned by the majority of onlookers wasn't exactly conducive to good will toward his slayers." Some of the "best people" in Miami were outraged at their favorite bootlegger's death. The case was diplomatically postponed for two years and when it came before the courts the Coast Guardsmen were exonerated. But it brought out a point: Miami appeared to consider herself outside the jurisdiction of the law insofar as Prohibition was concerned.

Politically Florida was still a dry state.

The Dawn of the Boom

THE UNITED STATES GOVERNMENT served notice that unless the City of Miami took steps to correct its haphazard system of naming streets, all U.S. Mail deliveries would cease. The government did not object to names like Hibiscus and Palmetto streets, but it objected with fervor to a half dozen of each. Perspiring mailmen were having small nervous breakdowns. What had happened was that the influx of new shops and small homes brought by the end of World War I was pushing the boundaries of the town as new land was subdivided and sold.

Despite this blunt warning, the City Council did nothing about the street situation. As politicians, not one of the group cared to tread on the toes of real estate operators and promoters of subdivisions who had a way of naming streets after their own tastes and often after themselves. A respected citizen and nonpolitician, Josiah Chaille, who had been selected to fill an unexpired term as a member of the Council, took the bull by the horns.

He took downtown Twelfth Street as a beginning and gave it a man's name, belatedly honoring the Father of Miami by calling it Flagler Street. He renamed Avenue D, calling it Miami Avenue. Next he began slashing names and substituting numbers. He found out what the weary postmen had known all along. A man would start walking down a street and every three blocks or so the name of the street would change. Chaille closed his eyes and wrote numerals. He made Brickell Avenue Southeast Second Avenue.

The government approved the new street system. It would have approved anything with the word "system" in it. After some pressure the City Council approved also.

123

Certain citizens, Charlie Leffler among them, raised a howl of protest. Leffler happened to live on Brickell Avenue and did not welcome the inconvenience of a changed address. Others had equally personal reasons for objecting.

Keeping calm, Chaille said, "Let the people vote on it."

Tempers were short and words hot. Chaille took to the hills of North Carolina to cool off during the heat of election. The people voted three to one to effect the change.

There are still a few people today who can recall the change of street names with irritation. A wag of the twenties drawled, "Joe Chaille says I live on Southeast Second Street." As for Leffler, he did not take matters lying down. He became a member of the boom-time "banker's commission" at the next election when Miami adopted the City Commission form of government. One of the commission's first acts was to change Southeast Second Street back to Brickell Avenue.

Later, smitten with the idea of changing street names, the clubwomen of Miami campaigned to change Miami Avenue to Tuttle Avenue in honor of the late Julia. Marjory Stoneman Douglas covered their activities in the *Herald*. Still on the opposite side editorially, the *Metropolis* pointed out that naming a "run-down commerical street for Julia Tuttle was a dubious honor." It stayed Miami Avenue to everybody's relief, especially the frazzled merchants.

On New Year's Day, 1920, the first automobiles rolled over the new county causeway to Miami Beach. A few weeks earlier Collins sold the wooden bridge which had seemed so extraordinary an achievement only seven years before. It was purchased by developers who planned to construct the Venetian Islands out of bay bottom, and planned a new toll causeway in connection with the development. Their advertising literature was fraught with delicious promise and hinted that "financial interests across the water are watching carefully and investigating thoroughly the Greater Miami district and the daring development of Venetian Isles, an investment absolutely incomparable."

Carl Fisher was writing welcome on the map of Miami Beach with the Flamingo Hotel, which cost a million and a half dollars and boasted a brightly lighted dome which ships at night used as a beacon. You were beginnning to be able to see Miami Beach from quite a distance. Fisher had merged with Collins and Pancoast, they supplying the land and he the money, and great plans were afoot for a giant tourist development with Fisher maintaining fifty-one per cent of the stock. He began to indulge himself, never for a moment unaware that his flamboyant schemes brought reams of publicity to Miami Beach.

He decided that Rosie the elephant should have a more colorful attendant than Yarnell and sent to India for a native trainer. The complications of transporting the fellow from Calcutta to Miami Beach involved his falling ill and requiring hospitalization en route. When he did arrive, Rosie took an instant dislike to him and chased him up the newly installed water tank. He remained the only mortal the gentle Rosie ever disliked on sight. Fisher gave the fellow his fare back to Calcutta. Rosie made the newsreels by caddying for President Harding when he golfed at Miami Beach, thus compensating for any trouble she'd caused.

One morning, Fisher decided he would like to see a lake at Miami Beach and before nightfall men were digging Lake Surprise. When it was finished, it looked so desolate he hired two men to drift around it all day in sailboats, one flying yellow sails, the other green. He shipped in a herd of cows from Wisconsin to supply his hotel guests with milk and cream and built a barn to house them where the Miami Beach Elementary School stands at Forty-first Street. He booked Italian singers to walk around the streets in velvet pants and feathered hats to serenade the people who built homes.

Charles Deering announced his private collection of exotic birds was for sale and Fisher seized the opportunity to purchase them and declare Miami Beach a bird sanctary. (Coconut Grove, drawing its skirts about it, had declared itself a town and was already a bird sanctuary by official edict.) Fisher's announcement made a great story and garnered praise all over the world, but actually most of the birds were caged in a museum. The ones set free instantly deserted the man-made paradise for the natural hammock land, portions of which were still intact across the bay.

Wealthy men like oilman James M. Snowden built palatial estates at Miami Beach, and Fisher built a yacht club on an island he created and named Star Island. Colonel E. H. R. Greene, the son of the financial wizard Hetty Greene with the bright gold hoard, later bought it and added to it until he had twenty-seven servants' rooms. Some *très gaie soirées* were staged on the Mississippi River showboat which he purchased and tied up on the bay alongside his estate. Greene was quite a character, popular with the entire police force because each winter on arrival he presented every cop in the area with a five-dollar gold piece.

Fisher's Roman Pools, built at a cost of three hundred and fifty thousand dollars (and dubbed "Fisher's Folly" by the doubting natives), began to be a smart place to swim at eleven o'clock of a morning, but a Miami minister preached a sermon damning the one-piece bathing suit worn by Carl's first wife as she mastered the Australian crawl. Before her death, she declared it was this incident that gave Fisher the idea of using bathing beauties to publicize his beauty spot.

Next, Fisher hit on polo as a good game to stir up interest when golf and swimming and tennis palled. He issued invitations to outstanding players and promised, "I'll have the stables ready in eighty days." He imported crack poloists from Europe at fifteen thousand dollars per man to show novices at his Nautilus Polo Fields how the game should be played. With his usual enthusiasm, he took up the game himself. To his polo fields came such players as Winston Guest and Billy Post. Laddie Sanford refused to permit his string of ponies to drink the Miami water and had fifty bottles of water shipped daily from New York to his stables. The parade of Harvey Firestone and his four sons with their string of ponies, grooms, and equipment from the lavish home they purchased from Jim Snowden was comparable to a parade of knights in full armor. They lived on the ocean and their stables were across the canal. This morning march was, according to those fortunate enough to have observed it, "something to see."

Fisher later built the King Cole Hotel to house the polo-playing set. To provide a Continental flavor, he decreed that English breakfasts served from sideboards start the day. All horsemen, visiting or home-grown, would breakfast in a horsy atmosphere.

Miami Beach, tailored for the tourist, boasted six hundred and forty-four residents in 1920. That was the year land began to move. By 1921 there were five hotels operating, the Wofford, the Pancoast, and the Breakers, in addition to Fisher's two, the Flamingo and the Lincoln. In that year the assessed valuation, which in 1916 had stood at two hundred and twenty-four thousand, jumped to five million, five hundred forty thousand, one hundred and twelve dollars.

At a meeting of the newly organized Miami Beach Chamber of Commerce, William Jennings Bryan, whose home, Villa Serena, lay across the bay in the direction of Coconut Grove, declared Miami Beach "the child of Miami." He added, "The child is the only rival a parent can welcome." This pre-Freudian notion that parents cannot be jealous of their children was not entirely so in this instance. Since 1915, the city of Miami had been spending money on nationwide publicity which E. G. (Ev) Sewell, brother of John, hoped would make Miami "a second Atlantic City." There was a dawning irritation in Miami at the tendency of Fisher's Miami Beach to force Miami into the role of commercial adjunct to its paradisical setup. There was not even a "colored town" at Miami Beach and black hotel and house servants employed there crossed and recrossed the causeway each day, crowding Miami's black neighborhoods during the winter season.

Plans for Coral Gables also relegated Miami to a commercial status merely by outlawing factories and other marks of commerce. The Merrick dream, nearer fruition, was still on paper, still involved the shaping of what was being called Miami's Master Surburb, not a resort area, but a spot where all life would be well ordered and serene, where everybody's house blended with his next-door neighbor's, where beauty and harmony existed in architecture and landscaping, planned by a master hand. Merrick, the master hand of the "Master Suburb," was proving himself a master at getting financial backing. His air of solemnity and solidity appealed to businessmen from afar. Organizations like the Jefferson Standard Life Insurance Company of Greensboro, the Misssouri State Life Insurance Company, and the Mortgage and Securities Company of New Orleans were evincing keen interest in his ideas.

Topnotch architects, designers, and landscape artists helped work out their plans while the marketing campaign waited. Not until they were complete would Merrick sell a lot. His city, he reiterated, must be "balanced" and must include room for people of modest means as well as people of wealth. There would be "the most beautiful country club in the world" in

Coral Gables, he promised. The first lots were sold on the front lawn of Merrick's home, *Poinciana Place* on November 28, 1921. The first street was opened and the first store building erected the following year.

In Miami, as the boom dawned, Bobo Dean, the "Bobonic Plague" to many a conniving politician in the early days, suddenly sold the *Metropolis* to James M. Cox, ex-governor of Ohio and unsuccessful candidate for president with young Franklin Delano Roosevelt as a running mate. The price was reputed to be a million dollars. Cleaning out his desk drawers, Dean allowed he was "weary of the fight." He took his money and put it in real estate.

Cox, renaming the paper the *Metropolis-News*, announced he would erect a million-dollar Spanish-style building to house the plant.

More than ever before, there was a feeling of great things to come in the Miamis. The stage was being set. Some of the players were ready to go on, letter-perfect in their parts. The rest would come.

Mary Brickell, shortly before her sudden death, looked across the bay at the man-made playland of Miami Beach and at the spoil banks which would grow into other islands and said ominously, "The sands pumped into Miami Beach will run out, like an hour glass . . . wait and see."

3 | Nightmare and Rude Awakening 1926–1930

B-o-o-m Spells Bedlam

I T WAS LIKE A FEVER that carried from person to person and place to place until finally no one remained untouched. The contagion center was Greater Miami but the fever spread to every remote Florida hamlet and deep into the Everglades. The fever involved the buying and selling of the land.

Most of the buying was not for land on which to build a home or start a business or raise crops, although there were instances of each. In its essence the fever involved the urgent need to turn land into hundreds, to turn it into thousands, to turn it into *millions.* They meant dollars.

In a frenzy to turn Florida sand into gold, men cut up fruit groves to make subdivisions, filled in swampland and planted coconut palms and Australian pines, setting the stage in the Fisher manner. Trees were props, nothing more, props to sell the land, occasionally serving the more physical purpose of holding up printed signs or advertisements.

A strawberry grower was stubbornly hanging on to his twenty-six acres of land just north of the new Seventy-ninth Street Causeway to Miami Beach, and people said he was "crazy" for having turned down a million dollars for it. He explained that he had made ninety-one thousand, five hundred dollars in fine strawberries over a four-year period and wanted "one more crop" before selling.

T.V. Moore's pineapple plantation became much too valuable to be used for fruit growing and was turned into a sixty-two-million-dollar development of twenty-five hundred acres known as Miami Shores and guided by the velvet hand of the Shoreland Company.

Sumptuous offices, following the wrought-iron and Spanish-Italian flavor of the period, were opened in the Shoreland Building. Neatly parked at the curb outside, awaiting the pleasure of the potential buyers, stood ten Cadillac touring cars. The buyers came. Americans on a traveling spree rolled along Dixie Highway in every make of automobile, with plenty of Tin Lizzies in the parade. Trains poured out tourists, who also came by Inland Waterway in boats and by the Clyde Line from New York and via the Baltimore and Carolina Line from Philadelphia. Real estate offices were established every few feet in downtown Miami as dairymen and farmers, haberdashers and bankers turned to the selling of the pineland and palmetto. During 1925, Miami issued seventy-five hundred real-estate licenses.

The people who came dismissed the land itself as "monotonous." This was the unique land that in its unspoiled state so excited foresters and botanists, the region of rock ridge and watery Everglades, of hammock and pine and mangrove, the land so lovingly translated by Charles Torrey Simpson down to the last gaudy grasshopper and land crab. Simpson called the region "an ideal spot for a naturalist."

A typical invitation of the time read: "Miami welcomes you with the song of the tropics. Leave winter behind, fling care to the icy winds, come to Miami and play at being eternally young again."

Answering the call, America came. It had trouble finding accommodations as apartments rented for unheard-of sums and men slept on part of a porch for twenty-five dollars a week, walking out in the soft evenings to look enviously at the glow of lamplight in houses and apartments and the bursting-at-the-seams hotels.

Orders for lumber went out and were answered by cargo ships from the Gulf ports, from the West Indies, from New York and New England. Discarded windjammers from far-off Oregon took to sea to bring the lumber to make the uncertain little houses, the jerry built structures whose only standard appeared to be that they hold up until they were sold. Skyscrapers began to rise against the blue-white sky and high on the scaffolding workmen gazed out over the harbor dense with ships like trees in a forest.

The people came with money to buy. Northern bankers, small- and big-town bankers, wailed that too many people were taking out their savings and heading for Florida as to the land where Dreams Come True. Farmers from Iowa and clerks from Illinois packed tents in the family automobiles and joined the cavalcade. All over the U.S.A. people who had been reading the full-page ads dreamed up by George Merrick and Carl Fisher hurried to the free, workless existence waiting in the Land of Perpetual Light where oranges grew on trees (along with greenbacks).

At the very crest of the boom the Shoreland people put the Arch Creek tract of four hundred acres on the market and buyers mobbed the offices at eight-thirty in the morning. The mangrove was barely covered by sand, but at eleven A.M. the office was forced to close its doors. The entire tract was sold for the sum of thirty-three million, seven hundred and thirty-four thousand, three hundred and fifty dollars. Shouting people had literally hurled their checks at the real estate men in a mass demonstration of their desire to buy, permitting the company to select the land for them. That was a sample of the temper of buyers. The cash and checks were carried to the banks at the end of a business day in barrels.

The Seminole Beach sale when N. B. T. Roney (his boomtime nickname was No Back Talk Roney) and ex-governor Cox purchased ocean-front north of Golden Beach for three million dollars was another sample of frenzied land buying. Without benefit of advertising, the news went out that the land would be developed. Two days later, a screaming mob formed at Roney's office demanding lots. In six and a half hours they purchased every lot, paying seven million, six hundred and forty-five thousand dollars. In a week, the land was resold again for twelve million. All this profit was "on paper." That is to say, it was held by a ten per cent deposit, the remaining fifteen per cent making up the first payment due in thirty days.

Miami was billed as a land of forgetfulness, therefore the real estate salesmen dressed informally, rakishly, in knickers and caps. The Miami *Herald* pointed out somewhat pettishly that wearing knickerbockers for business simply was not suitable, but readers wrote in defending the attire as proper playland regalia. The *Herald* was objecting to symbols. What it probably found irritating was the glib, fast-talking salesmen who wore the knickerbockers.

There was another form of life, more onerous, known as "the binder boys." These fellows in dirty white linen took up options on land for a small sum of money with a first payment due usually in a month's time. The binder

133

boys had no intention of holding on to the options but sold them over and over at a profit. This alone raised the price of property.

More pathetic but equally unpleasing were "bird dogs." They were the tattered and hungry, the hangers-on of both sexes who haunted railroad stations and docks in the hope of latching onto a genuine prospect. The general excitement, the auctioneering, the bands and the parades assisted these unfortunate people in eking out an existence.

The Florida boom had begun to form in 1921, and during the year 1925 nine hundred and seventy-one subdivisions were platted, one hundred and seventy-four thousand, five hundred and thirty deeds were filed by the county clerk, and four hundred and eighty-one hotels and apartments were constructed. Miami was spreading out toward the 'Glades with subdivisions consisting of sidewalks and entrance gates and a few palm trees—nothing more. Some of them would remain that way, too, for some time to come, like ghost cities, only worse, like lands of unfulfilled dreams, limbos. It would be two decades before some of these sidewalks would be rediscovered under the rank growth that covered them and become bona-fide cement pathways for flesh-and-blood people.

With a straight face, promoters of Poinciana, an inaccessible spot situated on the Gulf of Mexico, advertised their development as "The Coming Miami."

James Bright, a Western cattle man, bought land for two and three dollars an acre, then sold some of it to Glenn Curtiss for a flying field. Bright raised some cattle, but before he could go into it in a large way the boom began. Promoters asked for a slice of land for Hialeah Racetrack and in their wake came promoters of dog racing and the Spanish game of *jai alai*, gambling operators of all kinds, bootleggers galore. "Hialeah rye" was a specific Prohibition Miami drink. Plans for motion picture studios were in the wind. Hialeah was a jazzy settlement, set for the big circuit.

The operators of Curtiss-Bright ran into fresh, pure-tasting water when they dug an artesian well on their Country Club Estates, and the whole area benefited from that discovery. They renamed the settlement Miami Springs. Curtiss then turned to a newer subdivision which he named Opa-Locka and on which were constructed buildings with Moorish mosques and domes.

Fantastic? Nobody thought it farfetched. Others were constructing Chinese and Spanish villages.

Addison Mizner, the talented American artchitect and designer who helped create the modern Spanish trend in the state of Spanish origin, was accused of inventing a style "more Mizner than Spanish." His retort was that he "turned Spanish architecture inside out as you would a glove." Whatever his hand, gloved or ungloved, touched was stamped by beauty, which is more than could be said for some of his imitators. Mizner combined Italian and Moorish and Spanish in his architecture, and when combing the Mediterranean to accumulate doors, wrought iron, and tile became too burdensome he established a factory where he created these adjuncts in "the Mediterranean manner."

The Everglades Club, which he did for Paris Singer in Palm Beach, and El Mirasol, the estate of Mrs. E. T. Stotesbury, were his creations, and while other men conceived and created whole cities he itched to do the same. This itch resulted in the announcement of a proposed complete village with market places and homes and streets, Spanish in feeling, to be created between Palm Beach and Miami and to be named Boca Raton.

Backed by General T. Coleman Du Pont and with Jesse Livermore, the "boy plunger of Wall Street," as finance chairmen, the enterprise began. Wilson Mizner, the architect's witty and literary brother, was publicity man. The Mizners came to Flagler Street with the slogan "Pioneering with men of affairs," and while the urbane Wilson joined the ballyhoo artists of the time (Ben Hecht and J. P. McEvoy were press-agenting Key Largo), Addison supervised the erection of offices complete with ancient doors from an old castle (in Spain). The only time the hammers stopped was when the salesmen had their "fifteen-minute daily pep talks."

A boom-time magazine called *Hollywood* observed: "The Hispanic towers of a new Florida city will fling a proud challenge across the broad Atlantic to their prototype in old Spain."

Merrick's Coral Gables was now known as "the one-hundred-million-dollar development" and was being pushed by a vast sales force which spread out over the U.S.A. Smooth-talking supersalesmen in New York and Chicago did business in lavish Spanish-type offices. Buses emblazoned with the name

Coral Gables carried potential investors to the pineland from all over the country. Merrick was applying the same technique he had used in the preboom days in providing transportation from Miami to his development.

"The greatest orator in the world," William Jennings Bryan, who conducted "the largest outdoor Bible class in the world" on Sundays, spent weekdays spellbinding potential land buyers around the picturesque Venetian Pools cut from coral rock. For the droppings from his silver tongue Bryan received one hundred thousand dollars a year, half in cash, half in land.

Merrick's City Beautiful had already brought him recognition from Alphonse, the King of Spain. His art adviser, Denman Fink, who was his mother's brother, and architect Phineas Paist took bows along with him.

Douglas Entrance, a rock portal with arches and gates and including a block-long building, was the elaborate gateway to Coral Gables. One of several gateways from the Tamiami Trail, being cut across the Everglades to connect the west and east coasts of Florida, was not yet completed, but soon streams of autoists would approach Douglas Entrance via that route, it was promised. Plazas, fountains, and parkways with stone benches embellished the new city. People desiring to build homes meekly presented their plans for approval from the board of architects who demanded to pass on color, type, and placement of all structures.

Doc Dammers predicted modestly that "in eight years the center of metropolitan Miami will be west of Coral Gables." Jan Garber made the Coral Gables Country Club hum with a tune called "When the Moon Shines in Coral Gables," and Olympic champion Pete Desjardins gave diving exhibitions daily at the Venetian Pools.

Merrick cut the Coral Gables Canal through to Biscayne Bay and advertised "forty miles of waterfront." By day, sightseeing boats left Elser's Pier bound for the Gables. By night, gondolas manned by authentic gondoliers—imported by Merrick to inject a note of romance-filled the canal. With hotel man John McEntee Bowman he began to build the Miami Biltmore Hotel with its Giralda tower, a landmark for the future Everglades traveler, at an estimated cost of ten million dollars. It is figured that one hundred and fifty million dollars was made in real estate sales during this dizzy period by Merrick, who calmly used up one hundred million in building.

Dreaming of a Pan American University to attract students from Central and South America, a group of citizens headed by Dr. John G. DuPuis, were attempting to raise money for it. Merrick gave one hundred and sixty acres and offered five million dollars as an endowment fund providing the university authorities would raise a similar amount. Happily, they set about performing this small task. James Cash Penney started off the pledges with two hundred thousand dollars. Victor Hope pledged a million. A cornerstone was raised in a fever of academic activity. Thus, the University of Miami was born.

Rex Beach wrote a brochure in which he extolled the beauties of tropic nights in and around the Master Suburb of Coral Gables and went on to point out that "Miamians say they are not having a boom . . . its growth from a village of one thousand inhabitants to a city of one hundred and eleven thousand in twenty-five years is largely the result of the permanent productive resources at its door." Nobody said "Oh yeah?" and for the brochure Beach received twenty-five thousand dollars. Merrick thought so highly of it he had thousands of copies, rich with color paintings, printed in elaborate book form.

In eleven years the values at Miami Beach rose more than eighteen hundred per cent. Fisher's dream city had come true in a big way. The very name of Fisher was enough to sell land. Incessant rumors that he was promoting developments in other parts of Florida kept cropping up. Fisher spiked them by announcing in paid advertisements that he had no such intention but would continue to concentrate on Miami Beach.

The former land of the crocodile now had as a trade-mark all over the world the bathing beauty. Under the inspired touch of Carl Fisher a young fellow named Steve Hannagan attended to the flood of publicity that sailed forth each day.

Always on the lookout for the novel and spectacular, Fisher built fifteen motor boats exactly alike, then invited the fifteen leading auto-racing drivers of the world to race them on Biscayne Bay, demanding that they weigh in before the event to insure equality of opportunity. From Big Louis Chevrolet on down, they were all daredevils as well as completely inexperienced at the wheel of motor boats. The crash boat was active that day.

Large ocean-going vessels were eager to get into Miami. The Mallory liner *San Jacinto,* unable to enter the channel, sent a terse wireless to the Fleetwood Hotel: "Come get your orchestra." Fisher turned his attentions to this Peninsula Terminal project, where on the island just south of the ship channel at Miami Beach he visualized a great port. He had already encircled it with a twenty-six-foot cut and filled in much of the land. When Congress approved the Miami deep-water-harbor bill and agreed to deepen the harbor from eighteen feet to twenty-five and widen it to five hundred feet from deep water to the jetties, Fisher announced he was ready to build wharves and a turning basin. He would spend two and a half million dollars, he said. The first channel had extended from the foot of Fifth Street to Cape Florida with a depth of ten feet to accommodate the *City of Key West* for the Florida railroad. This was a decided improvement.

Ev Sewell had worked for the passage of this bill as the head of Miami's Chamber of Commerce and he had no intention of permitting Miami Beach to cash in on his glory. Sewell successfully opposed the filling of four hundred acres of bay bottom west and north of Virginia Key by its new owners "because it would spoil Miami's view of the ocean." Everyone understood it was to save the future of Miami's harbor.

During this hectic period Miami Beach made attempts to absorb within its city limits everything along the coast from the Broward County Line to the lower end of Virginia Key but got some stiff opposition from Miami Shores, which stopped the plan. From the Redlands, a cry went up for a Redlands County to contain the rich farming country south of Miami on the mainland en route to the Keys. That was squelched by Dade County bigwigs. Hollywood, north of Miami, was another development of the boom days and into this a Californian named Joseph W. Young plunked down forty million dollars. General G. W. Goethals, who built the Panama Canal, was called in to supervise the deepening of the harbor as well as the building of the "largest hotel in the world."

The boxer Gene Tunney, in between training, became sales manager for Hollywood Pines Estates, and dancer Gilda Gray provided a wiggle of excitement with the shimmy at a night club in that area. In Miami, where the hammers and riveters made their uneven sounds endlessly and the jabber of salesmen was the mark of the times, the city fathers offered a pious note by refusing the notorious Evelyn Nesbit the right to open a night club in Miami "in the shadow of the murdered Stanford White's Halcyon Hotel."

The exiled King George of Greece was sucked into the boom along with Mrs. Stotesbury, the grande dame of Palm Beach, whose son James H. R.

Cromwell (not yet married to tobacco heiress Doris Duke) dreamed up the Floranada Club north of Fort Lauderdale. John Pillsbury of flour fame climbed on the glittering land wagon.

Nothing was too good for Miami.

Mary Garden sang "real opera" in a tent in Coral Gables, Red Grange played his famous brand of football, and Paderewski was brought to a downtown Miami church, the White Temple, to give a concert. James Deering rose to the occasion by giving a beautifully appointed candlelight dinner in Paderewski's honor. His dinner partner reported the celebrated pianist showed a squeamishness about eating the bullet-like papaya seeds in the fruit put before him and that he shook his head in a kind of bewilderment, meanwhile murmuring, "What a fon-ny food." It was probably the end of a long, fon-ny day for Paderewski.

Deering, who was destined to die alone at sea on a return trip from Europe before the boom burst, is best noted for the stag dinner he gave at Vizcaya when the entire chorus of the Ziegfeld Follies was brought south for the entertainment of his guests. Two of the chorines elected to remain and marry Miami men.

Between them, Prohibition and the boom brought all the old vices back into the area. Gambling accelerated, jewel thieves roamed on cat feet. The Macon *Telegraph* described Miami as "a frontier town harboring criminals and rascals." The Ku Klux Klan offered to "police" Miami but its services were refused. Many considered it a sensible solution.

Boom-time sheriff was Henry Chase who appeared to be following the path trod by his former chief, Dan Hardie, in transferring his energies from fire to crime. Henry, who had grown up with the town, had his hands full. When he took over, the dog tracks were running on Sunday. He closed them, as he had promised to do in his campaign speeches and to the up-in-arms dog-track owners suggested that they put lights around their tracks and run at night. It was the beginning of nighttime dog racing.

When it came to casino gambling, the new sheriff had his worst problem. He closed all but two clubs, the Palm Island and the Tea House, on the theory that Ed Ballard would run them on the order of Bradley's at Palm Beach and as John Olive had done in the early days of the Seminole Club: no local yokels welcome. The dawn of the boom had brought many VIPs from around the nation to Miami as businessmen and some very fancy pressure began to be exerted on Henry Chase to let a few other gamblers slide in. He was holding tight the day the notorious Heywood Register of the Ashley gang staged a jailbreak, and in the subsequent gunfire two prisoners were killed. Chase had received word the remnants of the Ashley gang were "coming to take out their boy," and everybody around the jail was on the *qui vive* when Register made his break. The artillery response was immediate. Register pretended to be dead and saved his skin but two other prisoners were quite dead as a result of the barrage.

The *Metropolis* and *Daily News* demanded that Chase be removed from office. When Governor John W. Martin refused to take action until he was offered proof of the sheriff's guilt, charges of murder were brought against Chase.

With the seven deputies and six policemen who had all drawn fire when the jailbreak was staged, the sheriff of Dade County went on trial. All were acquitted. The power of the press had failed to accomplish a change of office in the sheriff's department, but boom-time Miami was something of a frontier town again despite the tall *News* Tower on Biscayne Boulevard and the baby skyscrapers rising all over town.

The Royal Palm Hotel withstood the boom. In fact through it all, its decorous opulence provided a note of substance in a world gone mad. It was inevitable that promoters should want to purchase it, but to offers of ten million dollars the Flagler trustees shook their heads. They had laid double railroad tracks into Miami and were counting heavily on getting back what had been spent. Furthermore, the Seaboard Railroad was laying tracks into Miami, and with the competition, the FEC wanted to hold on to the Royal Palm as a source of revenue.

New hotels had arisen to claim the attention of tourists, among them the Dallas Park Hotel built close by on Julia Tuttle's homesite. The ladies of the Daughters of the American Revolution decided to move the historic barracks over to Miami's Lummus Park.

Harry Tuttle, whose management of the Tuttle estate had been laced with strings of misfortunes including downright theft by crooked executors, determined to build a fitting monument to his mother's memory in the form of

140

the "exclusive" Julia Tuttle Apartment Hotel. At a cost of a million and a half dollars, he had it constructed in the Dallas Park section with sun parlor, tile roof, garden, and pipe organ in the lobby. Harry was a candidate to lose his inherited shirt, but he would be in good company. The trouble appeared to be that it was no longer possible for anybody to think in terms of less than a million dollars.

Ex-sheriff Hardie happened to be counting up the profits at the casino one day and found to his astonishment he was a millionaire. He decided to leave his casino and take a trip around the world. "I want to see the Taj Mahal," he told Fisher.

One day, Miss Belle Brickell went visiting a neighbor in one of the narrow wooden houses the Brickells had built on Southeast Sixth Street and while she sat rocking on the porch a fire truck clanged across the new Second Avenue Bridge and turned in at the old Brickell home across the avenue.

"Using up the taxpayers' money," Miss Belle grumbled. "No fire at our house."

A man came running up the street, waving his hands. He stopped. "A live wire," he called up to the people on the porch, "cut one of the Brickells spang in two."

It was Miss Alice, who had come to the wilderness, perhaps reluctantly, and to whom riches had brought only bitterness. Now there were only Miss Belle and Miss Maude, alone in the house on Brickell Point.

In Coconut Grove, land was put on the market at twelve hundred and ninety dollars and up for a single lot, but the burning controversy was sea walls vs. natural shoreline. Commodore Munroe was holding out against the former on the grounds that in severe storms the bay water would break with concentrated fury against the walls. Of the Commodore's valiant efforts to save the shoreline David Fairchild said, "There is something truly pathetic in the spectacle of one of the very oldest pioneers on Biscayne Bay having to stand up like John the Baptist crying in the wilderness, 'For God's sake save the beaches of the Bay.'"

The worst was yet to come. One feverish boom-time day when the bulk of Coconut Grove's residents were summering in the North, the city of Miami, greedy for her taxes, swooped down and gathered the Grove into its city limits. Coconut Grove was swallowed up "like a trout by a bass." Feeling ran high but in the babble of boom time the voice of Coconut Grove was not even heard. Whether they liked it or not the residents of the Grove were now part of the squalling, lusty city of Miami.

Having gathered the Grove under her protective wing, Miami proposed to extend sewers to the section. This suggestion created such a cry of horror that the idea was stopped. The Commodore called the idea of pouring sewage into the waters of Coconut Grove "revolting and impractical." Nobody in Miami or Miami Beach was concerned with what was pouring into their surrounding waters.

The final insult to the early Grove settlers was the proposal to build a series of artificial islands from Dinner Key to Cocoplum, completely cutting off the Coconut Grove waterfront. Verbally and in writing the people protested to the U. S. District Engineer and stopped that move. But it was time-consuming, distracting, aggravating. There seemed no way to keep out of the madness.

Mabel Dorn, big with child, drove off real-estate men who came to suggest that she cut up her South Miami grove-home, the land she had planted along with her husband, the land that was now hers in a way that had nothing to do with money.

One day she burst into tears. "Leave me alone," she shouted. "This is my home."

Other residents put up signs: "NOT for Sale." A few were aware that during this period of boom the "richer they grew the poorer they were" by way of increased taxes, complicated civic improvements, and increased cost of necessities in a population-swollen area.

People were still pouring into Miami but there was a warning cloud on the horizon. To have observed it would have been considered un-American. Federal men appeared at the courthouse to inspect the profits of certain speculators.

Without benefit of fanfare the last coontie mill in the area had gone out of business after the hurricane. The industry that had once flourished all over the region was no more.

The Beginning of "The Bust"

NORTHERN BUSINESS EXPERTS, removed from the heat of the subtropics, had begun to say as early as the summer of 1925 that the Florida boom had passed its peak. This rude remark was attributed to sour grapes by most Floridians who stoutly maintained that the best was yet to come.

Miami land deals continued to build up and up even in the face of the freight embargo the railroad was forced to put into effect in order to repair tracks and which saw builders smuggling supplies in as food in refrigerated cars. Each obstacle appeared only to whet the appetites of those determined to get rich. Some rare individuals took their enormous profits and departed. Others, flushed with victory, dipped back into the pot where sand was being turned into gold. In the end these predominated.

Miss Hattie Carpenter's nephew, sent home from college because of an epidemic of pink eye, took out a real-estate broker's license during his brief stay and sold a fifty-thousand-dollar house. With his commission, he went to New York and selected a Steinway grand piano. Few were as sensible as that. Bobo Dean's sons sold land Carl Fisher had given them and made a fortune, then turned around and purchased land that in the end they lost for taxes.

The bubble of the boom did not burst overnight. There were definite signs for those who cared to see them. The National Better Business Bureau, with the help of Florida units, started looking into fraudulent promotions and as these cases were made public it gave the general purchasing public pause. The stock market had a period of decline. The Breakers and Palm Beach hotels both burned to the ground at Palm Beach. All these events, added up, resulted in a psychological dampening of enthusiasm for Florida. Then on January 10,

1926, the barkentine *Prins Valdemar*, an old Danish naval training ship rigged up as a floating hotel, went aground at the entrance to the turning basin as she was being towed to Miami Beach to open up for the season. A northeast wind caught the four tall masts and over she went on her side, all two hundred and forty-one feet of her. More important, there she stayed for nearly a month, blocking the entire harbor entrance. Tempers flared like Roman candles as captains with boatloads of passengers and cargo remained locked in Miami. The passenger ship *George Washington* was just ready to leave for the North. Ten other large vessels were waiting to give up their berths to as many craft waiting outside to come in.

After considerable local chuf-chuffing, the U.S. Engineers began to dig an eighty-foot channel around the reclining *Prins Valdemar*, but first with acetylene torch and ax they removed the proud masts. Freighters edged in to the causeway to land their cargo, then, when the channel was filled with boats, the steamer *Lakevort* grounded across the outer channel. This held up at least fifty vessels beside the edge of the Gulf Stream. Some, attempting to get closer to the mainland, went aground on reefs. It was a seaman's nightmare.

It was also a boom-time builder's nightmare. It is figured that during this stoppage forty-five million feet of lumber urgently needed by builders was sitting outside the harbor while crews fished or took sun baths on enforced vacation. By the time the channel digging appeared completed, men were too exasperated to cheer. Just as well, because at that point the two dredges broke down and it was discovered that dynamite would be needed to accomplish the end of the job.

Commodore Munroe said later, "One can only wonder why the vessel itself was not immediately blown up."

The *Prins Valdemar* was eventually refloated and taken to the foot of Sixth Street and Biscayne Boulevard where it was converted into an aquarium and, for a time, became a Miami institution. Actually, by blocking further building, the *Prins Valdemar* prevented some men from getting into any deeper financial complications. It saved people a lot of money, but nobody ever said thank you.

The last transaction of the boom involved the creation of Biscayne Boulevard in which Roy Wright and Hugh Anderson, with a high disregard of expense, cut through homes and gardens, the Charles Deering Buena Vista estate, and a Jewish synagogue to make the wide, four-lane thoroughfare. It is estimated that the last eight miles of Biscayne Boulevard cost one million dollars a mile. J. S. Phipps lent seven million dollars to the promoters, and when the boom ended, the Phipps estate took over to protect the family's investment. It is difficult to visualize Miami without it.

Despite warning signs and even with the prone *Prins Valdemar* signaling a somber message, the people went jiggling along with their big boom. Galli-Curci came to the White Temple and Feodor Chaliapin sang at the completed Biltmore Hotel. Paul Whiteman played at the Gables Country Club and the Roney Plaza opened with fanfare. Miami started building "the tallest courthouse in the South," constructing it around the old courthouse with the cupola so despised by the Duke of Dade in order not to interrupt city business. The Venetian Causeway was opened and so was the new Olympia Theater, later to be called Gusman Center, the Columbus Hotel, the Everglades along the bayfront, and the Floridian at Miami Beach. The freight embargo was lifted. Perhaps with all this visible to the eye, it was impossible not to believe in the boom going on merrily forever.

The people were there that winter of 1926 (but the Gene Tunney-Young Stribling fight was called off because nobody would guarantee Tunney's fifty-thousand share of the purse). The music was as loud and the fun was as fast, but when it was over and the horse-racing season ended in March it was as though someone had turned a master switch. The town was suddenly empty. A lot of people liked it that way and said, "Thank heaven we won't have a summer like last one."

Nearly everyone agreed that now Miami could settle down to a nice, steady growth. Even the most optimistic were ready to admit that the boom was over. But they added that what lay ahead was something better.

The Big Blow

By THE TIME STEAMY SEPTEMBER, 1926, ARRIVED, Miamians were once more chattering hopefully of the season, the tourists, and real estate. They were also interested in the Dempsey-Tunney fight to be staged in Philadelphia, the opening of the first airmail service to Miami, the completion of the Tamiami Trail across the Everglades, and the fact that two dredges were back in Biscayne Bay, this time to start the new channel and harbor program. They paid no attention whatever to reports of a series of tropical storms playing about the West Indies.

On the morning of Friday, September 17, glowering skies and increased winds called attention to the fact that the latest report concerned a hurricane stirring about, with winds of one hundred miles an hour and headed straight for the Florida coast. Boat owners took steps to make lines secure and some went so far as to move their craft up the Miami River. It was only the old-timers who stocked up on drinking water and canned food and took the precaution of nailing shutters to their houses. People went to bed either frightened or uneasy as the winds increased but in any case unprepared for a hurricane. When it moved in on the Florida coast in the black night with its sighing and moaning and shrieking it was apparent to all that this hurricane was a granddaddy.

It hit the Florida coast soon after midnight, knocking out power lines and plunging the city into darkness. It lifted weather-recording instruments high in the air, tossed lumber about like matchsticks, played with the pretty tiles of the rooftops like a child with a game of jacks, plucked the man-placed trees and set them down on their sides.

147

In their assorted houses, so many carelessly thrown together by get-rich-quick builders, the people lit candles and mopped up the water that rushed down chimneys and leaked through roofs and crept under doors. They swept up shattered panes of window glass and hung rugs and stuffed rags in the open spaces where the howling, whistling, deafening wind raced.

And they prayed.

For eight hours in the black night the winds kept up the rushing, raging, shattering onslaught. In the morning, the people peered into the gray outdoors, unable to believe the sight of trees and shrubs uprooted and naked of leaves, houses vanished, and all the land a litter of debris. All at once there was a quiet. The wind stopped and the rain did too. A pale yellow-white sun began to shine. They flung open their doors and came out to find their neighbors and friends, look after their businesses, investigate the damage.

The last hurricane of any account had struck back in 1906 when the "extension workers" had met unsuspected death in the lull of that sweeping storm. A somewhat minor hurricane hit in 1910. In the intervening twenty years, minds had been centered on other matters than nature. This '26 hurricane swept in on the most ignorant of subtropical dwellers.

Old-timers and seamen could have told the uninitiated that a full-grown hurricane is a whirling doughnut of wind circulating about a calm center. This center or "eye" was at this moment passing over the area. The barometer stood at 27.75. It was the period known as "the lull."

Floridians went out of their homes and before they could get back inside the hurricane struck again, this time from the opposite direction. Once again concrete blocks and two-by-fours were tossed about like leaves in a northern September to the tune of the shrill, screaming wind. Houses which had managed to withstand the first attack collapsed under this second invasion.

It was late Saturday afternoon before the hurricane passed and people once more opened their doors. As night fell they took inventory. No electricity or telephone, no telegraph or radio. Miami and her sister city across the bay, which lay buried under from two to four feet of sand, were for the moment as isolated as the early settlers had been in the era of the bay, but the settlers of 1926 were not as happily situated, being without drinking water. No longer was it possible to dip a tin cup in the Miami River and come up with a drink of clear, sweet water. With flashlight and candles the people stepped over fallen trees, boats split in two, broken glass, and demolished houses. They began to count their dead.

Sunday-morning newspapers throughout the U.S.A. carried black headlines about the Florida hurricane. A typical headline read: "South Florida Wiped Out in Storm." A makeshift radio station was set up in Hialeah and a message was relayed to the world that Miami was down but not "wiped out."

The Blow received more national front-page attention than the Boom, but it was not the kind Miami promoters enjoyed. In fact, during the clean-up period, the efforts of some Miami boosters and bankers to soft-pedal the extent of the damage was a source of consternation to Red Cross officials interested in raising relief money for the thousands of Floridians in dire need. Despite this handicap, donations totaling more than three million dollars found their way to the American Red Cross for the Florida coastal communities hit by the hurricane. William Randolph Hearst dispatched a special train with one hundred doctors, nurses, and engineers carrying four chlorine water-treating units. This rescue mission labored for a week, day and night, from Fort Lauderdale, which was badly hit, to Homestead. President Machado of Cuba sent a gunboat loaded with doctors and medicines.

In Dade County, the known dead reached one hundred and thirteen while eight hundred and fifty-four people were hospitalized. Hundreds of others were treated at home. In Miami, two thousand homes were destroyed, three thousand damaged. In Hialeah and in the outlying districts where cheaply constructed homes abounded, the loss was staggering. Coral Gables, with its "planned construction," was hurt least of all. Miami's bayfront was a welter of broken boats and twisted material. The schooner *Rose Mahony* was swept up onto the boulevard along with smaller craft. The giant dredges stationed in Biscayne Bay to start the much-sought-after channel-deepening lay at the bottom of the bay. Ironically, the *Prins Valdemar*, which many felt was the first link in the chain of disasters which beset Miami, was the only vessel to safely ride out the Big Blow.

A puff of the hurricane had dented the steel girders of a rising skyscraper. A resident reported seeing a two-by-four being driven like a giant stake through a live oak tree by the wind's force. Nature had really been on the warpath.

149

The National Guard moved in early Sunday to help maintain order but there was little looting. In the steamy heat, a sober population was tackling the titanic task of mopping up. The invading wind and water had moved the streetcar tracks on the County Causeway from the center of the roadway clear over to the outer edge. Sheriff Chase stationed armed guards at the Venetian Causeway to prevent "undesirables" from prowling about Miami Beach as the County Causeway was closed to all traffic. He assigned guarded prisoners to open up other roads blocked by trees, pieces of houses, demolished autos.

Three hundred volunteer plumbers worked at restoring the drinking supply. Every hotel and apartment was opened to those left homeless. When the figures were finally tabulated it proved to be the staggering number of forty-seven thousand. A lost children's bureau was established and two hundred and fifty little ones were restored to their parents amid weeping and laughter.

Every hurricane has its amusing sidelights and this one was no exception. Looking out the window just as the eye of the storm passed over and the wind started blowing from the opposite direction, Sheriff Chase witnessed a man clad in a bathing suit attempting to reach home with his arms filled with bags of groceries. The wind-battered fellow sought to brace himself against a fence where he was unlucky enough to catch his bathing suit on a nail. As he staggered forward the entire suit ripped down the back. His frantic efforts to save the suit resulted in complete loss of the groceries and he ended up racing down the street stark naked and empty-handed.

Millionaire Charles Deering had grown deaf and his wife reported to a friend later that he slept through the hurricane at his bayfront home at Cutler. His bed was equipped with rollers and as the windows gave or the water spilled in Mrs. Deering quietly moved him from room to room.

As the hurricane lashed and bit into the town, tempestuous "Judge" Worley, Pope's ring and all, breathed his last. He had been seriously ill and the end was not unexpected. Everyone agreed it was a fitting way for the blustery, dramatic figure to make his exit even as they acknowledged that the curtailed funeral which followed, necessarily quiet and without processional, would not have been to his liking.

September is the month when anybody who can find a reason for being out of town finds it. From New York and North Carolina, New England and even California, Miamians streamed home. Joseph W. Young, the Hollywood builder, chartered a special train from New York and loaded aboard Mayor Ed Romfh, the Miami banker whose cautious handling of bank loans during the boom gave him a reputation for being "tight;" John Levi, Fisher's friend and Beach leader; and a bunch of politicians and businessmen. Their train broke a record, making the run to Miami in thirty-one hours.

Within a week, Mayor Romfh sent a prepared statement to the press that "Miami was almost back to normal." Miss Hattie Carpenter, who had turned her hand to magazine fiction after leaving the old *Metropolis*, took issue with this evaluation. Hurrying home from a summer vacation in North Carolina to inspect the damage to the family home, which was now the house Will Brickell had built for his bride on Southeast Sixth Street, Miss Hattie discovered that right next door what appeared to be a house of prostitution was going strong. This fact was clear to the forthright Miss Hattie, who demanded the eyesore be removed before her mother's homecoming from the Carolina hills.

Miss Hattie, with a quiet tongue but fire in her eye (as well as the threat of fire at the end of her pen), got immediate results despite the fact that the power behind the establishment led straight to the home of the son of a former mayor who was exhibiting a predilection for bizarre and shady enterprises.

The Miami Spirit

A writer for the Tampa *Times* visited Greater Miami following the '26 hurricane and declared he found Miamians referring to the Big Blow as "Miami's wonderful hurricane." A native Floridian, the writer hailed the extensive loss of shrubbery as a boon which now permitted visitors to view without obstruction the "private estates of celebrated people." He closed his glowing piece of fiction by commenting on "the Miami spirit," which made all things possible.

Any attempt to whistle off the damage of the storm while closing both eyes to the declining real estate values was pathetic in the face of the unfinished Roosevelt Hotel, which stood against the cumulous-clouded sky in silent testimony to the fact that the millions had run out. But Miamians were pretty good whistlers.

While Mabel Dorn accepted the chairmanship of a city-wide "beautification program" under the Junior Chamber of Commerce banner, with cash prizes offered for the best-looking gardens, Doc Dammers took a full page in the daily newspapers to run an advertisement inviting the citizens of Miami to "a talk."

"I particularly want to invite you cold-feet babies who thought Miami was gone," the ad stated. "Have you read of the terrible loss of life in the floods of Tennessee, of the hundreds dying of pneumonia and other winter diseases in the icebound New England states, of the freezing weather in France, and the earthquakes in California and you ask WILL FLORIDA COME BACK. FLORIDA NEVER WENT AND IT DOESN'T HAVE TO COME BACK. Sure some lives were lost in the hurricane but hurricanes come only once in a lifetime . . . "

The Miami *Herald* advised the populace to "look ahead to the future. The dead past buries its dead."

When a prominent citizen hanged himself in his garage the newspapers were quick to point out that his bond and mortgage company was in first-class shape and that he was not suffering any financial worry.

President Coolidge asked a Congress agitated mainly over poison liquor to approve emergency loans to Florida farmers out of tick-eradication funds. The Red Cross assisted in getting mortgages reduced. Somebody made the proud statement that Miamians were "not in need of charity but merely required aid and time to meet their obligations." The voice was drowned out by cheery words from Miami boosters.

All through the next two seasons they harped on the building figures of 1926, paying no heed to the fact that in other parts of the country men were beginning to show financial strain. Lou Tellegen went bankrupt in California and a New York financier committed suicide. Business was so poor that Burdine and Quarterman advertised a sale with "dramatic reductions" in January, and Gene Austin was hired to come to town to sing "My Blue Heaven" in three Miami stores to step up business.

Newspapermen gave N. B. T. Roney a new nickname. Instead of "No Back Talk" Roney of the boom, the promoter was now "Nothing But Trouble" Roney.

T. Coleman Du Pont, departing from Miami after a stop at the Cocolobo Cay Club, suggested that Miami drop the habit of using "extravagant phrases." He had yanked his millions out from under the Mizners, because of their flamboyant claims in advertising, and, unperturbed, was on his way to earning the title: Daddy of the Bust.

"You only need the unvarnished truth of the climate to attract desirable people here," he said. Du Pont, relaxed and fresh from a happy time at one of America's most exclusive clubs, could afford to be objective.

Likable C. W. (Pete) Chase, Jr., who handled Fisher's land sales at the Beach, personally saw to it that the forty-one club members led undisturbed lives, while at the same time being apprised of the daily stock market quotations as well as the weather reports from Northern centers. One day for lack of something more pressing to do, Pete sat down with pencil and paper to figure the aggregate wealth of the forty-one members. It came to five hundred million dollars, which even for Miami was a lot of millions. Banker-mayor Romfh was the happy president of the rich men's club.

Another exclusive club composed of local lads in the various professions as well as visiting millionaires was the Committee of One Hundred, and when Clarence W. Barron of the *Wall Street Journal* addressed the august body he stated reassuringly, "Florida is economically sound." There was heavy applause. Carl Graham Fisher, sitting in the audience along with John Collins, showed his famous dimples in a forced smile.

When the news of the hurricane was brought to him at Montauk, Long Island, where he had begun a development as fantastic as Miami Beach, he first said, "We built it out of nothing and we'll build it again." Then, in a flash of prescience, he jumped to his feet, exclaiming, "Securities, securities."

He had sold Miami Beach lots on sales contracts payable one fifth down and the balance over one, two, three and four years. He feared that the purchasers might be scared away by the hurricane from paying on their purchase contracts. That is precisely what was beginning to happen.

Feverishly, Miami turned to the arrival of the new Seaboard Air Line Railway and fifteen thousand people including Governor Martin and leading Seminoles lured from the Everglades for the occasion welcomed the Orange Blossom Special from New York. Arabs on snow-white horses guarded the minarets of Opa-Locka as the train neared the city. A celebration was held at the Pancoast Hotel at Miami Beach that evening, after a mammoth welcome in Royal Palm Park.

An official of the FEC Railroad made a public statement within the next few days that "business was increasing daily." Actually the FEC, which had pioneered in Florida, was feeling the pinch of having overextended itself by its track-laying.

Optimistic statements, all by individuals financially stretched to the last cartilage, littered the front pages. One headline said: "Bowman Sees Bright Outlook for Miami." Bowman, who had just finished the Miami Biltmore with George Merrick, was nervously wondering how to fill it and was headed irrevocably for bankruptcy. Merrick, sanguine to the final curtain, paid a visit to Washington, D. C., to look into the possibility of having the harbor-development program "moved closer to Coral Gables." On his return, he reported, "I found everywhere a growing faith in our future." He cleared twenty-five miles of bridle paths in the Gables and announced that fox hunting would be introduced as a wintertime diversion.

They whistled and they whistled and they whistled. A popular tune of the day was "Laugh, Clown, Laugh", and the children of Florida in a poll sponsored by the Federation of Women's Clubs wisely chose the mockingbird as the state bird. The Florida legislature ratified this selection, making it unlawful to molest the mockingbird.

Miss Jefferson Bell, *Herald* society editor, observed that the "social temperature was climbing steadily" as Ed Howe, the sage of Potato Hill, arrived in his flowing black tie. Will Rogers, loyal to the spot for a winter vacation, came, too. Gene Sarazen won the Miami Open Golf Championship with a score of two hundred eighty-nine. Streets were crowded again and Miami tried not to notice that the season of 1927–28 was nothing like boom time.

Young ladies in sleek flapper haircuts jingled slave bracelets and said, "Be yourself" at tea dances in the Oriental Gardens of the Flamingo Hotel. Mary Pickford played in *Sparrows* at the Olympia, and out in Coconut Grove a new four-hundred-thousand-dollar motion picture house opened with Adolphe Menjou in *Sorrows of Satan*. (Along with other big stars the suave Menjou had taken a drastic salary cut.) Hialeah Racetrack opened, Glenn Curtiss started an Archery Club, the Roney Plaza completed an ocean walk, and the University of Miami Hurricanes played Howard College at football.

Up in Palm Beach, the Mizners, Addison and Wilson, sat down with Mr. and Mrs. Arthur Somers Roche as guests of Irving Berlin to a simple dinner of wild boar. (The suit of Addison Mizner against Victor Searles to nullify the transfer of Palm Beach ocean front valued at a million dollars protesting the use of "fradulent seals" would come later. Closer home, in Miami, the Shoreland Company defaulted on a million-dollar note.)

As the disappointing season drew to an end, the Miami *Daily News*, which was now burying the word *Metropolis* in small type and soon would drop it entirely, declared in a burst of petulance that "the sugar bag hat from England looks more like the dust bag from a vacuum cleaner." It was an apt description of the latest in ladies' chapeaux.

When the last tourist shook the sand from his shoes, wihin the family circle and with the shades pulled down, Miami wiped off its big smile and decided the "once-in-a-lifetime" hurricane had frightened its tourists away.

By the fall of 1928 plans were being made by Ev Sewell to send two hundred and fifty agents representing apartment-house owners to northern cities to try to rent apartments. He was also asking for a twenty-five-thousand-dollar fund to publicize Miami in the North, meanwhile selling the home folks the usual load of hope. Headlines like "Largest Tourist Season Due This Winter, Inquiries Show" appeared with rhythmic regularity.

Dade County schools were facing a two-hundred-thousand-dollar yearly deficit as they prepared for a September 17 opening and seventy-one resignations "were requested" among teachers. Those staying on would be paid by the month "as long as the money lasted."

Stephen Cochran Singleton who wrote feelingly of "murmurous inlets and tide-swept bars" in his poem "My Florida" accepted a commission to go to San Antonio, Texas, to investigate the plausibility of starting colonies of bats as antimosquito agents. On his return, he strongly advised Miami to fight mosquitoes with bats.

The opening of the Dade County Courthouse, "the tallest building in the South," constructed at a cost of four million dollars during the flood tide of hope and planning, "raised its bold pyramids to the sky" on September 6. It was twenty-seven and a half stories high with a penthouse "escape-proof" prison. In the years to come, many a crook would successfully demonstrate how simple a matter it was to break out of the escape-proof jail.

That September as the calendar neared what would be autumn in the North, Miami waited for the first cool breeze of October and took heart from certain hopeful signs. Tex Rickard was enlarging and remodeling his North Bay residence at Miami Beach, Dr. J. H. Kellogg of Battle Creek, Michigan, inspected the city with a thought to opening a health sanitarium, and the exclusive Bath Club completed a seventy-five-thousand-dollar swimming pool with lockers, *cabañas*, and such for the coming season.

By way of the Associated Press from New York, Miami learned that Glenn Curtiss planned a new flying school in Miami as "a link in the first nation-wide air-taxi service." It was, the AP reported, a ten-million-dollar company. The sum had a nice familiar sound that drowned out the warning of Judge Edith M. Atkinson that in Miami "parental love was on the wane." She was concerned by the hundreds of cases of child abuse coming before her.

A new little company known as Pan American Airways announced it would move its operations to Miami from Key West's Meacham Field from which it had made its first flight the previous year and tested a Sikorsky amphibian plane for use in its first Miami-to-Havana flight. The company had been founded on a shoestring by Juan Terry Trippe, a Yale boy whose college days were interrupted when he enlisted in the Naval Air Service. When the war ended he went back to Yale and on graduation went into investment banking but continued to dream about aviation. In the spring of 1927 he applied for a government airmail contract between Key West and Cuba, and, in an empty room in Key West's La Concha Hotel, began the airways that eventually would stretch around the globe, putting the word "World" into his company.

Miami took Trippe and his high hopes for making the Magic City the "Gateway to South America" to her bosom. Plans for a Greater Miami Airport association and the All American Air Maneuvers were begun. Miami grabbed and clung to the idea of aviation as to a doorjamb in a hurricane-tossed house. Aviation was her support, her depression-child, her dreams of new fortunes all in one.

To give the lie to Doc Dammers' "once-in-a-lifetime" tag to the '26 storm, another hurricane hit on September 16, 1928, and this one claimed one thousand, eight hundred and thirty-six lives in Florida, with close to two thousand injured and the damage set at twenty-five million dollars.

Miami escaped any serious damage, being on the storm's edge, but her heart was with sufferers in Palm Beach, where the hurricane struck early in the night before moving into the Lake Okeechobee region, where floods accounted for most of the deaths. In the first few days, Miamians raised more than twelve thousand dollars, and before the storm had subsided a relief caravan was traveling toward Palm Beach, where water, gas, and power were wiped out and martial law was declared. A trainload of a thousand refugees, black and white, from the lake district were brought to Miami and tales of heroism were a dime a dozen. Thelma Martin, aged twelve, saw her mother washed away by the rising waters and her six-year-old sister knocked from her father's lap and killed as the water rushed into their small house. All through the night, pinned under the roots of a tree and badly injured, she kept the heads of her two-year-old brother and seven-year-old sister above water.

Miami gave benefits at the Olympia and listened attentively to the Indian superstition "when the saw grass blooms, danger comes." The Indians had all left their homes for higher land before the storm struck. The West Indian chant of the hurricane was heard again on people's lips: "June, too soon; July, stand by; August, come it must; September, remember; October, all over." Miami now had good reason to remember her Septembers.

The Associated Press accommodatingly filed a story reporting to the rest of the U.S.A.: "No hurricane has ever been known to hit the state from November to June."

Dwellers in the drowned lands blamed certain state officials with maintaining too high a water level on Lake Okeechobee and with the discontinuance of dike-building operations which might have prevented an overflow. Demands went up for joint state and federal control of Lake Okeechobee. John Sewell got in heated argument with the governor.

When September 19, 1929, brought still another hurricane with winds of one hundred and fifty miles an hour centered at Key Largo, the damage was cut to five hundred thousand dollars because of improved hurricane-warning service and because the uninitiated had learned how to live through what Miami learned to call "a tropical disturbance." But it heaped up more debris and more unwanted front-page publicity.

A lot of people were still talking in millions in the fall of 1928 when Governor Martin wired Sheriff Henry Chase, "Can you and will you stop racing in Dade County? Do you need help?"

Chase wired back, "I can and will and do not need help."

The racetracks were darkened and many people gave thanks, but some of the ones who agitated to close them would change their minds as they felt the pinch of the Depression, and ask to have racing restored. By the time the stock market crashed, the last optimist was willing to quit talking in millions.

The word "Boom" became socially unacceptable in most company. A lot of awfully nice people were awfully, awfully broke, but as Bobo Dean put it, "I wouldn't want to be rich with most of my friends wiped out."

Harry Tuttle, who had shot the works with the Julia Tuttle Hotel, had an ace-in-the-hole in the form of his mother's almost forgotten liquor clause. For signing his name to releases on land changing hands he could charge in the currency of the realm.

The Brickells had the same privilege in their land deeds which held the same restriction against spiritous liquors. However, the Brickell family was Gibraltar-like financially. All but Miss Maude. Word got out that Miss Maude had been swindled out of three hundred and twenty thousand dollars by a smooth-talking individual named N. H. Wheeler (alias E. Randolph Atkinson) at the very height of the boom. Along with two other fine-looking men he rented a Brickell Avenue home from Miss Maude and after making himself attractive to her produced a plan for "cornering the market on the stock of a copper mine." Innocent Miss Maude paid over the money in cash and bore her loss stoically until the county solicitor, hearing rumors, sent for her. When the story broke in the local press, readers asked how anybody could have been so foolish as to hand out so much cash money.

Early settlers recalling Mary Brickell counting out five or ten thousand dollars in bills from her apron to some businessman in difficulty (and asking no written note) were not surprised. They were just sorry Miss Maude had been duped by a stranger and a mythical copper mine. They felt it would have been better if she'd lost her money in the Miami land boom.

Villa Vizcaya, built in 1916

The Biltmore Hotel, built in 1926

Venetian Pool, built in 1924

The Biltmore Hotel, built in 1926

Overleaf: Cape Florida Lighthouse, built in 1825

Villa Vizcaya, built in 1916

Villa Vizcaya, built in 1916

Miami Beach residence, built circa 1924

The Barnacle State Historic Site,
Commodore Ralph Munroe's home, built circa 1891

Coral Gables House, George Merrick's home, built in 1899

Lord Jim yacht on Biscayne Bay, built circa 1938

Miami Beach Island from Biscayne Bay

Carl Fisher's former Miami Beach home, built circa 1930

Fisher Island, William K. Vanderbilt's home, built in 1929

Fisher Island, William K. Vanderbilt's estate, built in 1929

Plymouth Congregational Church, built circa 1917

The Spanish Monastery, built in 1141

Overleaf: Hialeah Park, built in 1925

Citation Statue at Hialeah Park

Miami Beach home, built circa 1938

Miami River Inn, built circa 1906

The Kampong, David Fairchild's home, built in 1928

Overleaf: Miami Beach residence courtyard, built circa 1934

Biscayne Bay from Villa Vizcaya at sunrise

Opposite page: Freedom Tower, built in 1925

Miami skyline, 1990

"Stay Through May"

AS THE SPRING OF 1930 APPROACHED, Miami coined a new slogan: "Stay Through May." It was a desperate invitation to tourists to remain through one of the most inviting calendar months in south Florida and with it went plans to attempt to develop a summer tourist season. The Clyde Mallory Steamship Line announced reduced rates. So did hotels and apartments. The indefatigable Ev Sewell asked for five- and ten-dollar offerings from merchants in order to publicize summertime Miami. In the spirit of the movement, Pauline Burdine scheduled a summer fashion show, and the Civic Theater, Miami's active little theater group, announced it would remain open throughout the summer. Alfred Barton would play the lead role, that of Prince Albert in *The Swan*. Joseph Cotton, the rangy, quiet-eyed classified-ad man from the *Herald*, would have roles in *Paris Bound* and *Green Goddess*. He was not yet ready for Hollywood but was being molded in the active laboratory of the Civic Theater.

The Three Score and Ten Club, where hearts were young and gay but where only the elderly were welcome, announced a "summer hop." The president-elect of the Advertising Federation of America handed Miami a slick compliment when he said, "There's gold in your sunshine." A sixty-piece boys' band, the Drum and Bugle Corps, drilled relentlessly for a nationwide tour that would bring them an audience with President Hoover and, they hoped, a handclasp from Admiral Richard E. Byrd, due back from his trip to the South Pole. By any means and at any cost, Miami, at the tip of the long peninsula, must be lifted high so the rest of the U.S.A. would see it.

Like a hang-over from the winy boom days came the announcement that drilling for oil had commenced out on Tamiami Trail. The company was headed by lumberman Gaston Drake, a respected citizen who had named a town in the Redlands, Princeton, for his alma mater. It was that old-time happy talk, that get-rich-quick kind of talk, that was native to the people. They needed an escape from reality, anyway. Miami was broke.

Suits filed to collect judgments were everyday fare. Efforts by a contractor to foreclose on St. Stephen's Episcopal Church in Coconut Grove to satisfy a claim for seven thousand dollars for repairs following the '26 hurricane failed in circuit court. The death of William J. Matheson on a fishing trip to Bimini aboard his yacht *Seaforth* was mourned but the bequests he left, to St. Stephen's, the Community Chest, and the like were fervently welcomed. Pages and pages of property listings in fine print, forty-one in one newspaper edition, were notices of land to be sold for delinquent taxes at public auction on the fancy new courthouse steps.

The city fathers decided it would be necessary to dispense with the traditional band concerts, curtail donations to both the university and the library. In addition, forty policemen and twelve firemen would have to be dropped from the city payroll. The *News*, considered brassy and addicted to "yellow journalism" by the *Herald*, came right out and said, "Miami Facing Lean Winter with Bond Maturities and Interest Greater Than Present Budget."

Miami bankers were asked to show their faith in Miami's financial future by subscribing part of the one million, three hundred thousand dollars needed to meet the principal on bonds maturing in the next twelve months. The hope was that New York bankers would furnish the remainder. In June, Mayor C. H. Reeder and L. J. Griffin, finance director, left for New York to arrange the city financing. All the way north they rehearsed the happy side of the picture, beginning with Miami's natural advantage of climate, and when they walked into the appointed bond house they were greeted by wary-eyed men who informed them that the Bank of Bay Biscayne had just failed. One of Miami's proudest institutions, this failure was a final, crushing blow for her people and a shocking surprise to the emissaries of Miami. They were able to float the loan in spite of it.

At home, Miami was learning that it would be necessary for the Everglades Drainage District to raise two million dollars in the Okeechobee

Flood Control District before the federal government would advance any further financial assistance. The millions, which once rolled off lips so liltingly, now stuck in the civic throat.

The Greater Miami Manufacturers pleaded with people to "buy at home" in an effort to sell Miami-made products, and the Dade County Juvenile Court pleaded with parents to go sell their own newspapers and send their children back to school. Diplomatically, the newspapers pointed out that "this was the practice of residents of *other* cities who had moved to Miami."

The town felt happy when Ethel Barrymore answered its advertising and came for an off-season visit to the Pancoast Hotel at Miami Beach but unhappy because she registered as Mrs. R. G. Colt and indicated she was a private citizen who wanted to bathe at the Roman Pools and go fishing on the Keys.

A violent outbreak of defacing of mailboxes began to plague post office officials. Hot tar was used to plug up the mail slots, trash was slipped in between the openings, and in one instance a live cat was forced into the box. Exasperated, the U.S. Post Office removed two public mailing boxes and threatened to remove more.

The blanket invitation to Stay Through May was accepted one rainy Easter Sunday by a well-known Chicago figure, who purchased a lavish home on Palm Island through a Miami lawyer. His coming brought out in sharp relief the fact that Miami was becoming a schizo-city. The *Herald* referred to him only when it was forced to and then as Alphonse Capone, but the *News* called him "Scarface Al Capone, alias A. Acosta, alias Al Brown, the notorious beer and brothel baron of Chicago." By front-page editorial and by slanting the news, the paper made it clear that it intended putting up resistance to Capone's residence in the Magic City. Many people felt this campaign to be in poor taste, taking the traditional Miami view that unpleasant fact was best covered up from the innocent eyes of the tourist and the outside world in general, which after all, was nothing but a group of potential tourists.

Just as they had spirited away the Negro help stricken with smallpox back in the early Royal Palm Hotel days and tried to soft-pedal the Big Blow even at the risk of circumventing help where it was dearly needed, there was now the tendency to let Capone live behind his walled palace on the man-made island on the banks of Biscayne Bay without quarrel. There was, speak softly, even the tendency to get acquainted with the overlord of gangdom and accept his "donations" in certain good causes. This led to a public policy on the one hand and a private policy on the other and brought about some embarassing moments for leading citizens.

The public policy, fed by the fury of the campaign conducted by the *News* and the awakening moral indignation of the people, was clear cut: it wanted Capone to go back where he came from. This idea was suggested to Capone by authorities. Flanked by his three Miami lawyers, Vincent Giblin, Bart Riley, and J. Fritz Gordon, the gangster stood on his constitutional rights. He had come to make his home, he told officials.

The Kansas City *Star* during this interlude headlined: "Chicago and Al Capone both breathe more freely while he fishes in South Florida."

Three of Capone's henchmen had been murdered in gangster fashion in Chicago the very day he arrived at Miami Beach. The climate in Florida suited the gang leader much better than the northern climate at the moment. He would, he said, "stay through May."

The American Legion came up with a beautifully simple plan for ridding Miami of the racketeer. Fifty legionnaires would surround the house, calling to Capone to "get out of town." When this happened the sheriff would call out the National Guard on the grounds a "riot" was in effect. Martial law would be declared. Under martial law, constitutional rights would be abolished. Capone would be given the old heave-ho. The beautifully simple plan, never made public, fell through when the governor understandably refused to send the militia.

When the notorious Chicago gangster Red McLaughlin was killed in Chicago and his body discovered drifting in a drainage canal, a Miami Beach police courtesy card was found in his pocket. People heretofore unaffected by Capone's presence began to scream that all this was "bad publicity" and it would "hurt real-estate values." This cry is known to observers of the Miami scene as the sharpest cry of all. City of Miami officials announced they would arrest Al Capone every time they saw him on the streets of Miami or "in a public place." With Attorney Giblin and his usual quota of armed guards, Capone attended the fights at the American Legion and the police promptly picked him up. On the trip to jail the gangster remarked on the "cheap touring car" the police officers rode in. Giblin got him out on bond and they returned to the fights.

The second time he was picked up, Capone spent seventeen and a half hours in jail and Giblin called it "an outrage and a breach of faith on the part of city officials." Capone, through his staff of lawyers, brought injunction proceedings against Police Chief Guy C. Reeve to prevent his arrest without a warrant and later "aimed his legal guns," as the News put it, at a group of citizens, including the mayor, the public safety director, a city commissioner, and ex-governor Cox.

The Miami City Commission in special session voted three to one to adopt the "vagrancy ordinance" making it possible to arrest any person unable to prove legal means of support. Labor representatives, claiming to have twenty-one union organizations behind them, growled ominously at this measure.

Ev Sewell, serving on the commission, wiped his brow and said, "I am supporting the ordinance even though the person at whom it is aimed has been a customer of the store with which I am connected." And everybody knew that when Capone bought he turned to his half-dozen armed bodyguards and said, "What'll you have, fellows?" They went for shoes from Sewell's or hats, silk pajamas or bathing suits. The six-foot, two-hundred-pound gangster was clothes-conscious.

The death of crime reporter Jake Lingle in Chicago put official heat on the Capone mob and gangsters in general and as Miami picked Albert, brother of Al Capone, up on the golf links, it was hinted that President Hoover himself had given the word to harass these criminals at every opportunity.

Miami brought suit against Capone in an attempt to padlock his Palm Island residence, claiming it was "kept and maintained as a harbor for criminals, crooks, gangsters, racketeers, and fugitives from justice." This gangster's retreat was a menace to the safety and well-being of residents, the suit maintained. Fifty residents were called to testify against the overlord of crime. Spectators crowded the circuit courtroom to look and listen.

Leading the parade of witnesses was Carl Graham Fisher, who testified that the presence of Capone was detrimental to land sales, that residents were uneasy having his trigger boys about. He denied it was his "order" that placed two Miami Beach policemen outside the Capone residence, but said he had suggested it would be a good idea. Giblin demanded the names of people who feared Capone's presence and Fisher recalled Mrs. Earl Kiser as one and Harvey Firestone as another.

There was something ridiculous in this demand, and the *News* pointed out in a front-page editorial "Giblin, one of the Florida lawyers representing the underworld, seeks to press witnesses for names. Capone has in a sense terrorized the whole country . . . and men have shrunk from the plain impulse of duty rather than come into the open and invite violence to themselves and their families . . ."

Capone, wearing a powder-blue serge suit and diamond stickpin, "sat for five minutes without a break and glared at the witness with all the ferocity of an infuriated beast," the *News* reported. Carl Fisher returned the gaze unblinkingly. A resident of Palm Island testified that "every time a tire blew" neighbors were certain gang warfare had broken out. A Baptist minister declared that one morning he overheard one of Capone's henchmen issuing an order for a case of champagne and two cases of Scotch to be sent to Fred Pine, candidate for the county solicitor's office.

Where had this conversation been overheard? Why, at Capone's bastion. The minister had gone "to try to rent Capone an automobile."

The editor of a weekly newspaper attempted to turn the trial into a vaudeville performance and succeeded in his small way. He claimed he met Capone "same way he met Hoover." He was, of course, referring to the president of the United States and he was throwing the president and gangster Capone into the same category. It came out that Capone had given a dinner for fifty, a dinner at which engraved invitations were exchanged at the front door for tiny lapel American flags. At this dinner Capone was presented with a fountain pen by his guests, who welcomed him to Greater Miami "as a new businessman."

It was apparent that a good many hangers-on were drinking Capone's liquor and giving him advice on how to capture hearts in the Magic City. Naïvely, Capone had hopes of becoming an accepted member of the community. Possibly the most all-around embarrassing testimony was that of Roddey Burdine, the well-liked head of the department store. Burdine and insurance man George Stembler paid a call on Capone as members of the executive committee of the Community Chest to secure a contribution. They went at ten in the morning, spent several hours, accepted a morning libation of champagne, and left with a check for a thousand dollars—plus the pointed suggestion by Capone that Burdine "arrange a little party." Capone had a specific place in mind for the party—the country club of which Burdine was president.

Perspiring profusely, Burdine admitted that when certain workers of the Community Chest learned of the check they threatened to quit and demanded the check be sent back. It was.

It seems apparent that a good part of Miami was streaming to Capone's door asking for contributions of one sort or another. When J. Fritz Gordon left town "presumably as a result of a nervous breakdown," the National City Bank tried to collect on notes which he owed them from Capone, using as grounds for this unusual behavior the fact that Gordon was Capone's lawyer. The Miami Civic Tourist Club split wide open on whether to accept a check for twenty-five hundred dollars from Capone; the president resigned in protest. A curt letter from Vincent Giblin assured the organization that his client had no intention of donating any sum whatever.

The padlock case was eventually dismissed, and Capone wore a victorious smile for a brief period one morning. By noon, perjury charges were brought against him as an outgrowth of the case. The office of the lawyer preparing the perjury evidence was broken into one weekend and important documents removed. No telltale fingerprints were left behind to assist in the apprehension of the thieves, but it was fairly clear who had committed the act.

During the thick of the feeling against Capone, Marjory Stoneman Douglas and lawyer Bill Muir co-authored a play about a gangster who was mobbed by the citizens of a city in the last act. Called *Storm Warning* it played to packed houses at the Civic Theater. Capone did not attend but some of his henchmen did. Their presence in the back of the theater added an extra tingle for the audience on opening night.

Giblin fought Miami with every trick in the legal bag for Scarface Capone and in the end Capone reneged on the bill rendered. Giblin got a court order to attach Capone's furniture and marched over to Palm Island while the gangster was in Chicago. That brought about a speedy agreement of fees.

Both Giblin and Gordon later became Dade County Circuit Court judges. Giblin narrowly missed election to the Florida Supreme Court. His failure to win the race brought gentle scoldings from both newspapers to the

167

voters. Giblin, they pointed out, had speeded up trials by disposing of technicalities and opposing delays and was well qualified for the job to which he aspired. The Dade County Bar Association thought so, too.

So did his press agents, who split up their publicity firm over a quarrel when the votes were counted.

Giblin and Governor Fuller Warren also quarreled colorfully all through the campaign and Giblin replied in one instance, "I haven't learned to steal or to lie. I haven't learned to doublecross my friends or to hypocritically evade issues. I haven't learned to get fabulous sums from racketeers for campaign purposes."

Miami was never able to move Capone out of town. Federal men finally took care of his imprisonment. His family went on living at Palm Island. His son attended St. Patrick's School at Miami Beach, married a classmate and then proceeded to live quietly in the area.

The *WPA Guide to Miami* compiled in 1941 listed the Capone residence as a "point of interest" directly under the Flagler Monument. Today, tour boats still cruise by the house.

It was more than "a point of interest" for a while.

While the Capone trial was in progress, Dr. Charles Torrey Simpson wearing his faded khaki trousers, torn shirt, and canvas shoes, and carrying a stained bamboo staff, conducted a "wading trip" to Cypress Swamp for nearly one hundred embryonic botanists. At eighty-four his step was as light, his eye as sharp, and his kindliness as bright as ever.

Joyfully, the party collected botanical treasures, rare native orchids, and the like, but when they reached the Dade County line on the return trip all the specimens had to be abandoned. Cattle tick inspectors, stationed at the border, classified them all as "shrubs" and the law said no shrubs could be brought in that might carry ticks on them to endanger the cattle.

Kirk Munroe was unable to take the "wading trip." Munroe, who had been so debonair when he took a walking tour across the continent at seventeen and when he founded the League of American Wheelmen, was now gray and bent and ill and would die before his eightieth birthday. There were only a few left to remember the good old days when his first wife got into rip-roaring fights at the Housekeeper's Club. She had died in 1922 and he had remarried.

The Commodore still sat on the veranda of The Barnacle and looked out through the old spyglass, but he was not at peace. He worried about the man-made islands and the fact that the '26 hurricane had brought so much water with it. Right after that storm, which had taken his boathouse and ruined his fine old trees, he had gone to Jewfish Creek to see what the water had done there, and he had been more afraid than ever of the solid dikes of the railroad construction.

"Some day the water will rush over the Keys, drowning everybody," he predicted.

That June, when the yellow-and-white Royal Palm Hotel was condemned as unsound, even the less aware of Miami's citizens recognized that an era had come to a close. Ridden with termites, the one-time symbol of hope and riches to come had outlived its usefulness and must come down. The people came and took little and big pieces of it away. Something was going from the scene and everyone felt it.

4 | REALITY
1930–WORLD WAR II

A Tree is a Tree

ONE DAY IN THE EARLY 1930s Harry Tuttle parked his car on Flagler Street and went to keep a business appointment. When he came back there was a ticket on it for overparking.

At the police station Harry told the desk sergeant that he was "a pioneer."

The sergeant, a Georgia boy, said coldly, "Then you oughta know the law."

Harry dug down to pay his fine. It was a day of reckoning for many.

The closing of the proud Bank of Bay Biscayne was the final, stunning defeat in a series of acts by God and man that sent Miami to her knees. The few cautious souls who had refrained from speculating saw their savings swept away, and heard reassuring explanations and promises dwindle away into public indignation, meetings and court trial. In the end, depositors realized a negligible amount of their savings. Mrs. William Jennings Bryan sued the Coconut Grove Bank and regained through the courts the full amount of her savings. Other depositors, not so fortunate, realized a mere fifteen cents on the dollar.

The Blow had precipitated Miami into the national depression before the rest of the country. Now it seemed the bad days would never end. Greater Miami, which in 1920 had boasted a population of two hundred, ninety-nine thousand, five hundred and seventy-one had in 1930, one hundred twenty-eight thousand, four hundred and sixty-three souls to struggle through the lean years.

On the streets of Miami, volunteers went about with boxes for the

Dade County Welfare Board pleading for "a penny a day to keep hunger away from somebody out of a job." In Coconut Grove, the women formed the Volunteer Nursing Service to distribute food and clothing to the sick and destitute. At a rummage sale sponsored by this group, vivid reminders of the past showed up in chauffeurs' uniforms and butlers' white coats.

The want ads offered nothing but sales jobs "on commission." Sewell Brothers, oldest of Miami business houses, filed a petition for bankruptcy. Fifty ex-soldiers prepared to leave Miami in a boxcar to join the hunger marchers on Washington in a demand for payment of the soldiers' bonus bill. Before leaving, they marched to the courthouse to deposit absentee ballots in the heated election which would bring about the defeat of Congresswoman Ruth Bryan Owen, stately daughter of the Great Commoner who made the error of misjudging the temper of her constituents and straddled the Prohibition issue. The country was in a mood for change that year of 1932.

Local post office officials announced that no officials of its branch would be "forced into the army of the unemployed," despite the fact that U.S. postal revenues were depleted by more than a hundred million dollars. In Miami nobody could hear the word million without wincing.

The University of Miami cut its staff to the bone, abolishing the departments of physical education, writing, aviation, and architecture.

A campaign to license auto drivers for one dollar on the basis of a paper questionnaire but requiring no actual test so ired the people that they stormed the city commission chambers to demand its repeal or "the resignation of the commission." The excuse that the funds were to be used to "feed the hungry" brought no change of heart. The Miami Realty Board pointed out that it disapproved of "obtaining the revenue by subterfuge."

In Chicago, Mayor Anton Cermak, happily unaware of his imminent rendezvous with death in Miami's Bayfront Park as the result of an assassin's bullet intended for Franklin Delano Roosevelt, called for financial help to weather the depression. "Unless you send relief in the next six months you will be sending troops," he wired President Hoover.

Judge Samuel Seabury, speaking before Washington and Jefferson College, warned that "public apathy paves the way for corrupt officials."

In Miami, citizens were not apathetic. They were up in arms on the matter of taxation. Taxes, harder and harder to collect, were still being held at a high level because city officials were unwilling to admit a collapse in realty values by making adjustments in assessments. The rumble of dissatisfaction was growing louder and louder while the city commission dallied. Five thousand citizens meeting in Bayfront park formed the Citizens Taxation Committee in a mass protest against the "apparent lack of leadership of the mayor and city commission in the present taxation crisis."

Alexander Orr offered a plan which called for reduced taxes, more employment, and relief from tax sale regulations which "deprived home owners of their holdings by placing them at the mercy of tax certificate sharks." The meeting lasted three hours during which Orr declared he "did not charge any city officials with dishonesty," but suggested that they were "damnably stupid and their best is not good enough."

That June night under the Miami moon while the wind rustled through the palms the townspeople called for the county and city to begin spending their "surplus funds," asking for fifty thousand dollars for the repair of the causeway as a specific beginning. Mayor R. B. Gautier, presented with this plan, declared it would "leave Miami like a rudderless wreck on a stormy sea." Orr tartly suggested that the mayor resign.

In their demands they were just a little ahead of the New Deal which Democratic presidential candidate Roosevelt was promising and which he would deliver to the people with a burst of blue eagles and rhetoric in the National Recovery Program.

While their northern brothers and sisters resorted to apple-selling on windy corners, Miamians learned to be grateful for back-yard grapefruit and avocados, summertime mangoes, and key limes, Surinam cherries, guavas, and bananas. People repeated to each other a new phrase, "A mango is five times more nourishing than a whole steak." Newcomers discovered what old-timers had always known: the sea grape made a delicate lavender jelly. A tree once more assumed its rightful role in a beneficent nature.

Dr. Gifford went on patiently preaching his familiar Back-to-the-Land sermon, suggesting five acres of land, tropical land, as the right-sized working plot. A Coconut Grove man stepped forward to say he had realized eighteen hundred dollars from the yield of seventy-five four-year-old avocado trees. Emphasis was turned to the unique land of south Florida in this realistic day of appraisal. The men who had shuddered to see the luxuriant Miami hammock disappear under the builder's ax along the rock ledge leading to Coconut Grove and who had witnessed the killing of the pineland in a scarification program of subdividing now saw with satisfaction the people's deepening interest in the land.

Through the late, turbulent twenties a man named Ernest R. Coe had been tirelessly pushing the idea of turning part of the strange saw grass country of the Everglades into a national park as a sanctuary for plume birds and animals and to preserve the wild growth, the orchids and palms and mangrove.

Now, in the thirties, he had realized the satisfaction of hearing Congresswoman Owen sponsor in the U.S. Congress a measure to create the Everglades National Park.

Coe, who knew the cause was not yet won, said, "Now it is time to ask for contributions." It was a poor time for a good cause.

Others were occupied with planting and preserving the land. George Brett, president of Macmillan Publishing Company, bought sixty acres of land south of Coconut Grove on which to build a seventy-five-thousand-dollar home called Journey's End. He wanted to try his hand at growing tropical plants. In Connecticut his activities in gathering pines and spruces into a pinetum had been taken up by another man of means, a Manhattan accountant named Robert H. Montgomery. Montgomery followed Brett south and built a home in the same area and began establishing a palmetum filled with rare palms.

In the mid-thirties, Montgomery proposed founding a botanical garden and naming it the Fairchild Tropical Garden in honor of Plant Explorer Fairchild. It was created on a tract of land adjoining Matheson Hammock Park and to the dedication services came celebrated botanists like the world's great herpetologist Thomas Barbour, author of *That Vanishing Eden*. Dr. Barbour had helped select the tract of land with Brett and Montgomery and in doing so discovered that the chosen area was the best, if not the only, spot on the mainland of the U.S.A. in which to grow tropical plants.

Six hundred willing and enthusiastic assistants attended the dedication and heard George Merrick speak out for the project. Broke but unbeaten, the builder of Coral Gables said, "This garden must prove actually to be as a great compounding cauldron for the actual magic that stirred, impelled, and motivated . . . the host great and small, that have builded and for those who will build true to the greatest destiny of south Florida."

Unheralded, as many important incidents often are, was the establishment of the University of Florida Experiment Station at Belle Glade. Here for the first time in the history of the state man set about to discover what made up the various soils of the Everglades. Until this happened, man's only interest in the Everglades had been to drain it, make it salable land, land on which to build or grow wintertime vegetables. Ever since 1882, when Hamilton Disston, the wealthy Philadelphian, bought four million acres of swamplands for a million dollars and put engineers to work, the idea had been to drain, change, bend to man's purpose. Nobody had tried to find out what the Everglades actually were. So that when the Everglades began to burn, sending choking smog over Miami, and when, because the water table had been lowered by overdrainage, salt crept into the drinking water, there would be people on hand who understood the involvements of the relation of soil to fresh water, the matter of evaporation and run-off and salt intrusion. Then the public would come to understand that the reckless dynamiting of the rocky ledge of the Miami River in dredging canals for farmers to get to market back in pre–World War I days had helped upset nature's delicate system of holding back the salt water from the fresh water of the 'Glades, and that local treatment of drainage had resulted in the shrinking and burning of the soil. This was all in the future, but the first step in the right direction had been taken.

The cause of conservation would win a round in the abrupt halting of Florida cattlemen bent on a deer-killing rampage by the unexpected figure of the almost-forgotten Seminole Indian.

Hysteria against the tick had been mounting and finally the center of attack shifted from shrubs to the deer. In Osceola County, everything, including rats, squirrels and deer, had been tested for ticks. The deer, it was announced, had more ticks than the others. Kill the deer became the battle-cry of the thirty-million-dollar cattle industry. Hundreds of deer were slaughtered by direction of the Florida legislature, which authorized fifty thousand dollars to bring this about. Taxpayers and conservationists protested, but the mass killing went on until the slaughterers reached the Indian reservation at Big Cypress. There, the Seminoles refused point-blank to permit any deer killing on their twenty thousand acres.

It was a great surprise to many to find that the state of Florida had nothing to say about this matter. When appealed to, Secretary of the Interior Harold L. Ickes demanded proof that the massacre of the deer was necessary. Finally, the matter was referred to the Audubon Society, which investigated, only to find that *all* animals carried ticks and the mass deer-killing was quite an ineffective method of dealing with the problem. The Indians saved their deer.

Later, the development of the program to study the porous rock and the water of the Everglades, the black muck of the saw grass country which dried in the sun and was ruined by over-productivity would result in the recommendation that the small islands and hammocks of the Everglades be replanted with hardwoods. A tree would have its place in the picture. Scientists would say so, not just landscape men or promoters of new subdivisions.

"Let's Go Miami"

LEGALIZED GAMBLING RETURNED TO THE RACETRACKS and the underground had it that Joseph E. Widener, the new owner of Hialeah, spent fifty thousand dollars getting the bill passed at Tallahassee. Widener, who had transformed Belmont Park into an area of swank and beauty, turned his magic wand on the boom-born Hialeah track and by elaborate landscaping and the laying of a grass track, turned Hialeah into a year-round park which attracted visitors even in the summertime when the ponies were running elsewhere.

Claude Pepper, who would one day be known in Congress as the champion of the elderly, represented the Miami Jockey Club and Tropical Park in obtaining dates from the State Racing Commission. Every time the question of dates came up, a delegation of merchants would appear to plead for a shorter season. These were the same fellows who wanted gambling back because it was "good for business." They would never adopt a policy about gambling and stick to it.

It was the era of kidnapping and the sinister growth of the underworld. Alarmed by what he saw and read, General John J. Pershing spoke out, calling on the U.S.A. to "mobilize its citizens against corrupt politicians." While the Seabury investigation of Mayor Jimmy Walker proceeded in New York, Miamians turned to their own kettle of corruption and heard testimony damning Sheriff M. P. Lehman, who had beaten Henry Chase with the backing of the W.C.T.U. Acting Sheriff Windham, a deputy under Lehman, declared on the stand that his old boss had ordered him "to leave slot machines alone." Lehman's former secretary disclosed she was advised by the sheriff to "tip off" a gambling establishment in the Halcyon Hotel, after a delegation of citizens appeared to demand the sheriff close the place, which could be clearly heard operating as you walked along the sidewalk. The sheriff, it was brought out in the trial, had spent fifty-five thousand dollars in office although his salary was a mere seven thousand a year.

Meanwhile, Fred Pine, the county solicitor, went on trial on charges of obstruction of justice and malfeasance and a man who had run for the city commission told his experiences while trying to muscle in on slot machines. He had been referred by the sheriff to Pine as the "slot machine boss." The trail led to the county solicitor's office by various routes but the case ended in a mistrial. It had its fiery moments as when Pine's lawyer, Bart Riley, threatened to "jump on the stand and break your neck" when one of the witnesses testified he had received three warnings not to appear against Pine in court and that Riley had sought to "purchase affidavits."

The supreme court sustained the reinstatement of police chief Guy Reeve after his removal by a former city manager and replacement by Hardy Bryan. In the case of H. Leslie Quigg, removed as police chief in 1928 and who sought reinstatement with full pay, the Tallahassee tribunal held with Judge Paul Barns against Quigg's contention, thus sustaining Reeve's right to remain in office. Quigg would be reappointed police chief in 1937.

The election that ushered in President Roosevelt and the New Deal brought rotund, jovial Dave Sholtz as governor of Florida and a new sheriff to Dade County. The people, weary of disclosures of crookedness in office, had by a sweeping majority carried Dan Hardie, now fifty-three, back to office as sheriff. Hardie, who had returned from his round-the-world trip after the Blow but in time for the Bust, had suffered from the bank failures. Like many of his townsmen, he was broke—but still incorruptible. The people knew it.

Dan Hardie went back as sheriff in the era of three-point-two, with Miami curb girls getting a cut from beer distributors—a penny for every beer cap. Dairymen were crying into their milk that thirteen cents a quart was insufficient recompense for their product, Colonel Montgomery was fighting the idea of an army air installation at Chapman Field near his estate of palms, and big northern yachts were being fitted for southern cruises after two years in wraps. Somebody in Miami figured that "one large yacht entering the harbor to base for the season is worth a whole trainload of excursionists." The

Bank Holiday the previous season had emptied Miami overnight as tourists hurried home to count their cash. This next season had to make up for it.

On Miami's thirty-seventh birthday the *News* declared editorially, "Miami asks no special favors, only that it be free of unreasonable handicaps; that it be given a chance to run its race."

It seemed likely that any reasonable handicaps would be removed and that the race would be run.

Mayor Ev Sewell of Miami and Mayor Frank Katzentine of Miami Beach left together with broad smiles for Washington, D.C. to press the area's request for a thirty-foot depth for the Miami channel as recommended by the Army Corps of Engineers. Despite the affable smiles of the mayors, Miami and the Beach were near the parting of the ways over the first attempt to cooperate on a combined advertising program.

The family of President Gerardo Machado of Cuba, wife, daughters, sons-in-law, and grandchildren, changed cars in Miami as they fled their country's revolution. FDR dispatched Secretary of the Navy Claude Swanson to Cuba aboard the *Indianapolis* as cries of "Down with Sumner Welles" filled the Havana air.

The U.S. ambassador to Cuba was in a hotter spot than ex-Congresswoman Ruth Bryan Owen of Miami, now U.S. minister to Norway. The first of the lady diplomats posed for photos with the Flying Lindberghs in faraway Oslo. To show her feeling for the Danes, the daughter of the Great Commoner would change her name to Rohde by marrying a gentleman-in-waiting to King Christian X.

Miami went to the polls to vote for the repeal of Prohibition that October as newspapers urged citizens to "renovate, decorate, beautify." It was the song of fall, the song of the coming season. Everything pointed to a good one.

Mayor Frank Katzentine of Miami Beach declared he would take a census of all criminals during the winter ahead, registering everybody ever convicted of a crime in an effort to keep watch over thieves and gamblers.

Mutterings of discontent with Sheriff Hardie began to infiltrate through the public prints. County solicitor Fred Pine declared there would be "no further prosecution of trivial offenders in the county courts."

Sheriff Hardie replied, "Miami and Dade County will get a crime cleanup even if the prosecutors turn the offenders out every morning. It may not be apparent to some but the people are demanding that law enforcement officials put a heavy foot down and I shall do just that."

Pine replied, "It costs the people of Dade County one hundred dollars to try a case in the county courts in the first instance. In view of the high cost it is the policy of my office not to file informations against minor vagrancy cases . . ."

He referred to Hardie's policy of picking up "women of the streets" but also had in mind the raiding of racehorse booking joints, it was said.

Before the county commission Hardie explained, "I shouldn't have to do this work, but I must. The police won't do it."

The *News* itemed: "Police bickering that may lead to bitter controversy is under way between official sanctums in the courthouse. Today's petty feud concerns the rights of the county solicitor to release the sheriff's prisoners. Hardie has consulted his attorney for a ruling on who's boss in determining the release of prisoners before they go to trial."

Sheriff Hardie objected to "letting criminals walk around in the custody of shyster lawyers and bondsmen and giving the impression we will allow criminals to stay here." There was, he charged, "not enough attention paid to the criminal after he is caught. When there is, the police and sheriff's forces may be cut in half."

Dan Hardie continued to be outspoken, even violent, in his determination to wipe out lawlessness.

While President Roosevelt was winning from Congress what amounted to a limited dictatorship with the agricultural adjustment act and revolutionary industrial reorganization, Dan Hardie went on making arrests. His critics said he was hot-headed. They said Dan Hardie dramatized. They said his leap from the stage at Bayfront Park to seize Zangara, the deranged killer of Mayor Cermak, was "overemphasized." They said he was "a fanatic."

To the latter charge Hardie said, "Some people are trying to make me appear as a fanatic or reformer. I am neither. I am trying to be a dignified sheriff and do my duty as I see it. Just now I see the cleanup of the town as my duty. I believe I have the backing of a substantial element of the county."

They made him appear ridiculous in stories like the one about Sheriff

Hardie and his deputies rushing a store in the black quarter on the tip of a bolita game, advancing into a dark room, and finding themselves in a chicken hatchery. They said he was old-fashioned and out of date. If honesty was those things, then he was.

Governor Sholtz, in derby hat and carrying a stick, visited Chicago to speak before wealthy members of the Committee of One Hundred before they made their trek southward to Miami Beach. He was really in Chicago to dedicate the Florida Tropical House at the Century of Progress Exposition. When he arrived at the fair grounds he received a nine-gun salute. At home, some citizens were calling for a special session of the legislature to plan a relief program, but Sholtz said there was no need.

"It will all turn out all right," he said with a wave of a chubby hand.

On the way home he paid a five-dollar fine for speeding in the town of Luna, Georgia, and Governor Talmadge of the neighboring state reprimanded two small-town police chiefs for permitting this to happen. One of the first things Sholtz did when back on the job was to suspend Dan Hardie as sheriff of Dade County. The charges were "lack of sound judgment and mental stability."

One of the principal critics of Hardie was lawyer James M. Carson who said, "I make no charges against him of corruption or dishonesty because I believe him to be sincere." It was a subtle campaign waged against a forthright man who was ousted as "incompetent."

Hardie said, "I've been the best sheriff in the U.S.A. in view of conditions. I've been sheriff ten months and during the first two months I was offered as much as two hundred and forty thousand dollars in bribes. My house will be foreclosed on next month. My casino at Miami Beach has gone under the hammer. I'll have to borrow money to eat.

"The trouble is, the gamblers want to run this county and I haven't allowed it. I guess the old methods are out of date. When I was sheriff before, I showed the gamblers the way out of town at the end of a .38. Apparently they don't do it that way any more."

After a hearing in Tallahassee that proved to be a mere formality, but during which Hardie produced a psychiatrist who testified that he was "perfectly sane," this proud and able man bowed out of the arena for good. His sons rallied around. Dr. Dan Hardie, Jr., was fined ten dollars in court for knocking down a scandal-sheet operator who said on Flagler Street that "the sheriff got what was coming to him."

Another son, William Hardie, ran for sheriff against D. C. Coleman, who was appointed by Governor Sholtz. Coleman won. The "unreasonable handicap" had been removed. Miami would "run its race." The gambling lid was off and everybody knew it. Miami, following the removal of the sheriff, planned to celebrate "Let's go, Miami" week.

"Something of the Big Top"

THE COMBINED Ringling Brothers and Barnum and Bailey Circus came to town and was hailed as "bringing sixteen hundred people and some two hundred thousand dollars which will be paid them in Miami." The *News* said editorially: "There is something of the Big Top in Miami's blood."

There was indeed. At the moment the center ring was occupied by a new performer, a sharp-eyed, goateed Santa Claus named Henry L. Doherty. A public utilities magnate, he was investing heavily in Florida property, having taken over the Miami Biltmore, the Roney Plaza, and the Key Largo Anglers Club as well as the Alba at Palm Beach, which he rechristened the Palm Beach Biltmore. "Colonel" Doherty had hired the publicity firm of Carl Byoir to manage his properties, dubbed the Florida Year-round Clubs, and a Miami Biltmore charity ball at New York's new Waldorf-Astoria ushered in the winter season that despite the effort to instill the words "year-round" in the national vocabulary, began in the middle of January and reached its peak on George Washington's Birthday.

Doherty, whose every move was followed in the Miami newspapers, stressed the need for "burning Miami into the public mind." Byoir set about accomplishing this. His methods included inviting Gentlemen of the Press from all over the country (wire service boys preferred) to come and bask under a palm tree with lodging and free booze on the cuff. All sports figures were welcome. Olin Dutra, National Open Golf champion, was hired to lend a helping hand with knotty problems in form on the Biltmore golf course. If you had a "name" you were good for a free ride at the Biltmore or the Roney. Names made news.

185

Doris Duke, spare and wistful, came to the Roney Plaza at Miami Beach and said tiredly in an interview on the sands, "Just tell your readers that I wore peacock feathers and strutted down the beach." She failed to say that, with her companion, she was on her way to Palm Beach to meet Mrs. Stotesbury's boy, Jimmy Cromwell, to become his bride. It goes without saying tobacco heiress Doris Duke was a paying guest. So was oil man Mike Benedum, who prodded a flamingo with his cane in the palm gardens and meditated on his millions.

Clare Boothe Brokaw, not yet Luce, declared her intention of "writing plays" from a chaise longue at the Roney while her mother, Mrs. A. E. Austin, beamed approval. Max Baer carried on a romance. Raquel Torres decorated a cabaña. Yvonne Printemps and Pierre Fresnay sipped dubonnet and whispered in their native tongue at the Roney's Café de la Paix.

Still there were empty rooms, especially at the Miami Biltmore out in what once had been "the sticks." The order went out to "light them up every night" to give the impression of success and activity. The brilliant Miami Biltmore tower twinkled at travelers crossing the Everglades on the Tamiami Trail.

Tying the ocean with the pineland, Doherty ran luxurious buses, called aero-cars, between the Roney and the Biltmore as an accommodation for guests, offered helicopter rides in the afternoons and vaudeville acts with dinner. An act of two comedians gotten up to represent a horse was side-splitting the first couple of times, but British columnist Nat Gubbins, on a news-exploring expedition in the U.S.A., resorted to having a tray sent to his room after fourteen sustained evenings of it. It was Gubbins who introduced the half-port, half-brandy cocktail with twisted lemon peel that became popular as a preluncheon drink.

Carl Fisher's former home, The Shadows, was now the Beach and Tennis, a night club with back-room gambling, while at the Surf Club ladies and gentlemen from Indiana, Michigan, and Minnesota, as well as northern New York found it pleasant to avoid the rigors of winter by sunning and ocean-dipping in walled seclusion.

Alfred Barton, who had been a correct little boy back in the days of Miss Smith's Private School in the early 1900s and later an actor in the Civic

Theater, now became a kind of majordomo and entrepreneur combined. He began to stage some expensive hoopla beside the beautiful sea in the form of Saturday night "galas" which the conglomerate mixture that made up Miami Beach "society" took to its thumping heart. You never knew what the subject would be: A Night at the Circus Gala brought a big top to cover the patio, live elephants, cotton candy, and all the trimmings. In the midst of all this carnival, solemn and rotund members of both sexes waltzed or rhumba-ed. People who had been making fortunes were now learning how to play. A few celebrities were always on hand to lend authenticity to the manufactured "glamour." Alfred Hitchcock dropped in on his way to Hollywood, California, providing something of a detour for himself. Lily Pons, Katherine Brush, and Rudy Vallee put in appearances. Rich food, rich regalia, rich setting stamped these evenings and in the midst of all the planned play the lack of natural spontaneity was accentuated.

The more discriminating preferred the sedate Bath Club, but a seasonal visitor who wanted to be in the social swim learned to join the Surf, the Bath, and the Indian Creek Clubs, the latter for golf.

Floyd Gibbons paid a quick visit to Miami Beach and was so taken with the spot he purchased a home on North Bay Road and with his sister Zelda Mayer's help set up housekeeping. He gave a party in his garden overlooking Indian Creek and to it came night-club entertainers, millionaires, local politicians, writers, strolling musicians, and indefatigable bartenders. Next morning as he sat under a palm tree with closed eye and wearing scanty shorts in an invitation to nature to erase the signs of the previous evening's wear, Gibbons heard a loud voice, like the sound of a radio turned up very near at hand. Squinting into the morning sun he beheld a sight-seeing boat sliding up the water. It came to a full halt while the captain bellowed through a megaphone, "There is the residence of the famous radio commentator Floyd Gibbons—and there he is sitting under that palm tree."

While the three-ring circus was in motion, a Lion, in the form of organized big-time gambling, was let loose under the Big Top. The Lion belonged backstage but he wandered into the center ring, noisily upsetting the show.

The season of 1934–35 was known as the season that "no wheels turned" because of a series of violent events that prevented the go-ahead signal by politicians. It actually began when a small-time Miami gambler named Skeets Downs, who was said to have once "told off Al Capone," was taken for a ride into the Everglades and peppered with bullets. His body was found by early-morning hunters. In the circles where such things were known, it was whispered that the Chicago syndicate headed by Marty Guilfoyle had been given the gambling go-ahead by Miami officials and that Downs "wouldn't listen to reason" at the new setup.

Earlier, another small-time gambler named Leo Bronstein had been mowed down by bullets as he answered a telephone call in a Miami Beach apartment lobby one night. These two killings called for a grand jury investigation that ran all season while gamblers champed at the bit.

M. L. Annenberg bought the Miami Beach *Tribune* and ushered in a flamboyant period in Miami annals during which veils were pulled aside and officials attacked in cartoon and phrase. Mayor Sewell was "Windy Ev" to the *Tribune*. The *Herald* and Frank Shutts were *Big Tammany*, the Cox-owned *News* and Cox's former son-in-law Dan Mahoney constituted *Little Tammany* in the the *Tribune's* lexicon.

The *Tribune* turned the light of public inquiry in large-scale fashion on city hall. The people ate it up and circulation figures jumped. Finally the *Tribune* outstripped the entrenched *Herald* and *News* in circulation. Meanwhile Governor Sholtz, aware of the "unfortunate publicity" emanating from the Magic City, ordered Sheriff Coleman to "round up gamblers, racketeers, and undesirables." The result was a token arrest of unimportant shady characters, but the big-time racketeers were let alone waiting for "the nod."

Into this electric atmosphere the grand jury brought in a true bill against Judge E. C. Collins of the Criminal Court of Record on charges of embezzlement and accepting a bribe. The judge heard of it at Deland where he was attending the Florida Baptist convention as head of the Men's Bible Class at Miami.

His trial, which was permitted to be "continued" indefinitely while he resigned as judge, brought forth charges of "fixed jurors" by the *Tribune*, charges which editors later proved quite conclusively in court.

Nobody was happy: politicians, gamblers, or legitimate businessmen.

It was during the season when "no wheels turned" that an event occurred out at Colonel Doherty's wigwam guaranteed to "burn Miami into the public mind."

At the cocktail hour one January afternoon a pair of masked hoodlums entered the Miami Biltmore suite of Mrs. Margaret Hawkesworth Bell of New York and at gun-point relieved her of her jewels, bound her hands and feet, and those of Harry Content, her guest. They then departed. The jewels were of some interest to Lloyds of London, being insured to the tinkling tune of one hundred and eighty-five thousand and five hundred dollars. Lloyds immediately dispatched Noel Scaffa, insurance company detective, and his Miami representative, Charles Harrington, to the scene to aid in the search for the criminals.

Before they were apprehended, a complicated piece of fantasia was worked out in which public officials, Lloyds detectives, and several gangsters were all to receive a piece of change while the jewels shuttled between New York and Chicago and finally back to Miami. When finally unraveled by the FBI, it became clear that the robbers were Charles Cali, alias Jimmy Williams, and Nicholas Montone, alias Little Nicky. They had been brought to Miami to run gambling operations at the Embassy by Albert J. Contento, alias Al Howard, and gambling having been temporarily shut down by the rude glare of the grand jury inquiry, had turned their hands to a stick-up job.

Before blown apart by the interference of the G-men, the payoff plans went like this: the sum of thirty-five hundred dollars for Sergeant Eugene C. Bryant of the Miami Beach police; two thousand dollars to gangster lawyer Ben Cohen; fifteen hundred dollars to certain law enforcement officers for the "squaring" of the case and the "vindication" of Montone; one thousand dollars to Harrington; and the sum of seven thousand to "other officials of Miami and Miami Beach." These monies were to be taken from the fifty-thousand-dollar reward fund Scaffa received from the American representative of Lloyds.

Federal subpoenas calling for the appearance of Dade County solicitor Fred Pine among others lent excitement to the trial in New York. Dade County officials went free mainly because the "reward money" had never been paid.

From the stand, Scaffa said calmly, "You talk about fixing prosecutors down there just as you talk about taking a drink. It's not unusual, in Florida."

189

Space does not permit going into the ramifications of crookedness among law enforcement agents nor the exposés in police matters then in the hands of Sam McCreary as director of public safety and acting police chief. But in every instance the exposé was followed by a wave of public indignation, hearings, and dismissals. Nobody went to jail. Fred Pine resigned finally as county solicitor and joined the law firm of Vincent Giblin. Eventually he would be indicted on charges of white slavery growing out of doings at La Paloma Club and sent to prison.

The following winter, the season of 1935-36, was a distinctive period of which national gambling figures moved into Miami in a big way. "Big" Bill Dwyer who operated the Latin Quarter, once the Palm Island Club and a stone's throw from the Capone mansion, took over Tropical Park. With him were Frank Erickson, one of the biggest bookies in the country, and Johnny Patton, one of the top three Capone men, as well as the notorious Owney Madden and his brother Marty.

Robberies reached a new high in the Miamis and no woman in her right mind would wear jewels to night clubs or the races. During this period, Governor Sholtz received a letter from the National Crime Prevention League informing him that special investigators would be sent into Dade County if something was not done at once to curb the activities of gamblers and racketeers. The governor wrote to Sheriff Coleman asking for "a report on the gambling situation."

The *Tribune* said editorially that the "governor was in a better position to compile a report on gambling . . . in view of the frequently publicized fact that 'the Governor's man' had to be seen by anyone who contemplated running a gaming place in Dade County."

The Miami Beach City Council held a secret session and the next day gambling was shut down at the Beach—but only temporarily. Miami continued to operate until Governor Sholtz got another word from the National Crime Prevention group. By that time the season was over anyway.

One of the laughs of the period concerned Art Childers, who as a member of the Miami Beach Council voted to outlaw gambling at the Beach, while operating his own gambling establishment, the Royal Palm Club, built close by the site of the old Flagler hotel across the bay, thereby eliminating competition.

Lucy Cotton Thomas Magraw, who had bought the Deauville Hotel and rechristened it Beautiful Deauville, got caught in the company of the gambling fraternity when indicted by the grand jury. Beautiful Lucy, who had shaved her head to please her then husband Bill Magraw and was wearing wigs, had leased the gambling room to a pair of New York gamblers, Frank Zaccarino and Harry Werner. State Senator Hays Lewis, said to be the state "fixer" for gamblers, was also indicted.

The grand jury reported: "Officials are allied with organized racketeers and have been engaged for some time in assisting and protecting them in their widespread and vicious assault upon our community. Their passive indulgence toward the program of organized vice and in some instances their encouragement of it, and participation in it, are generally known. We are convinced that enormous sums have been paid to officialdom for protection."

That was the winter when federal agents killed Fred Barker and his mother, "Ma" Barker, in a house at Ocklawaha, Florida. They also found that Alvin Karpis, public enemy number-one, had left the hideout for Miami thirty-six hours before they raided it. The whole thing began to smell in a way that was not appealing.

Police raided a garage apartment at Miami Beach, recovering about one hundred thousand dollars in stolen jewelry and arrested three men. Two were members of the Owney Madden gang of Tropical Park and got off free. The third was given a fifty-year sentence at Raiford. In Miami, it paid to be in with the right gangster.

Despite the handicaps thrown up by the men they put into office, some of the citizens of Miami were aiming toward good government and on March 1, 1939, the city's first recall election threw out of office "the termite administration." The Cox-owned *News* won for its part in the recall activities the coveted Pulitzer Prize "for the most disinterested and meritorious public service rendered by an American newspaper during 1938."

In 1937 the *Herald* was purchased by John S. Knight of Akron, who took the precaution of also buying out the morning competition of the *Tribune* and scrapping it. The *Tribune* had provided some grade-A political excitement during its brief stay. Under Knight's hand the *Herald* blossomed forth as Florida's leading newspaper.

191

The Road That Goes to Sea

K EY WEST WAS THE SAME DISTANCE AWAY FROM MIAMI, but it no longer took a night and a day to reach it by sailboat. Pan American Airways had a triweekly flight between the two cities and Flagler's train rolled out along his Overseas Extension down through the Keys. Physically connected, the cities were as separated as ever. Time had reversed their positions. Miami, which had been a wilderness, was now a city with all the external marks of affluence—the click of the gambling wheels, the dazzling jewels and orchids, the champagne and *cabañas*, the ocean-front estates that stood against the milk-white, clouded blue sky as concrete evidence of wealth.

Only those who understood caught the strained smile of the small businessman of the thirties as he sold his coconuts carved into heads, his shells and knickknacks, or read the anxious faces of small homeowners seeking mortgage refinancing. These things were hidden from the tourist along with the fact that children were turning up for school barefoot. Miami was a play city dedicated to supplying entertainment to the nation. Poverty never would be as apparent in Miami as elsewhere in the country. In Key West, it was apparent.

Desperate, the city signed over its voting power to the Federal Emergency Relief Administration and formed the Key West Administration by an act of the state legislature. The City of Key West and Monroe County were in the red to the sum of five million dollars. People had left, saying Key West was "a dying town." When the drastic FERA measure was adopted, there were about twelve thousand people living in the island city. Julius F. Stone, who headed the FERA, had the notion that he could sell the tourists on Key West,

193

but Floridians generally hooted the idea, claiming he would "have to provide the tourists, too."

The natives and residents of Key West had nothing to lose. They set about a cleanup program—a program that struck every yard, back and front. They planted trees, swept their beaches, and burned their trash. They opened a bureau to list rooms and houses for rent and started training classes for servants so that people who came to rent houses would find competent household help.

Stone began to dream of constructing a highway to Key West. Why not, if Flagler had built a railroad? He envisioned the concrete path as a future link with the Pan American Highway, just as Henry Flagler had. They began to talk about this highway in terms of Public Works Administration funds and got an unexpected boost from Washington. Faced with the problem of what to do with the veteran hunger marchers who were at this time encamped in the Civilian Conservation Corps working for a dollar a day and food, clothing, a roof over their heads, and medical attention, the government said: why not send twenty-five thousand of these men to build the Overseas Highway?

President Roosevelt, who posed for the newsreels eating steak and potatoes at one of these Northern CCC camps, considered it a sound idea.

Just as Flagler had brought in his crew of men from everywhere to work on his extension, the government brought in veterans from New York and New Jersey, Pennsylvania and Ohio, among them the ill, the hopeless, the dejected. Most of these men were in their forties. The first group reached the Keys in the winter of 1934–35. While they waited for the roadwork to begin they were put to work constructing living quarters.

It is doubtful if any of them had ever heard the Bahamian warning . . . September, Remember. Those who lived beyond September 2, 1935, would have reason to recall it the rest of their lives. When a tropical disturbance was reported as early as Saturday, August 31, moving west-northwest at about sixty miles east of Long Key in the Bahamas, Miamians noted it but otherwise went about their business. There are so many blows that never hit it would be futile to mark each one as a threat.

By Sunday afternoon, high winds were felt in the Miamis and by Labor Day morning, the day the storm was destined to hit the Keys, it was squally. Nevertheless, the Labor Day parade was held as planned in Miami, although the all-day picnic, as well as the sports and evening program at the American Legion home, were canceled. The Weather Bureau reported that the hurricane "might enter the Florida Straits."

Authorities at the Key camp telephoned Washington to discuss the situation on Monday morning, but nobody felt that mass evacuation was indicated. General arrangements had been made before the arrival of the first encampment for the railroad to remove the men in the event of a hurricane.

By noon, it was blowing hard. Through the gray and gusty afternoon, tension increased as the Conchs of the Keys boarded up. Finally an assistant director of the veteran's work on Matecumbe Key telephoned Jacksonville about two P.M. to ask for an evacuation train. The train left Miami two and a half hours later at about the time the Keys got official notice that the storm had turned and was headed for the Keys. A few truckloads of men were evacuated then.

By the time the train reached Islamorada, the winds were blowing so furiously all its cars were overturned. The engine alone stood to face the gales. It was too late for help. The hurricane moved in like a giant mowing machine and leveled everything. Surprised men, feeling the impact, tried to find something to cling to. A man from McKeesport, Pennsylvania, holding to the railroad tracks with two comrades, decided to attempt to crawl to a nearby clump of trees. With an embarrassed laugh, he said, "Well, fellows, if I never see you again, so long . . ." He reached the trees and turned in time to see his companions swept out into the Gulf of Mexico by a fifteen-foot wall of water that men said later was a tidal wave.

Men, women, and children all over the area were swept away by the hundreds. Some who clung to trees with all their might survived the first half of the storm only to be picked up and carried out to sea after the lull when the storm hit from the other direction. There were a total of six hundred and eighty-four men at the three veterans' camps, Number 1 on Windley Key and camps 3 and 5 at each end of Lower Matecumbe. Less than half of them escaped death, one hundred were injured.

The story of the losses unfolded slowly as rescuers advanced into the Keys. It was midnight Tuesday before the first rescue party crossed Snake Creek on barges and stepped ashore at Matecumbe Key. Bodies were everywhere, even hanging grotesquely from the tops of mangrove trees. Not a

195

trace of the camps remained. The loss of camp records complicated the work of identifying the dead. Many veterans had been on holiday leave in Miami and Key West and were mercifully saved from the fate of their comrades. They had to be located as the work of identification went forward.

While Coast Guard seaplanes continued to search for signs of life along the Keys, the American Legion and any volunteer with two willing arms and a strong stomach set about the task of moving the injured and sorting the dead. Miami doctors and nurses worked around the clock in the recreation hall of the First Baptist Church in Homestead as survivors were brought in. One was a ten-year-old girl, stripped clean of clothing by the wind, the only one left of a family of seven at Tavernier. Clinging to beds, using mattresses as overhead cover, the people of the Keys had watched large rocks roll about like pebbles, buildings crumple like houses of cards, water lift up houses and carry them off.

Fingerprint experts were sent down from Washington to help in identifying the dead. The deterioration of bodies from water and sun made the work impossible. In the end, and pathetically, the best means of identification proved to be from tattoo marks on arms and legs.

President Roosevelt ordered separate coffins for each body and Miami undertakers did a landslide business for a day or so until health officers called a halt and refused the removal of any further bodies. September weather was against this individualized treatment of the mass dead. The danger of epidemic was too possible. Because of the unique earth, the porous rock that defied the shovel, burial would have taken too long. Cremation was agreed upon. They piled the unknown dead together in a gigantic funeral pyre and while a Jewish rabbi, a Catholic priest and a Protestant minister took turns reading their separate prayers for the dead the smoke curled skyward. It was remembered by the Conchs that long ago the Indians had named Matecumbe "a place of weeping."

In Bayfront Park, twenty thousand people turned out to honor the dead at a community service. The president's wreath was laid upon a replica of the tomb of the Unknown Soldier. Planes dropped flowers from the sky. There were muffled drums. The survivors said they would rather face the guns of war any day than face again the fury of that Labor Day hurricane. Investigations followed the burials. State's attorney George Worley, Jr., absolved the railroad of any charge of delay in reaching the camps. Criticism of the Weather Bureau ran high, the general opinion being "an old-timer looking at the sky with a barometer and rheumatism" could have guessed better.

Arthur Brisbane, who had a winter residence in Miami, writing in his Hearst-syndicated column that appeared on the front page of the *Herald*, asked objectively: "When will men find a way to control the savage outbursts of nature?"

The investigations closed with the judgment that the hurricane was "an act of God" and that the "responsibility does not lie with any human factors concerned." That wasn't the way the Conchs on the Keys had it figured. They were bitter about the tragedy that they said "need not have happened."

If Flagler had listened to Commodore Munroe and others when he was laying his Overseas Extension and put up arched bridges instead of elevations of filled land, there would not have been all that water that men called a tidal wave, they explained angrily. If the War Department had listened during the winter of 1913–14 when the matter of reopening the fills was aired throughly in public hearing, it would not have happened. Through the years the people who knew the region had patiently explained that there must be bridges instead of fill for the waters to have free sweep through to Florida Bay in the event of a hurricane. If the railway fills hadn't given away when they did and let the water flow through that Labor Day there would not have been a soul alive on Upper Matecumbe Key, they said.

They had tried, those people, to get the idea across. When, twenty-five years before, the railroad closed the last two openings without government permission, a man named Gene Johnson took matters into his own hands. He crept out that night and spaded a small hole through the fill. By morning all the fill was washed away. But the railroad filled the area again and then, after the hearing, it had a right to do it. Now Gene Johnson was dead as the result of the very thing he had tried to prevent—along with seventy-six members of his family. The original Johnson had come from England a couple of generations before. His brother Johnny, postmaster at Islamorada for twenty-nine years, lay in his bed in the recreation hall at Homestead with his face to the wall.

When a reporter asked if he would return to Islamorada he said, "There is nothing to go back *to*."

Another Conch, refusing to comment for the press, explained, "The thought of what we've been through is enough to drive a normal man crazy."

A man named Alonzo Cothran, in the midst of the raging storm, took the pains to measure the rise of the water by the clock. At seven-thirty, it began to rise. At eight-thirty P.M., it was fifteen feet above the high-water level and covered the whole key. The moment the fill across Whale Harbor washed away, the water began to fall rapidly. At nine-thirty, there was still wind but no water. This, the natives said, was their proof.

Now the ones who were left said in effect, "This time we won't let the railroad put in fills. There must be bridges over the natural waterways."

It seemed unlikely that the Florida East Coast Railway, twisted and cut and lifted into the air by the giant hand of the hurricane, would ever run again. The railroad was too broke to repair the sections that lay crumpled under the sun.

The idea of the Overseas Highway did not die with the veterans brought in to construct it. Alert Engineers pointed out that the bridges and trestles of the railroad were undamaged and suggested building the new Overseas Highway over the old railroad bed. The idea took hold at once.

The FEC sold to the Overseas Road and Toll Bridge District the right-of-way from Florida City to Key West for six hundred and forty thousand dollars and the cancellation of three hundred thousand dollars in city, county, and state taxes. In order to swing it, the district sold three million, six hundred thousand dollars in bonds. The Reconstruction Finance Corporation lent three million dollars for the building of the highway. Two years later in 1938 the Overseas Highway, one hundred and thirty-nine miles of roadway crossing the heretofore inaccessible Florida Keys, became part of U.S. 1 and opened up Key West to motorists.

Carl Graham Fisher, who pioneered in the automobile industry and trail-blazed the Lincoln and Dixie highways, rode down along it. He was near the end of his trail-blazing, but he could not stop dreaming. Ill and living on a modest income, he was planning the Caribbean Club at Key Largo—a fishing club for men of moderate means with dockage for boats, a family club where a man could come and bring the children, a poor man's retreat. He built it, but after his death in 1939 it became a gambling establishment.

They erected a bronze bust of Fisher at Miami Beach, slouch hat and all. These words appear under it: "He carved a great city from a jungle."

For the men who were lost at the CCC camp that terrible Labor Day there is another monument, at Islamorada.

There is no monument for the "unidentified" dead, Flagler's extension workers, the men of the "tattered battalion," the tough, the drunken, the brawling—the Greeks and Bahamians, the Swedes and the Irishmen who lost their lives on the job. They made their contribution to the building of that ribbon of roadway that ties the Keys into an unbroken path to Key West and is called "The Road That Goes to Sea."

In all, it probably cost in the neighborhood of one thousand lives to build.

"Even the Stone Deaf . . . "

THE NEWS OF PEARL HARBOR hit a Miami poised on the brink of the Season. After the inital shock wore off, the first tourists, Miami's number-one business in war and peace, had drifted south for their winter tans. From then on everybody was very busy seeing that they had a good time.

The predictions of pessimists that Miami would become a deserted playground for the duration were lost in the ring of the cash register, the beat of the rhumba, and the splash of the surf off Miami Beach. Miami Beach never had it so gay as titled European "refugees," wartime manufacturers, and government bigwigs crowded the night spots, attended the horse races, and brunched in *cabañas*. Shipwreck Kelly and his wife, ex-debutante Brenda Frazier, took a home on Pine Tree Drive and entertained as their first houseguests Howard Hawks of moviedom and his bride, Nancy. Senator Hiram Johnson checked in for a vacation and so did Al Jolson, Benny Fields, Orson Welles, and Lee Shubert.

At the Surf Club when tired millionaires gathered the word was out to soft-pedal lavish parties as being in "bad taste" during wartime. It never occurred to anybody to spit that taste right out of their mouths. Playing was the area's prime business, and some tourists sold themselves on the idea that it was "patriotic to keep fit" by continuing the practice of vacationing in winter.

In the accelerated play pattern of a nation at war, bathing beauties painted their fingernails red, white, and blue, jingled bracelets that spelled out army or navy, wore diamond V-for-Victory pins, or the more available copies in junk jewelry. Lou Costello, minus his sidekick Abbott, auctioned off a man's "Victory Suit" minus cuffs and vest, to supply the necessary note of patriotism for a fashion show. Kate Smith, "the Songbird of the South,"

201

broadcast her God-Bless-America from the privacy of an ocean-front suite. Sonja Henie and Sabu, the Elephant Boy, paraded down Flagler Street to help sell defense bonds. It was as though the war was picked up and used as a theme on which to hang the Miami Season.

Arthur Murray, barefoot on the Roney Plaza sands, predicted a boom in ballroom dancing as "the natural expression of a people at war," and Betty Grable and Jack Oakie came to Miami Beach to preview their *Song of the Islands.*

Billy Rose and Ben Bernie teamed up for a golf tournament and were assigned beautiful chorines to act as caddies while Bernarr Macfadden, who had taken over Beautiful Deauville and renamed it Macfadden–Deauville, announced the opening of a new *cabaña* club, with carrot juice on the house.

When *Life* magazine showed a picture of Mayor Val C. Cleary of Miami Beach being kissed by a bathing beauty and called him the mayor of Miami, nobody was pleased. Miami and Miami Beach, despite separate publicity campaigns, were faced with the dreary fact that the rest of the U.S.A. refused to recognize that they were two separate cities connected by three separate causeways.

One of those causeways was about to have its name changed. In a burst of patriotic fervor, the *News* succeeded in getting public opinion aroused to rename the County Causeway in honor of General Douglas MacArthur, the man of the hour.

For some time now, merchants had failed to see eye-to-eye with Philip Wylie, who since the late thirties had been plugging away, first in letters to the editor, then in columns appearing first in the *Herald,* then in the *News,* against particular aspects of life in the Magic City, mainly in the field of public health. Wylie, who had become a hero by writing his Crunch and Des stories in *The Saturday Evening Post,* thus advertising the area with his tales of deep-sea fishing, had inexplicably turned traitor and begun calling attention to such things as unpasteurized milk, the high rate of venereal disease, unsanitary conditions at the then city-owned Jackson Memorial Hospital, polluted water in black neighborhoods, and the like.

This unheard-of procedure of a resident Miamian turning on his own city was a piece of treachery comparable to matricide. The flow of lucid, graphic phrases from the Wylie typewriter turned dyed-in-the-wool Miamians apoplectic. The old, unspoken rule about hiding Miami's defects from the eyes of tourists did not hold with this prolific, hard-hitting upstart.

Wylie's one-man cleanup campaign proved an effective light in the darkness, eventually bringing the Public Health Department into the Miamis for a thorough survey. The reforms which followed were never fully appreciated by politicians and merchants. Until the rude glare of Wylie's searchlight got in their eyes, dwellers of ocean-front palaces had failed to consider the fact that the servants who kept their homes and often nursed their babies were crossing the causeways every evening on their way back to toiletless squalor in shameful slums. Wylie had a new tune every month as he sang his song of cleanup, exposing the incidence of hookworm and malaria, the lack of any records whatever in the cases of communicable diseases, the need for modern sewage disposal.

As Germany invaded Holland and Belgium and France, author Wylie turned his battery of typewriter keys on the dangers of Hitler and Mussolini and aligned himself with William Allen White's Committee to Defend America by Aiding the Allies. When he pointed out that Miami was vulnerable to attack from the air, the anti-Wylieites, the Miami Concealment Squad, were speechless. This Jeremiah, this Judas, was trying to ruin the Season, they said.

Miami was not alone in looking after her tourist interests. The various chambers of commerce of resort cities in the country took a poll to see how the war would affect their territories. It resulted in the glad news that all hands were expecting banner seasons. Atlantic City pointed out that World War I had zoomed business, why not World War II?

His Royal Highness, the Duke of Windsor, was not so sanguine and flew to Miami from Nassau to confer with highranking U.S. naval officers and members of the British consulate to see what he could do as governor-general of the Bahamas to keep business bobbing along during the war days. Wallis, his duchess, a popular figure in Miami, remained at Government House. In lieu of reporting her costume, a ritual with the local press, the papers gravely noted that the duke was wearing "a gray pin-stripe suit, blue shirt, and tie."

It began to dawn on clearer-thinking Miamians even in early February, the proverbial "height" of the Season, that war was bound to bring changes in the city's economy. State Senator Ernest R. Graham, the practical politician who had cleaned out the gangsters and hoodlums at Tropical Park and gotten a slice of racetrack money for the Florida aged in addition, came back from Washington and made a prediction.

"I am thoroughly convinced that Greater Miami must join the all-out war effort, and I predict a great change in the method of living hereabouts." He offered to serve without pay in the nation's capital as liaison man to see that Miami got her share of war contracts.

The Miami *Daily News* joined the chorus with a call for "fewer tuxedos and more overalls" as well as "more planning for year-round productive living and less nail-biting over the Season." It warned, "Even the stone deaf cannot sleep through a war."

Michele Morgan of the Hollywood cinema industry and late of Paris, France, said it another way: "Miamians live in a paradise."

President Roosevelt named Leon Henderson for the post of Price Control Administrator and delivered a fireside chat in which he said, "From Berlin and Rome and Tokyo we have been described as a nation of weaklings, playboys who would hire British soldiers or Russian soldiers or Chinese soldiers to do our fighting for us . . ."

Miami Beach society was up in arms because the FBI seized one of its members, Prince Girolamo Gioeni-Rospigliosi, and one indignant lady said, "Why he's a lovely man. I had tea with him only yesterday."

Miami had changed beyond recognition in the years between its country's conflicts. In World War I it had been all smalltown patriotism. Back in the Spanish-American War days it had solemnly expected to be attacked by Cervera's fleet, but that oddly assorted group of militants known as the Miami Minute Men never got a chance to exchange fire. In February of 1942, war seemed very far away, yet one moonlit night it washed right in on Florida's golden beaches.

A man named Adolf Hitler rang down the curtain on the Season by dispatching submarines to the Gold Coast, and the sound of the torpedoes hitting Allied merchantmen was louder than the rhumba bands and the dice games and closed the swank Brook Club, the Old Forge and the Sunny Isles Casino. The German U-boats that had been waging a devastating war in the North Atlantic moved into the shipping lanes off the Florida coast on the night of February 19 when the tanker *Pan Massachusetts*, loaded with one hundred thousand barrels of gasoline, oil, and kerosene, became a flaming torch after being struck twenty miles south of Cape Canaveral. It lit up the ocean for a full mile. The eighteen survivors of the thirty-eight-man crew were picked up by a British passenger vessel that also loaded aboard many of the dead and headed for Jacksonville.

Within the next week, the Nazi wolf pack struck again and again up and down the coast at the merchant ships moving in slow procession, hugging the coast to avoid the Gulf Stream with its tugging current. Unseen, ghostly, these subs lay on the sea bottom close to shore ready to fire on the unarmed vessels—American, British, Cuban, Swedish, Mexican—which were as vulnerable as ducks in a shooting gallery.

Frightened tourists left by the thousands as the military ordered first a dim-out for Miami, then a blackout. The lights of the playground of the nation blazed away six miles out to sea and although German subs were probably operating on the highly secret mechanical device known as radar, it was safer to douse the lights. Authorities never were able to do a thorough job of it.

The sinkings managed to convince "Season Nail-biters" that the Miamis were in the war, but it still seemed inconceivable that Hitler's subs were on the prowl right off Miami. Where they were refueling was immediate cause for conjecture. Men badly burned, quiet and moaning men, were filling the hospitals along the coast. Amateur nurses, Red Cross First Aiders, got in some good licks in the way of service. There was the story of the youthful novice attempting to bathe the inches of oil from a sailor and covering her embarrassment by making conversation. "Is this your first visit to Florida?" she asked politely.

One of these survivors wrote home, "You can't fight submarines with potatoes."

President Roosevelt had signed the law to arm the Merchant Marine before Pearl Harbor but it had not yet been accomplished when the Germans struck. Now before an adequate defense could be built two dozen ships went down, the bulk of them American. To a man, these survivors lifted their fingers in the Churchillian salute of the V and shipped out again on another trip. They cursed Hitler, Hirohito, and Mussolini roundly; they were afraid to drop off to sleep at night. They kept shipping out.

One admitted, "It is a queasy feeling to be shadowed by those bastards."

The oil which stuck to the skins of merchant sailors also clung to the skins of voluntary bathers, and daily dips either in the ocean or Biscayne Bay became unpleasant affairs toward the end of that eventful season, which cut the nation's gas supply in half and brought about gas rationing.

By May, Miamians believed what they saw when the *Portero de Llamo*, a Mexican tanker, was hit south of Fowey Rock and turned water into fire. All the next day it drifted north along the Gulf Stream, a smoking reminder of what lay in the once tranquil waters. Within a week, another Mexican vessel, the *Faja de Oro*, was torpedoed off the Florida Keys. Shortly after, Mexico declared war on Germany.

Two Miamians, Dr. F. E. Kitchens and Dr. R. Smith, played the role of twin rescuers in the sinking of the *James A. Moffett, Jr.*, one dark night off Tennessee Reef down on the Keys. The regular Coast Guard craft assigned to the area was laid up for repairs and in their two cabin cruisers these two men saved forty-one of the crew of forty-two.

The vessel had attempted to beach after the first shell hit it. After the second, the Nazi sub surfaced and fired ten more shells. One of the five navy gunners assigned to the ship found himself in the unhappy position of swimming around within earshot of the Nazis. Fortunately for him, it was a pitch-dark night, no moon, and with the stars hidden by low clouds. The Miamians rescued all but the captain and went back to the burning ship at the request of the engineer for the ship's dog.

The cry "wreck ashore" that had once meant adventure and provender for the Conchs now meant tankers afire, lining the coast, and floating dead men and singed and injured living ones. The war was piling up new wrecks on coral reefs, but there was no joy in the canned food, the raw rubber that could be exchanged for money, the rum and the flour, although washed up by the same old sea without benefit of ration points.

Citizens with every kind of old fishing scow, motorboat, and sailboat, millionaires with elaborate yachts, all answered the screams of the injured and dying, and now these men who knew the coastal waters volunteered to form a Coast Guard auxiliary to report submarines. Yachtsmen from the area—men like Wirth Munroe, son of the pioneering commodore, and Hugh Matheson who had come to Coconut Grove as a schoolboy and who was now the commodore of the Biscayne Bay Yacht Club—kept the watch. So did fishermen and old retired sea dogs and young boys. They were a homemade outfit and they paid for their own fuel, and one day a German sub commander who surfaced face to face with one of them said angrily and in impeccable Americanese, "What do you think you're doing here? Scram!"

Commodore Matheson, whose four sons were in the navy, moved into the Coast Guard Reserve and became a chief petty officer assigned to the waters he knew so well. He was invaluable in helping train the boys from the Submarine Chaser Training Center, which was hastily assembled and which instructed in the art of handling P.C.'s and S.C.'s in group formation. Those boys who attended class learned to display nonchalance as they passed by the lifeboat exhibited without words at the Sub Chaser School. It was filled with machine-gun bullet holes and caked with dry blood.

As in the Spanish-American War, Miamians were screaming for coastal guns. Cries went up all over the nation asking where the United States Navy was. Secretary of Navy Knox answered that question with the quiet reminder that the U.S.A. had a one-ocean navy to fight a two-ocean war.

While the Coast Guard auxiliary kept a sharp eye out for submarines, sending back radio warnings to shore, the Civil Air Patrol stood guard from the air. As on the water it was the same story of a stopgap outfit, men without uniforms spending their own money on fuel, holding smoke bombs in their laps ready to heave them out as signals if they sighted a sub. Lloyd Fales, who had learned to fly back in 1917 in the early Miami Beach days, was base commander. These pilots, too old or too young for the war and known as "the Flying Minute Men," had a wry name for this volunteer period. They called it "the boom."

The Gulf Sea Frontier was organized with headquarters first in Key West and later Miami to cover Florida, a piece of the Bahamas, most of Cuba, the Gulf of Mexico, and the Yucatan Channel. Its equipment in the beginning was pitiful.

The first sinkings were reported freely in the newspapers and then the information was censored for security reasons. That's when the Miami rumors began. Two Nazis were picked up in a submarine and had Flagler Street movie stubs in their pockets, one rumor went. Another was that German sub commanders were getting daily milk deliveries from a local dairy. Ominous barbed-wire fences lined lonely stretches of shore and citizens looked hard at every passing sailor.

J. Edgar Hoover, after the submarine menace was ended, declared that from January, 1942, until May, 1943, his office investigated five hundred reports of refueling enemy submarines and they were all false alarms.

The landing of saboteurs at Ponte Vedra, Florida, was not a false alarm, and these men were later caught and executed. It was no rumor either that the FBI picked up twenty-nine German, Italian, and Japanese aliens before February was out. They were all neatly ensconced close by the Naval Air Station at Opa-Locka, equipped with guns, cameras, binoculars, and spyglasses.

As the *News* had pointed out earlier in the month, "not even the deaf could sleep through a war."

Before the submarines were driven out of the Caribbean, a not-so-somber and nostalgic note was supplied by the natives of Cocoa and Titusville when the British vessel *Paz* was hit off Cape Canaveral. Hurrying to the spot, they first saw to the safety of the crew, then proceeded to lighten her cargo by four hundred cases of Scotch whiskey before the official salvagers moved in to take inventory.

The day of the first sinking, the Army Air Corps announced that it would train enlisted men to become officers at Miami Beach and billet them in hotels. The very next day, the first five hundred arrived with duffle bags and Officer Candidate School was launched. The first group bunked at the Boulevard Hotel, while the Miami Beach Municipal Golf Course was leased for a dollar a year and set up as the school's headquarters and drill ground. Eventually eighty-five per cent of the Miami Beach hotels were taken over by the army and the happy hunting ground for gay divorcées became ready-made if somewhat glorified barracks for America's future officers. The simple act of shifting from tourists to soldiers saved the government the vast expense plus the delay involved in building encampments. It was one of those beautifully simple plans that worked. Owners stripped their hotels of furbelows before leasing them to the army but even so one officer candidate wrote home, "Dear Mom: The army has gone very swell."

Among the men who trained under the hot sun, sweating off pounds on the greens, was Clark Gable, who was given an official veil of anonymity by the army that served as a countermaneuver against aspiring Miami Beach hostesses.

The University of Miami had already begun under lend-lease to train young Englishmen in celestial navigation, and in Coral Gables, British boys were constantly being amazed at the "lemonade" which people drank and called "iced tea." They were also learning to navigate and returning to England to fly and die on bombing missions over Germany. One does not forget these young men easily.

The Submarine Chaser Training Center brought Russian sailors, chunky and pink-faced and clear-eyed, marching in formation up Biscayne Boulevard, where hotels were turned into quarters for the navy. Even then they had their orders: no fraternizing with the natives. Despite plenty of invitations, the Russian boys were eternally "unable to come."

Other nationalities were represented in the training units. Norway and France and Cuba, Chile, Uruguay, and of course Great Britain were all learning how to attack Nazi submarines in the waters surrounding Biscayne Bay and strolling along Flagler Street in the evenings, crowding the movies, the bars, and recreation centers.

South of Miami was installed the Richmond Lighter-Than-Air Station, second in size only to the mother station at Lakehurst, New Jersey. From these hangars a blimp rode out to patrol one day, only to be shot down by a bold Nazi U-boat riding on the surface. A natural phenomenon occurred another day when a dark cloud was blown into one of the enormous Richmond hangars and proceeded to let loose with rainfall. In Miami during the war anything could happen and did.

The Air Transport Command had farmed out cargo-ferrying to the various airlines—Pan Am and National and Rickenbacker's Eastern Air; all the big lines were represented. Regular ATC men and these nonmilitary fliers kept aerial roadways filled from Miami to Natal to Dakar, to Ascension Island, to India and Persia. One of these missions carried the Russian diplomat, Litvinov, back to Moscow. He requested a day's tour of Palestine en route. The captain and crew obliged but when Litvinov left the plane in Tehran, he did so without so much as a nod of thanks, let alone the customary handshake.

Throughout the war the wounded were flown directly from the battlefields to Miami. Out in Coral Gables, George Merrick's dream hotel, the towered Miami Biltmore, was turned into a mammoth veteran's hospital. On being landed in the United States the wounded who were physically able made a ritual of kissing the ground.

Then there was the contrasting figure: the winter tourist aquaplaning on black-market gas in the waters of Biscayne Bay.

The bulk of Miamians heeded the call for "fewer tuxedos and more overalls." Consolidated Vultee manufactured airplane parts, hiring up to four thousand men and women at its peak. Other small firms converted to wartime manufacturing. Shipbuilding became an important industry. Tantalizingly backward in growing up to its responsibilities, Miami took several giant steps forward as a result of the war. It is doubtful if anything but a world cataclysm could have turned her away from her self-preoccupation and frivolous disregard of proper values.

The skeleton of the unfinished boom-time Roosevelt Hotel, disappearing under a covering of mortar and concrete blocks and converted to a round-the-clock workshop for mechanical trainees for wartime crafts as the Lindsey Hopkins Vocational School, was a striking symbol of the change. Fifteen stories of brightly lighted activity, that institution rocked and buzzed and hammered its way toward belated preparedness under the National Defense Training program, becoming at war's end "the skyscraper school," a technical high, and "poor man's college" wrapped in one.

Over at Miami Beach, the women turned the Million-Dollar Pier where Minsky's burlesque shows had lightened prewar days, into the Servicemen's Pier. They ran it on businesslike lines, working in shifts. Volunteers from Coconut Grove, Coral Gables, Miami Shores, and other sections sliced sandwiches and waxed floors, handed out stationery and arranged dances. They did a remarkable job. Eighteen thousand volunteers headed by Katherine Pancoast, wife of John Collins' grandson, Russell, entertained more than four million servicemen over a four-and-a-half-year period.

The military prodded in the field of sanitation. To some of the more stubborn dairymen (the ones who ran the milk through the pasteurizer but did not turn on the current, *par exemple*), the army said, "Clean up or we will ship in outside milk." This effected a reform in the milk industry—a reform for which Philip Wylie and the Miami *Herald* had long fought.

The military closed all houses of prostitution, among them Gertie Walsh's. The only American madam who had been permitted to run a house of prostitution in Havana, Gertie Walsh had become a political influence in the state of Florida. She began operating in a Victorian mansion on Flagler Street and moved later to a more modern place on the Miami River. (The old place has since been turned into an undertaking establishment.) Her new place was known all over the United States as the bordello with a berth for yachts. Gertie Walsh always had a waiting list of from fifty to a hundred girls, and when the legislature was in session in Tallahassee it was her habit to bring her fairest to the state capital to make friends with the legislators. Several of her call girls married men of some position.

It has been said that it took the army, the navy, the air corps, and the marines to close Gertie Walsh's. The military order in World War II was to close all bordellos and Gertie Walsh's fell with the others.

The military closed the houses of prostitution and Miami teenagers turned prostitute in Bayfront Park, plying the oldest trade for small sums of money. Early park closing and extra policing failed to stop this mass prostitution until all shrubbery was ordered trimmed and thinned from the bottom. Some fine old trees and hedges were sacrificed, but it put a stop to the situation.

The youth of Greater Miami lost their lives in flaming planes, on remote atolls, in strange waters. Boys who had never seen snow died in it. Miami gave her blood and opened her homes to wives of boys from the Sub Chaser School with orders to be shipped to the Pacific (many never to return) in order to provide one last visit. Miami women worked in war plants and drove trucks and manned the Army Information and Filter Center. But none of that makes a story.

What does, and an unforgettable one, is this:

The wounded from Anzio—men in traction, amputees, the mangled and hurt—lying in the temporary hospital established in a hotel on Collins Avenue were not getting well. They were restless and uncomfortable. They were angry and bitter. Day after day they watched the goings-on in the hotel next door, still open to civilian use. They watched sun bathers having cocktails and lunching under umbrellas. They saw the line of luxurious automobiles drive up to take them to the racetrack in the afternoon. At night, they listened to the band play music for men who were dancing in the patio below. They couldn't sleep until the music stopped along about two A.M. The head doctor paid a call next door to see if the hotel manager couldn't put a curfew on the dancing.

What the hotel manager told the doctor was, "Nothing doing."

5 | New Growth, Old Problems

The Facts of Life

THE UPHEAVAL OF WORLD WAR II, following the pattern laid down by World War I, resulted in another mass migration to Miami. Men who trained on the Miami Beach golf links and those who received instruction in the waters of Biscayne Bay and their wives and sweethearts and parents and assorted relatives who came to visit began this big parade to Miami at war's end. Damon Runyon, who made his winter home on Hibiscus Island, one of the man-made islands of Miami Beach, once wrote a piece about getting "sand in your shoes." The theory is that once you have trod the golden Miami sands you are marked and will never be able to stay away.

It was, all over the country, a time for turnover as restless, seeking men and women looked for something better in the way of living. They chose Miami for her sunshine and the informality of dress, and for the glamour associated with the name, perhaps. They also chose it because they could get a piece of land, build their own homes, enjoy outdoor living, swimming, and tennis and back-yard barbecues. They fanned out all over the place.

South Miami, once a sleepy, somewhat down-at-heels community, enjoyed a new look of prosperity and busyness. New shops of every description sprang up to answer the needs of the people. Ranch-type or Colonial homes went up in many areas, and in many more, tract homes for ex-GIs, small identical dwellings different only in color: yellow and orange and gray, coffee and chartreuse, pink and blue took over woodlands. Apartments rose all over the area. So did motels.

The bulldozer, arch-enemy of those who love the land, mowed down the pines and palmettos south of South Miami and north of North Miami, as

215

new little subdivisions and accompanying grocery stores and juke joints made their appearance with typical Florida suddenness.

Miami was bursting at the seams. Schools were packed. Miamians began to long for life away from the bustle of the city and they began to look at land that once had gone begging. Once George Merrick had been unable to convince investors of the worthiness of Coral Gables because it was so far west. Now, with the increased demand for new homes, developers began pushing out into the Everglades.

Not for the first time, Miami began to face the limitations of its environment. Some postwar settlers who moved into trim little houses along the western fringes of the city found all too unhappily that the land was too low, and learned to their sorrow that they would always be flooded in seasonal rains. And growth was forcing two issues that had long been ignored: fresh water to drink and how to dispose of the effluents that growing urban centers specialize in.

It had been during the war that the people who had come to live on the rim of the rock ledge adjacent to the Everglades first were forced to take a long look at what they had inherited.

Two things happened. First, during a long dry period that endless prairie of water and grass began to burn. The other was that the drinking water, the sweet, endlessly flowing water which had once bubbled up even in Biscayne Bay, was endangered by salt intrusion.

People said that cigarettes tossed from training planes and from automobiles crossing the Tamiami Trail to the west coast started the fires. Without rain to put them out, they raged out there in the wilderness, sending a choking smog over Miami, the area touted as a haven for asthma and hay fever sufferers. The rains finally put out the fires but salt continued to infiltrate into the drinking water, and a lot of people were beginning to ask intelligent questions about drainage. As a merciful providence would have it, for the first time in the history of Florida, scientific answers were available since the federal government had begun a survey to ascertain the exact nature of the Everglades as part of a study of national resources in connection with soil and water conservation.

Now as the people coughed and wiped the smoke from their eyes, spit out the salty stream from their faucets, and resorted to bottled mineral water, they got their answers.

The picture was this: man's insistence on draining off the water of the Everglades, opening up more and more of the watery saw grass country as inclination and development dictated without considering the nature of the region, was madness. Soil analysis proved that various areas had different types of soil, even different types of rock. The same treatment did not apply to all the land from Lake Okeechobee south. Some of the Everglades land would not only never be good for making subdivisions or planting beans or strawberries, some of this land if not returned to something approximating its natural state at once would play its part in destroying the whole modern civilization man had created at the end of the long peninsula, where rainfall supplied all fresh water. A modern city without drinking water would soon become a deserted city.

Miamians, listening hard to the hard facts of life, learned that the porous rock on which they lived, the oölitic or Miami limestone, was shaped like a tapering teaspoon. Imagine, said the geologists, that the spoon is filled with fresh water. Now dip the spoon into a teacup of salt water (the sea) and you have the picture of the position of the two liquids. The rain water, the region's source of all fresh water, stored in the limestone of the spoon, and the salt sea water (in the cup) are held separate within the same rock rim by maintaining a fresh-water level. Drain off or lower the fresh water enough and the sea rushes in through the porous rock. "Developers" of the region had been tampering with that delicate balance of fresh and salt water. Too late Miami learned that dynamiting the rapids of the Miami River had done more than spoil the picturesqueness of the stream. It had broken a natural dam between the fresh water of the Everglades and the salt water of the sea.

Remember Ingraham declaring in the magazine *Success* back in 1904: "Flagler decided there was nothing to prevent the water of the lakes from flowing into the ocean and leaving the land drained if vents could be made in this long ledge of rock . . ."

"Nothing to prevent" except a prearranged plan of nature upset by tycoons and land promoters as well as farmers and cattlemen. With the people applauding, these men fixed their eyes upon the profits but not ever on the region itself with even a tiny question in their minds as to its limitations. Ever since Florida entered the Union as a slave state in 1845, she had been trying to drain the Everglades, which men said "couldn't be surveyed until drained."

Only one man, Stephen Mallory of Key West, in all the military and

217

state officials of that time ever suggested that the investigation of the Everglades should come first and a conclusion about it follow. Revived by the government's Great Swamp Lands Act of 1850 which saw five hundred thousand acres of swampland come under the state of Florida, drainage was interrupted by the Seminole Wars and the War Between the States. The idea was never far off. Drainage was the magic word that meant opening up new land, making the Everglades the winter vegetable garden of the U.S.A., open sesame to riches. Now, for the first time, all the scientific facts available were laid before the public.

Still, knowing what the problem was didn't mean it would easily be resolved. Cattlemen, farmers, and dairymen throughout the state weren't interested in "Dade County's problem of salt intrusion in the drinking water." They felt it didn't concern them but of course it did. Nor, for that matter, were some Dade Countians interested in such a plan. Letting go of the powers to drain as they pleased to improve their individual lands was a hard thing to let slip through the fingers.

Coral Gables fought hard the damming of its canal which was being planned there. That waterway along which boats moved was the same canal Merrick cut through to the bay to advertise his "forty miles of waterfront." (Some said to get his forty miles he measured both sides of the canal.)

There was another hidden reason for fighting the damming. Sewage from some of the exquisite homes lining the canal banks was pouring into the waters. Damming would make a most unpretty sight as people sat on terraces sipping cool drinks or stepped into their power boats or merely sat. Whenever the matter came up somebody declared the sewage from the towered Veteran's Hospital, which started life as the boom-time Miami Biltmore, was fouling up the canal. This wasn't so. In 1944 the army installed an effluent plant.

Shouts had been going up for some time about the sewage pouring into the once-glittering waters of Biscayne Bay. When Philip Wylie first began calling attention to this dangerous situation in words that left nothing to the imagination, the keep-it-quiet philosophers, so long a part of Miami's pattern-making, nearly blew their tops. Wylie, who had heretofore confined himself to writing locally about the things wrong with his town, aired them in a national magazine in a picture spread under the title, "Polluted Paradise."

It moved the city fathers to action. In 1946, Miami voters agreed to require homes to have septic tanks. Then in 1952, with sewage floating in Biscayne Bay and fishermen complaining fish were dying, voters approved issuing bonds for the city's first sewage treatment plant.

It would be many years before the bay would be returned to a relatively clean state, and even then it would never be as beautiful as when the first settlers arrived.

Uninvited Guests

THE MOST VICIOUS CRIMINALS IN THE U.S.A. were now making Miami Beach their winter capital. The bathing beauty, traditional Miami Beach trademark, was in danger of being replaced by the figure of the gangster—thick-lipped, heavy-lidded, wearing a coat of tan and smoked glasses along with his custom-tailored "play togs." No longer dependent on violence to achieve their ends, these overlords of crime were expertly wielding the weapon labeled "corrupt political influence." Their racket was organized illegal gambling, the operation of bookie joints, the most highly organized racket since the bootlegging twenties. In *cabañas* and hotel lobbies, in office buildings, these bookmaking parlors operated all over the area.

A group of citizens formed the Crime Commission of Greater Miami "in order to encourage more widespread respect for laws and better law enforcement in Dade County." They hired Daniel P. Sullivan, an ex-FBI man, as operating director to run their office. All through late 1948 and through 1949 and early 1950 the group fought hard against corruption, while newspapers cooperated in printing photographs of the Miami Beach and Coral Gables mansions occupied by leading figures of the Capone gang in Chicago, the Costello gang in New York, the Purple gang in Detroit as well as representative criminals from Cleveland and Philadelphia.

Several of these big-shot hoodlums were proving more successful in assuming positions of semirespectability in the community than Al Capone had been. They were infiltrating into legitimate business, into the building trades, hotel and night club fields, liquor and the like, usually the fields in which blackmarketing operations sprang up from time to time. With wealth accumulated along the trail of lawlessness these men were buying political patronage, sending their children to Miami's schools, digging in for a lifetime of pleasant living under the sun.

The Crime Commission filed complaints about the operation of the bookmaker establishments with the sheriff's office. So did private citizens. So did a grand jury. Nothing ever happened. The sheriff was one Jimmy Sullivan, a former downtown Miami traffic cop whose smile and good humor were contagious. In a city not noted for its courteous police officers, Jimmy Sullivan helped old ladies cross the street, gave directions to school children, turned back jaywalkers with his own personal whistle and broad smile. He made a host of friends on that corner. One day it occurred to him to cash in on his popularity and he ran for sheriff. He was overwhelmingly elected.

It is supposed to be an accepted saying that "one term of office as sheriff of Dade County and a man can retire." Jimmy Sullivan didn't retire. He got caught by Estes Kefauver and his special committee to investigage organized crime in interstate commerce, and resigned under fire.

Before Kefauver introduced his resolution before the U.S. Senate to investigate crime in interstate commerce, Director Sullivan of the Crime Commission conferred with him in Washington, offering evidence that Miami was the wintertime hub of organized crime. When the investigation opened, all files and evidence accumulated by the Miami Commission were placed at the disposal of the Kefauver Committee, thereby saving weeks and months of investigation. The main worry of the Kefauver Committee was whether it could prove the interstate connection. The Crime Commission insisted it could and so it did in closed hearings that preceded the public hearings.

The public hearings threw the glaring light of "unfavorable publicity" on the Magic City in many people's minds—but the citizenry on the whole was so thankful to be exposing the racketeers and corrupt officials that for once it didn't care. New citizens who had never thought about the operation of the sheriff's office heard Jimmy Sullivan squirm verbally over radios in their own living rooms as the public hearings unfolded. They heard him admit that during his five-year tenure of office his assets had increased from twenty-five hundred dollars to "well over seventy thousand dollars," no small sum in those days.

Sheriff Sullivan admitted that he was in the habit of keeping thousands of additional dollars wrapped up in a blanket and also in an old fishing box at home. Three ex–deputy sheriffs testified that the sheriff had forbidden them to make arrests for bookmaking. The foreman of the grand jury which sat in Miami offered the suggestion that law enforcement "had broken down" and that bookmaking, card games, roulette, bolita, and other rackets were operating with the sanction of the police.

This governmental X-ray into organized gambling brought to light the fact that in Miami Beach a group of five local gamblers, known as the S and G Syndicate, had controlled the racing wire services and the bookmaking establishments, operating with the full protection of the Miami Beach Council, which in turn controls the police department absolutely, until a member of the Chicago Capone mob was cut into the lucrative Miami Beach field under highly suspicious circumstances. The entrance of the Capone mobster, one Harry Russell, came about only after a bit of expert arm-twisting which was traced, many felt, to the executive mansion in Tallahassee.

The event went like this: Before Russell was accepted into the syndicate an investigator appointed personally by Governor Fuller Warren, newly elected to office, arrived in Miami and, with the help of the heretofore unwilling sheriff's office, raided several S and G bookie parlors. This investigator was getting his information from Russell with whom he conferred during these raids. He also conferred about gambling activities with William H. Johnston, horse and dog track operator in Florida and Chicago, who happened to be a friend of Governor Warren, a friend who had contributed one hundred thousand American dollars to the governor's campaign fund.

During this period of applied pressure, the Continental Press Service, distributors of racing wire news, cut off the service to Miami Beach for ten days, a crippling act not without intent. The S and G Syndicate saw the light and accepted Russell. Next, a Jacksonville lawyer, John A. Rush, another friend of the governor as well as Johnston's attorney, received for his services in drawing up a simple instrument calling for the legalizing of gambling the sum of ten thousand dollars from the S and G.

All this was brought out by the cast of characters which paraded before Kefauver, who also subpoenaed the books and records of night clubs and hotels in both Dade and Broward counties. The Wofford at Miami Beach was clearly established as the meeting place for notorious racketeers from all over

223

the country and had been bought by gambler Frank Erickson with Abe Allenberg, an attorney, as a front. Erickson's operations in Florida included concessions at the Roney Plaza, Boca Raton, and Hollywood Beach hotels and active illegal bookmaking activity at the racetracks. The sum Erickson had put into Tropical Park back in 1935 was declared on the witness stand to have been two hundred and fifty thousand dollars.

The world was now informed that the New York gangsters stopped at the Wofford and Boulevard hotels, the Detroit mobsters at the Wofford and the Grand hotels, and the Philadelphia underworld characters at the Sands Hotel. They nearly all congregated daily between eleven A.M. and noon at the corner of Twenty-third and Collins, like show people of vaudeville days meeting by the Palace to swap trade information.

Some interesting testimony concerned the sheriff of adjoining Broward County, Walter Clark, and his brother Robert and the combined monies garnered by them during the former's term of office. Sheriff Clark, whose official income was sixty-five hundred dollars a year, augmented it by partnership in a "novelty company" which was another way of saying operations in bolita and numbers games. He was also investor in numerous other small businesses. In an enterprise representing the investment of thirty-five thousand dollars, he transacted business with five- and ten-dollar bills. His brother's income rose from eighteen thousand to three hundred thousand. And so it went.

The Kefauver investigation in Miami and subsequent investigations elsewhere touched off some speedy action by the Bureau of Internal Revenue which took steps to cut in on ten per cent of the monthly gross take of horse books, punchboards, numbers rackets, everything but gambling casinos, by putting a tax on betting. Kefauver, it is said, was not in accord with this law which he interpreted as making the Treasury a partner of gamblers. Nevertheless it was passed by Congress and made part of the Internal Revenue Code and became the lethal weapon for wiping out bookmaking. By demanding that bookies register publicly, it opened up their doors to law enforcement officers and tax men. It killed the horse books and the S and G Syndicate was forced to fold at Miami Beach. Members were subsequently brought to trial to explain the disparity between the income of four hundred sixty-six thousand, five hundred and four dollars declared and the twenty-six million dollars in bets Kefauver had estimated passed through their hands in one year.

The next winter the shady characters were missing from Twenty-third and Collins and from Copa City Night Club and the *cabañas* by the beautiful sea. Some were in prison on tax evasion. Others soon would be. Some were being investigated to see if deportation might be arranged. Others had taken their operations to Cuba, Haiti, Puerto Rico, to be welcomed with open arms.

Their time would come.

Facing Up

THE STATE DEPARTMENT, coldly insistent in the matter of suitable hotel accommodations for not only diplomats but "all people of color coming from abroad," prodded in the field of human relations all during World War II. In the face of the federal government's Good Neighbor Policy, which heretofore Miami had used as a kind of trade slogan, who could fight such insistence? Temporarily, local prejudices and local voices were stilled as for the first time important matters were removed from the frequently bungling hands of local policymakers. The sardonic humor of observing individuals attempting to draw the line between skins that were Negroid and Indian was lost in the realization of the tragic stupidity.

But after the war, some of the Miami hotels which "cooperated" with the State Department as a "wartime measure" returned to banning the visits of darker-skinned visitors. Newspapers in various corners of the U.S.A. pointed accusing fingers at Miami in the matter of minority and racial prejudice.

Ignorance and violence would sway. In 1951, a black settlement known as Carver Village was bombed, as were a Catholic Church and the Jewish Centers. Authorities say the first bombings in April were by student thrill-seekers but the Carver Village bombing and later explosions, none of which claimed lives, were marked by more sinister implications. Crude signs with Nazi and Ku Klux Klan symbols figured in the later acts of violence; and in December, 1952, three Klansmen and the vice-president of the Edison Center Civic Association, a woman, were indicted by a federal grand jury for "lying" during the earlier investigations.

The Dade County sheriff asked Governor Fuller Warren to call out the National Guard because of "inflammable conditions."

The governor, saying that Miami had always enjoyed better-than-average racial and religious relations, felt the bombing incidents were sporadic outbursts and not worthy of calling out the militia. Further, he took no action on the Anti-defamation League of B'nai B'rith's suggestion that a conference of law enforcement officials be called to adopt a coordinated program to cope with the acts.

Jewish leaders stormed police headquarters to demand action of some sort. Miami Beach was and still is one of the largest Jewish communities in the world and Greater Miami claimed good minority-group relations until this strange outbreak which began in April and ended in the tragic death on Christmas Eve of Harry T. Moore, state coordinator of the National Association for Advancement of Colored People, and the fatal injury of his wife in the small town of Mims in Lake County. The murder of the Moores brought the FBI into the situation and wrote "period" to the local interim of gathering tension.

Before the climax of this period a Protestant clergyman offered to supply armed men from his congregation to watch over synagogues. The Jewish War Veterans, after considering similar action, voted against it. An organization known as the Coordinated Committee Against Bombings was formed.

There is no doubt that in the case of the Carver Village bombings the basis had to do with mounting tensions between blacks and whites over housing problems. Blacks in Miami had always lived in substandard housing and the slum clearance programs offended many whites, who felt their homes were threatened by public housing programs. Blacks were making gains. Most liberals agreed that the gains were not fast enough.

The governor had pointed to Miami as the scene of "good" racial relations. But in fact race relations had always been tense. One hundred and twenty years ago a good many white men on the bay threatened any black who attempted to move in. "Don't let nightfall catch ya," was the expression they used to scare the blacks. Yet there were examples in Miami of racial cooperation. Perhaps the most noteworthy happened in Coconut Grove. It was the cleanup of the black Grove, the old section settled by southern blacks and Bahamians who sailed over in the days when Miami was a peaceful wilderness.

Coconut Grove was as guilty as the rest of Miami in ignoring its slum conditions, in refusing to allow the blacks to expand, in closing its eyes to the shocking lack of sanitation. It was as though the poinciana trees and the mangoes, all the dooryard planting that made art studies of shacks, covered up the awful truth. Occasionally a white woman would get exercised about the living conditions of her laundress or maid and quarrel with a white landlord, but twenty-seven per cent of these blacks owned their own homes.

Still, they had few toilets. Outside privies were the norm. They were still using wells, long since polluted, for drinking water. Their garbage was not picked up because seldom was it put out in proper containers and there was a city law about requiring uniform containers.

It is likely that nothing dramatic in the way of a reform would have occurred if it hadn't been for one woman—tiny, blue-eyed Mrs. Vladimir Virrick, Kentucky-born wife of a leading Russian-born Miami architect. In 1948 she led a crusade to clean up the slums. It started when she went to a meeting and heard a black Episcopal minister, the Reverend Theodore Gibson, say expressively, "My people are living seven deep." All night the words reverberated in her mind and next morning she presented herself at Father Gibson's home.

"What can I do to help?" she asked. Her only daughter was away at college and she was prepared to plunge into the task ahead.

This is what happened, and at once: A group of twenty-four whites and blacks met at Mrs. Virrick's home. There were ministers, a black policeman, a lawyer, a welfare worker, a writer, a housewife among the group. They made plans. They sent out posters calling for "an old-fashioned town meeting to form the Coconut Grove Citizens Committee for Slum Clearance." It was summertime—August. Two hundred Grove-ites attended the meeting.

The campaign began with black women—block leaders—inspecting garbage pails. There were forms to fill out. One block leader classified twelve garbage pails as rejected, nine fair, and six good. The committee bought pails and offered them at wholesale prices. They set about checking screening, sponsored a rat-killing campaign. The black men worked at night clearing a dump and converting it into a playground. A big rally was set for Columbus Day and prizes ranging from printed stationery to a septic tank were offered for the cleanest grounds. Everybody came to the rally. The George

Washington Carver Negro School Glee Club sang. There was a band. The whites were more excited that night than the blacks.

In November they began on the plumbing. At night, when it was too dark to disturb the eyes, the city was in the habit of sending "the honey wagon" around to remove excrement. This work cost the city ten thousand a year. The Citizens Committee worked vigorously to persuade the Miami city commission to pass a law ordering the people of the slum area to connect with the city's water mains and to install flush toilets, sinks, and septic tanks. White landlords fought this move undercover. But the city commission passed it. They went to work setting up loans for blacks to buy them. Legislation alone would not bring sanitation. The Coconut Grove Bank agreed to lend owners on home mortgages. Plumbers swung other loans with credit agencies.

The committee set up its own fund borrowed from sympathetic whites and lent money at two per cent interest. The Bank agreed to take care of the collections at half-price. Some residents paid as little as five dollars a month.

One woman telephoned Elizabeth Virrick to thank her for her "first bath."

Next the Citizens Committee fought for rezoning, the root of slum conditions, and here they stepped on many white toes. Individuals who would profit enormously by multiple housing were attempting to push through apartment-type housing, expensive and worse, housing which would eventually increase the slums. Hammering its point home and fully backed by leading architects who lived in the area, the group insisted on zoning being altered mainly to single-type dwellings.

Heated discussions before the city commission with distinguished winter visitors, some of whom had been coming to the Grove for forty years, kept the commissioners aware of the continued zeal of the workers. Despite all this in a last-minute typical double-dealing act the commission voted to permit two builders to put in multiple housing. There was talk of a "fix." Fighting mad, the Grove citizens resorted to their right to an initiative election and set out to get the required number of signatures of registered voters to bring this about.

It was the first time in Miami's history, or in the history of Florida, that the citizens took over their right to an initiative election and carried it to a successful conclusion. Milkmen and newsboys, doctors and lawyers, took the petitions and got signatures. It was a period of consolidated citizenry and the voters on the whole were entirely sympathetic. The ordinance went on the ballot for the following November and was voted law by the people.

Meanwhile the committee was busy supplying free adult-education classes in reading, writing, and arithmetic for blacks, some of them elderly. It worked for and got the Board of Public Instruction to purchase an additional two-and-a-half acres adjoining the George Washington Carver School, the last chance at land for adding on badly needed classrooms. In working for sanitation the committee kept unearthing new evidence of things not right in other fields. The school, for instance, was fifteen years behind other Dade County schools in curriculum and materials, although nine teachers had master's degrees.

This work, begun as a sanitation campaign, eventually became a year-round project with a day nursery and a summer entertainment program for children, including classes in creative dancing, baseball, folk dances and storytelling, garden-club information, tennis, Ping-pong, and basketball.

Elizabeth Virrick received the fame from her work that she deserved. The Voice of America, eager to counter the Soviet Union's broadcasts about American racism, sent a reporter to Miami. The librarian at the Miami *Herald* once remarked to her, "You have more clippings in your folder on slum clearance than any other group except the racketeers."

But for all of Mrs. Virrick's energies in Coconut Grove, little changed overall in race relations in Miami. Miami's largest slums in Overtown were neglected. The hard lines of Jim Crow laws were strictly enforced.

Bryan O. Walsh, now one of Miami's most influential clergymen, recalls how in 1955 he was turned away from the Florida A and M Orange Blossom Classic because he had "a black ticket."

Recently arrived from his native Ireland, the young priest was living at the parish of the Holy Redeemer in Liberty City, one of Miami's largest black neighborhoods.

The young Fr. Walsh explained at the gate that he expected to sit with his black parishoners and that the ticket had been given to him by a black friend.

231

"No," the guard explained. It was "a rule." Obviously the Irish-born priest was a foreigner and did not understand the customs of the good old U.S.A., Miami version.

Miami's race relations would remain a flashpoint for many more years to come.

Miami Beach: Tourist Heaven

IN THE 1950s the spit of swamp and mangrove between the ocean and the bay turned into a shining city. Forget Smith's and Hardie's Casino with its high-flying flags; forget Fisher's Miami Beach which was, for all its grandeur, small, intimate. Now there were miles of modern shining hotels, every shade and shape, block after block of colored monuments to tourism, rimming the broad Atlantic, curving as the land curves, each a contained little world designed for fancy living.

The millions of tourists who flocked to Miami Beach expected glamour and they got it.

At a convention of travel agents in the early fifties, someone sat down and figured that Miami Beach had built more hotels since World War II than the rest of the resort world put together. Nothing in Great Britain, France, South America—the combined world resorts— came up to it.

Miami Beach, all seven square miles of it, was a play city, highly organized to offer every type of entertainment man craves. Industries were outlawed, there was no black settlement and therefore no white-created slum area. Even railroad tickets had to be picked up over in Miami, and until railroad offices were opened on the Beach, there was a going trade in black-market tickets.

The summer business became brisk with North and South Americans mingling—and advantageously at reduced prices. Delta Air Lines took advantage of the lower summer rates to offer economical packages called "Millionaire Dream Vacations." They were particularly popular among young women office workers, who may have been attracted by the possibility of romance, though the statistics argued against it: seventy-five per cent of the dream vacationers were single young women, either traveling alone or in pairs. The other twenty-five per cent were either single men or families.

The tourism boom sent the hotels marching, gobbling up ocean front without so much as a civic squawk. A leading American travel agent pointed out sadly that the area had sacrificed "the preservation and beauty of its greatest and most valuable single asset in an eagerness to transform precious waterfront land into tourist dollars." The *Herald* rose to the occasion editorially with the thought that "there is still time to salvage some of the frontage farther north that is not yet cumbered with concrete, steel and neon lights."

Sunning and swimming came first with tourists, but as the fifties unfolded shopping, too, came into its own. Lincoln Road, named by Carl Fisher for his idol, Abraham Lincoln, came to be known as the Rue de la Paix of the South, the Fifth Avenue of the South, and in the slogan-loving language of its merchants the Most Beautiful Shopping Lane in the World.

On Lincoln Road double sidewalks, separated by cool green planting, permitted window shoppers to dawdle without impeding those on business bent. Rows of royal palms towered above the walks, and under the shaded awnings visitors peered at displays by Hattie Carnegie, Peck and Peck, De Pinna's, Saks Fifth Avenue, *et al*. Ladies bought gowns and men, if they were in the mood, could buy diamond bracelets, rare china, handsome rugs, exotic fruit—and occasionally exotic play clothes for themselves. Men's slacks in cerise and high yellow, shirts that dazzle, were purchased—and worn—under the influence of the soft air, the brilliant sun, sky, and foliage. Following former President Truman's uninhibited example at the Little White House at Key West, men went overboard for wild shirts and shorts.

Full undress was the rule, enough so that the Miami Beach Council even passed a law to ban scantily clad tourists strolling along Lincoln Road. It required a robe over your bathing suit. The council even tried to extend the law to cover women from shoulder to knee. This provided an interlude of hilarity until it sensibly decided against overextending its powers thusly. The law said "no bathing suits."

The Beach of the 1950s was full of tales of *nouveau riche* excess. Nevertheless, a photographer for a home-decoration magazine reported setting up his camera to take pictures in one of the colorful waterside villas. The scene in the living room looked singularly set so he proposed placing an open book on a coffee table. It was not his intention to throw the entire household into a tizzy but that is what happened. Three comic books were presented and rejected by the photographer before the cook came forward with a hard-cover cookbook, the only book in the house. Then there was the house with the fake books lining a whole wall of a "den."

Another typical Beach tale concerned Jocko, a Brazilian marmoset which was brought regularly by its mistress to a Twenty-third Street beauty parlor for a manicure and pedicure.

Carl Fisher's Miami Beach had disappeared in the new growth of hotels and homes and night clubs and restaurants. His home, the Shadows, which had become the Beach and Tennis during Prohibition days, was moved and put to use as a restaurant.

Fisher's first wife, Jane, divorced from the developer in 1926 and subsequent party in a series of marriages, applied to the courts after Fisher's death to resume using his name. Then she embarked on a radio career of reminiscences about early days on the Beach and wrote a book about Fisher. It is a measure of how quickly the town forgot that she was now referred to in Miami newspapers as "the widow of Carl Fisher." A glance at the telephone book would have convinced a reporter that Carl's widow, the former Margaret Collier, had been dwelling quietly in the area all those years.

Jane's last husband was a man known at the Surf Club as Alberto Santos. As Alberto Guimares he was questioned by police in connection with the murder of Dot King in the early twenties in New York, and admitted the murdered beauty had given him ten thousand dollars within a brief period of time.

When Jane and Alberto parted company he sued for two hundred and seventy-five thousand dollars on the grounds she had agreed to pay him ten thousand a year at the time of the marriage. It was pointed out that he was figuring his desserts on his life expectancy. The suit was thrown out of court and Jane went back to being the widow of Carl Fisher. Santos-Guimares died in 1952 at the age of fifty-six, his life expectancy unfulfilled.

Hotels were in the entertainment business in a big way, offering stars like Lena Horne and Edith Piaf, Sophie Tucker and Joe E. Lewis, a great alltime favorite whose "Sam, You Made the Pants Too Long," never failed to bring down the house.

Night clubs like Ciro's and the Latin Quarter went their merry ways and the Five O'Clock Club was a must for a drop-in visit for cocktails. Joe's Stone Crabs continued to gain in popularity.

A supply of neckties was kept on hand to present to gentlemen who appeared without them. In private clubs like the Bath, Surf, and Indian Creek, it was regularly black tie.

A visit to Miami Beach was tied up with the Miami moon, the Atlantic Ocean, swaying palms aglow with indirect lighting, swaying rhumba dancers, gallons of sun-tan oil, gallons of frozen daiquiris, Bloody Marys, and dry martinis. Gallons of Chanel Number Five. Gallons of everything.

Recording it all "for Mr. and Mrs. America and all the Ships at Sea" was radio's number one news broadcaster, Walter Winchell. He called it "Heaven." When Miami Beach merchants said their prayers they always thanked the Lord for sending them Winchell. A drum-beater for the spot as well as an attraction at the Roney *Cabaña* Club, Winchell not only wrote about Miami Beach, he staged his Sunday night broadcasts from the area. Top entertainers and movie moguls, newspaper publishers and government officials, press agents and publicity seekers, all stopped by and said "hi" to Winchell as he sat sunning himself at his winter headquarters on the pool deck.

It was a time of glamour, as shimmering and fragile as moonlight on the bay.

6 | Living in Miami
1953–1990

Ring Out The Old

NOT EVERYBODY TOOK THE TIME to read the paper that New Year's morning. At the Biscayne Bay Yacht Club, flags were raised along with eggnog cups before members took off for the Orange Bowl football game between Oklahoma and Syracuse.

The Miami *Herald's* page one headline shouted: KING ORANGE TO BE JUICIEST YET. Those who caught the banner headline rejoiced to read: HAPPY '59 — EAL STRIKE ENDS. That would be Eastern Air Lines. (Three decades later in 1989 another acrimonious strike would shatter Eastern, reducing its size and producing a no-win situation.)

Down at the bottom of the page in very small type, a wire story, clearly a space filler, reported that "United States Senator John F. Kennedy was released from the New England Baptist Hospital after suffering a virus infection."

Relegated to page two, another headline announced: BATISTA TROOPS/ POUND REBELS/FROM PROVINCE. Stern words followed: "There will be no New Year's holiday and no truces or respites for the rebels." It reported that "a Roman Catholic priest harbored two hundred rebels in the town of Cruces and came out crying for peace while carrying a machine gun in his garments."

Buried at the bottom of the story were these words: "In Havana, a group of government officials and lawmakers sought visas from the American Embassy to go to the U.S. Families of some prominent Cubans already have left for the U.S."

Actually, there was no reason to notice this story. There were always deposed Cuban leaders with their followers taking refuge in Miami. President

Carlos Prio, knocked out of power by Batista in 1952, was residing at Miami Beach at that very time.

What was noticeable in Miami on New Year's Eve was that street celebrations were prolonged. Unless you were in the thick of downtown or Cuban nighborhoods, however, you did not hear the cries of "Viva, Castro" which rang out repeatedly, while horns honked and loud cheers ushered in the New Year.

Putting the holiday behind them, Miamians went to bed New Year's night with no more than passing interest in the fact that the dictator, Fulgencio Batista, had been deposed and that the thirty-two-year-old revolutionary, Fidel Castro, had claimed power.

Far more interesting was the fact that Alaska was about to be declared the forty-ninth state in the union and that the European Economic Community, or Common Market, had gone into effect that day.

Who would ever have imagined as 1959 dawned that Miami had been put on a course that would lead it to becoming what the former president of Ecuador, the late Jaime Roldos, would be calling "the capital of Latin America" and Ralph Renick, the dean of Miami television commentators, would term "the exile capital of the world"?

Who would ever think to connect the ailing young Senator Kennedy with the lives of so many Cubans who in turn would change the course of history for Miami, U.S.A.?

La Causa

A S FAR BACK AS 1891, Cuba's revered patriot, Jose Marti, was in New York drumming up support for the revolution to extricate his country from Spain and organizing groups to help him give voice to *la causa*. There were two hundred in all, seventy-six of them in Florida, sixty-one in Key West alone, where the Cuban population numbered three thousand. In Tampa, fifteen organizations held forth among the thirty-five hundred Cubans. They all raised money to ship guns to their homeland. Cigar makers were handing over ten per cent of their earnings for this purpose, and the guns were being shipped secretly out of Fernandina and Cedar Key as well as Key West and Tampa.

A century ago, certain Floridians were raising questions. What if Cuba became part of the United States? Wouldn't this cause "unwanted competition" in the marketplace?

It would take Fidel Castro to accomplish that.

Castro had come to Miami in 1955 looking for money for his July 26th Movement, and deposed President Prio had given it. Miami was the place to come for plotting both the rise and fall of Cuban leaders. General Gerardo Machado made a hurried exit to Miami in order to avoid capture in 1933 when his government fell.

The young Castro moved quickly after the fall of Batista and on January 2 proclaimed a provisional government headed by Dr. Manuel Urrutia, while he claimed the role of head of the military. On the seventh, the United States recognized the new government and on February 16 Castro became premier of Cuba.

In Miami in the days following the fall of Batista, many Cubans were beside themselves with excitement as they prepared to drop everything and return to Cuba. In some instances, they left so suddenly they failed to have the electricity turned off or dispose of possessions. Getting passage back to Cuba was their first aim and the airlines were swamped. There were instances of arriving supporters of Batista running into trouble with departing Castro enthusiasts, causing enough friction at the airport to call for extra police to handle the situation.

A Havana family, fleeing to Key West on their yacht the day after Batista fell, was met with uncertainty by officials who had no instructions as to how to handle them. That being the case, they were held for ten days until a policy was adopted and they were released.

In mid-April, Castro, set out on an eleven-day goodwill tour which landed him in Washington and New York and included a visit to the home of Vice-President Richard Nixon as well as audiences with Secretary of State Christian Herter and U.N. Secretary General Dag Hammarskjold. On all sides, as he expressed his democratic leanings, he was greeted warmly, garnered newspaper and TV interviews and made favorable impressions.

Later it was established that five hundred Batista supporters had been executed in the first three and a half months of his regime.

Recognizing the growing ties between Russia and Cuba, in July 1960 President Dwight D. Eisenhower took steps and announced a ninety-five per cent decrease in Cuban sugar imports. Next, he warned the Soviets that the 1823 Monroe Doctrine was still U.S. policy and not to meddle in this hemisphere.

On October 28, 1960, the United States declared in a note to the Organization of American States that Cuba had been receiving shipments of arms and technicians from the Soviet bloc and warned of a plan "to give armed support to the spread of revolution in other parts of the Americas."

In the November elections, the forty-three-year-old John Fitzgerald Kennedy won the presidency over Richard M. Nixon with a small margin of one hundred thousand votes.

Now it was his turn to deal with the Cuban situation.

Exactly two years after Castro came to power the United States broke off diplomatic relations and announced restrictions on travel to Cuba.

In a May Day speech Castro abolished free elections and declared, "I am a Marxist-Leninist and will be one until the day I die."

Miamians seemed to look at Cuban affairs over their shoulders at the time because they were busy with their own affairs.

Air conditioning was turning South Florida into what Colonel Doherty's press agents had touted in the 1930s as "Florida Year Round."

Miami Beach was marching forward, with two glitzy new hotels, the Fontainebleu and the Eden Roc, helping maintain its reputation as a tourist paradise. A lasting quarrel was begun over the fact that the Eden Roc had deliberately stolen the Fontainebleu's (usually pronounced Fountain-blue) view of the Atlantic.

With bulldozers turning farmlands into shopping malls and families moving into the suburbs, a call for a consolidated form of government had gone out. Turned down in 1953 by voters after bitter opposition from municipalities unwilling to give up power, officials turned to the University of Miami to try to come up with a solution. The University study resulted in the home rule bill passed by the Florida Legislature, giving Dade County the power to create a metropolitan form of government, provided voters approved it.

Nixon Smiley observed in his book *Knights of the Fourth Estate*, "Never was an experiment in government, outside of communism or fascism, more bitterly condemned or more stubbornly fought by its enemies." Even so, the voters approved this experiment in government, referred to as a "two-tiered system" because it functions as a municipal authority for unincorporated areas as well as a county system. It turned the nation's eyes toward Miami in a new way.

In the years 1920 to 1950, greater Miami had gone from a population of forty-two thousand to four hundred and ninety-five thousand and was on the verge of one million. There was reason for Miami citizens to cheer.

It took about six months for some of those who had rushed back to Cuba to realize things were not as promised and they began the trickle back to Miami, the trickle that turned into a flood.

The Cubans were designated as political refugees and their cases were

243

processed at the old Miami *News* Tower. Miami's first newspaper had moved out of the landmark building and into a modern, more efficient plant on the Miami River. The *News* Tower was given a new name: Freedom Tower. It was there that each family was awarded the sum of one hundred dollars a month and food stamps from the United States government.

There would be other name changes. The old Riverside section of Miami, between Tamiami Trail and Flagler Street, became a Cuban neighborhood. Rents were cheap and the exiles moved in, generously sharing quarters with each other as new refugees arrived. Tamiami Trail became known as *Calle Ocho* or Eighth Street and the area took on the name of Little Havana.

It goes without saying that not all Cubans were alike any more than all Miamians were alike. The first wave to come ashore brought their family wealth with them, having departed their island home with jewels and bank accounts long established in the United States and abroad. They moved into the homes some had already purchased and took up their social lives where they had left them off in Havana.

The arrivals who excited the admiration of Miamians were the professionals who left their lives behind and arrived with the scant five dollars permitted and the clothes they were wearing. Their remarkable performance proved history-making.

The spirit with which these transplants made their way, performing menial jobs with zeal, advancing in the job market, starting small businesses, working toward resuming their professions, served as an education for entrenched citizens of Miami. Their family solidarity was unmatched.

There was the Cuban senator who borrowed five hundred dollars from an established Miami family, found a place for his own family and furnished it with second-hand pieces from the Salvation Army. He then picked up a beat-up station wagon and went early each morning to pick vegetables in the field after which he went door to door selling the produce in order to make a living.

The University of Miami Medical School assisted physicians from Havana in building up credentials in order to eventually resume their professions. A flow between Havana and Miami already existed in the medical fraternity and assistance was offered unstintingly in many cases. Mercy Hospital did its part, as did others.

Some Cubans elected to stay in Cuba and fight to regain their government.

Parents who wished to remain worried about the fate of their children when rumor had it that Castro planned to send them to Russia for "training."

The parents appealed to the CIA and the State Department through underground channels, whereupon a plot was hatched to spirit the offspring out of the country and bring them to Miami.

Bryan Walsh, the Irish priest refused in 1955 the right to sit with his black parishioners at the football game, was approached to assist in the program, which had its dramatic baptism on Christmas Eve 1960.

As head of the Catholic Welfare Bureau, he was plunged into a mission achieved with the help of the British Embassy and the Colonial Authority Administration in Jamaica, through which the children were flown. It was kept dead secret for a period of two years by the news media which dubbed it *Operation Pedro Pan* after the ban was lifted.

Before it ended, the clergyman, now a Monsignor and head of the Catholic Community Services Inc. covering both Dade and Broward Counties, had shepherded fourteen thousand, five hundred children of assorted ages. The operation was unique in many ways, only one of which was the strict record-keeping. Today, anyone seeking information as to the whereabouts of any of those children can locate it in the Monsignor's files.

Plans are afoot to turn the files over to Barry University, that fifty-year-old success story out in Miami Shores, where they will be readily available for research.

No need to search out files to locate Armando Codina, who arrived at the age of fifteen knowing two English words: Coke and hamburger. He is highly visible as the 1990s race into the twenty-first century.

Codina is the first Cuban president of the Greater Miami Chamber of Commerce which, thoroughly reorganized in the late 1960s to meet the demands of a community in travail, plays a vital leadership role. Codina, the man, rides in a telephone-equipped Mercedes-Benz, with a walkie-talkie just in case, and a driver to get him to appointments on time.

When President George Bush was vice-president under Ronald Reagan and Codina was politicking for the Republicans, he was told that Bush's son Jeb and his Mexican-born wife, Colomba, wanted to leave Houston for

Miami. Codina promptly offered him a job. Later, Jeb Bush had a cabinet post in the Florida State government. Today, the president's son and Codina work closely together in various real-estate developments in Miami.

Cubans are big Republicans and big contributors to campaign chests.

It all started with what has become known as the Bay of Pigs. Until then, Cubans believed their Miami stay was temporary.

They were encouraged in this belief by the CIA, which had started on its way to assuming the proportions of a Miami industry. As late as 1972 Cubans would be cast in lead roles in the Watergate break-in, the event that toppled a Republican president and which left the lead players out in the cold.

The Bay of Pigs operation was supposed to be a secret, but any number of people were entirely aware that the CIA was behind the exiles training in the Everglades. The plan was to invade Cuba and oust Castro.

The group was composed of seasoned military figures, professional men, young idealists, patriots all. They were flown to Guatemala for more training and while there, Carlos Rodriguez, a member of the group, was killed. His number was 2506 and thereafter these men, calling themselves Freedom Fighters, gave themselves a new name: *Brigade 2506*. They numbered just over twelve hundred.

The date engraved in the hearts of exiles and their families is April 17, 1961, when the Brigade landed on the southern coast of Cuba, close by the Bay of Pigs.

Reams have been written about how the United States failed to supply air support, without which victory could not be achieved.

Those who died fighting and those who drowned when their ship sank, one hundred and seventeen in all, earned immortality, but all Cubans felt the United States had let them down. The word "betrayed" is most often used. Many of the one thousand, one hundred and eighty captured were wounded.

Jose Perez San Roman, who served as military commander of the operation, was captured and thrown into prison for twenty months, along with the rest. They were released after the U.S., attempting to make amends, paid out sixty-two million dollars for tractors and medical supplies delivered to Castro in exchange for the prisoners held in Cuban jails. Eleanor Roosevelt and Milton Eisenhower were among those serving on a *Tractors For Freedom Committee* which helped bring about their release.

Perez San Roman, still brooding over the failure of his command and the loss of his comrades, killed himself September, 1989, in Miami. For him, the burden proved too great.

The failed Bay of Pigs operation told Cubans they would not be returning to their homeland anytime soon and changed their focus.

When the road to Cuba was closed for them, they simply changed direction and brought Cuba to Miami.

Contrary to the expressed belief of some, however, they did not invent Miami.

Miami had its own history.

Miamians learned about the missile crisis first hand by waking up one fall day in 1962 to the sight of convoys of military trucks and extra trains filled with soldiers decorating the landscape. Next, tents were erected on the fringes of town and reports of missile installations in South Dade open spaces were whispered about.

This news was received with natural alarm.

Was Miami about to be invaded?

Just as Nazi submarines lurking offshore had brought World War II to South Florida, this new crisis in Cuba carried with it a deepening awareness of the world political situation.

Some people packed up and fled, as some had during the Spanish-American War. Others battened down and discussed the possibility of bomb shelters. On the whole, Miamians responded as they always had to hurricanes—by laying in extra supplies of food and drinking water.

At Doctors' Hospital, where blocks of beds were being set aside in case of emergency, one influential lady was most insistent about installing her elderly mother for safekeeping. She was turned away.

On October 22, 1962, President Kennedy went on television to explain why the United States was being placed on a wartime alert.

Reconnaissance planes had reported that Russian missile pads were being installed in Cuba. World War III was not an impossibility.

247

Things remained tense for six days before Nikita Kruschev agreed to remove the missile stockpile, but he exacted a condition, one that would not surface as public information for twenty years: the United States would not invade Cuba nor would it encourage others to do so. For many Cubans in Miami, it was an agreement that would earn President Kennedy lasting hatred.

In late 1962 the prisoner exchange was made and President Kennedy came to Miami to pay homage to the men of the brigade at an emotionally charged ceremony in the Orange Bowl.

It was attended by cheering Cubans, thirty thousand of them, waving American flags. Twenty months after the Bay of Pigs disaster they presented the president with the Brigade 2506 flag. He promised to return it to them "in a free Havana." Today, it remains in storage in Washington, its delivery unmade.

Security was very tight on President Kennedy's next visit on the night of November 18, 1963, when he arrived to address the Inter-American Press Association.

Newspaper executive Lee Hills met Air Force One and escorted the president to Bal Harbour and the Americana Hotel where he changed into a tuxedo. At the dinner he told the newsmen gathered that "for the United States, Latin America is the most important area in the world."

He apologized for having to return to Washington immediately, explaining he was due to leave for a swing through Texas.

He had a historic rendezvous in Dallas.

After his assassination, the nation went into mourning while television made the terrible event all too real.

Two years later the U.S. State Department negotiated with Castro, who agreed to allow two planeloads of Cubans to take off every day for Miami. They were called Freedom Flights and continued until 1973.

These flights brought one hundred fifty thousand additional Cubans to Miami so that at the end of the 1960s, it was estimated, there were four hundred thousand refugees in Dade County.

By their overwhelming presence, extraordinary enterprise and energy, the Cubans gained political and economic power in a short time. Other refugees from Central American countries were on their way.

The Cubans turned to the United States for citizenship, became staunch Republicans and opened up an entirely new way of playing politics in South Florida, with passions unleashed and no holds barred.

Miami became a hotbed of plotting and terrorist activity by extremist Cubans bent on ridding the world of Fidel Castro and stamping out communism all at the same time.

Bombings and shootings were part of the scenario. Confrontations between extremist political factions were the norm.

On the gentler side, but still political, a network of *municipios* were set up by Cubans to provide aid and comfort to transplanted Cubans from similar locations in Cuba.

Miamians began to complain of feeling like displaced persons.

Douglas Fairbairn, a novelist who grew up in Coconut Grove, wrote a book called *Street Eight* that the New York *Times* called "a gripping piece of work." After spending time in Little Havana, he told a friend with awe, "This is the first time that a foreign country has taken over an American city."

It was an astounding part of the continuing unfolding drama begun in Miami in 1896.

There Goes The Neighborhood

A DIFFERENT IMMIGRATION hit Coconut Grove in the 1960s, a steady stream of a new breed of wanderer called "hippies."

They spoke of "flower power," were homeless by choice and wandered in from all over the U.S.A. The real name for them was runaways.

They slept in Peacock Park, wore out the grass of St. Stephen's churchyard, where they lounged when not walking the streets of the village, asking for handouts, quite clearly stoned out of their minds.

They raided fruit trees all along the bayfront, and, in the former home of Dr. Leo H. Baekeland, the inventor of plastics, Helen Ross awoke one morning to observe several long-haired peace-lovers engaged in denuding the banana trees she had been watching come to full growth after careful nurturing.

When she inquired what made them think they could steal her bananas, they declared that Nature provided the bananas for all. They were Nature's bananas, not hers.

Some preferred cooked food. A sixteen-year-old runaway girl prepared one hot meal a day over an open fire for her lucky friends. Some of them pitched tents on Bird Road.

Wirth Munroe lay quietly on the upper veranda of The Barnacle, the place his father, the Commodore, had built and where he had been born. Looking out over the familiar waters of Biscayne Bay, where he had learned to sail and later tested his skill as a yacht designer, he was getting ready to die. His wife, Mary, dealt with the hippies who regularly strayed over from Peacock Park.

251

"Go back to the park," she would call out through the late Commodore's megaphone. Once it had summoned the boy Wirth and his sister Patty in for meals.

It was the end of an era.

A decade later the old family place was sold to the State of Florida for a museum and, in the accelerated pace of today's Miami, it remains a refuge for eyes and spirit and a reminder of the early days before the railroad chugged in to connect Miami with the outside world and started it on the road to all its tomorrows.

The man who set the stage for the first dramatic change in Coconut Grove was George Stanley Engle, a Kentuckian who made his first million in oil before he cast his first vote.

Engle had set out on horseback searching for oil leases when he was seventeen after inquiring of a fellow who drove up to the Engle general store in Berea, Kentucky, in a Stutz Bearcat where he had gotten the money to buy the car.

The fellow told him he was in the oil business and that was all the young Engle needed to know.

Engle discovered the Grove one afternoon when he and his Texas-born wife, Dorothy, were invited to a bayfront estate for tea. He had been visiting Miami since the days of the old Royal Palm Hotel, but the Grove had escaped him until the 1950s.

That day he asked his hostess point-blank if she would consider selling him her house. Unblinking, she said yes, she would, and they signed an agreement the next day. (This house today is the Coral Reef Yacht Club, next door to the old Biscayne Bay Yacht Club.)

By his own admission, George Engle "fell in love with Coconut Grove because it was no Coney Island." Then, like many a lover before him, he immediately set about changing the face of the beloved.

He moved swiftly with the construction of the Engle Building. Some people growled at giving up what had become bank parking space; others growled about the architecture of the building.

The building completed, Engle stocked a fancy drugstore and staged a grand opening with free ice cream. He was proving himself to be a blend of the homespun and sophisticated. His early background in his father's general store was beginning to show.

The drugstore carried jewelry, top-line beauty products and flashy, high-priced gifts such as a brass tea cart in which rhinestones glittered.

Upstairs, Engle had a suite of offices to conduct his oil business. One of his investors was Marlon Brando.

On trips to New York he managed to find time to "personally select" items to sell in his Florida Pharmacy. It all fit neatly together.

One day in the spring of 1955, he excused himself from lunch at his drugstore. Back in ten minutes, he said he had just purchased the shuttered movie house, a landmark which had been under construction when the hurricane of 1926 hit and had weathered many a Saturday motion picture matinee for Grove children as well as occasional stage productions.

He explained that his plan was "to bring Broadway to Coconut Grove." He did just that.

On January 6, 1956, he unveiled a jewel of a theater that he called the Coconut Grove Playhouse. It contained lavish living quarters for stars, a private barber shop, and, oh, yes, gold plumbing fixtures in some bathrooms. In certain cases, toilet seats were sprinkled with rhinestones. First-rate dining rooms and bar did not detract from the scene.

Broadway came.

The Playhouse was considered an intrusion by some and one bayfront estate dweller declared grandly, "I shall simply plant it out." Another hoped the "place would burn down."

But who could plant out theater figures like Judith Anderson and Tallulah Bankhead, Bea Lillie, Katherine Cornell and Tennessee Williams who came to the Coconut Grove Playhouse at Engle's bidding?

Who would be mean enough to want to burn down a theater that gradually began to affect the economy of the Grove? Understandably, the merchants were the first to recognize that.

Besides, sprinkled around the Grove were seasoned theatergoers who were happy to spend an afternoon or evening at the Playhouse. It made a pleasant change from their own company, albeit that was of an excellent caliber.

Many were highly literate, privileged individuals with an appreciation for nature and the simple life and a high regard for privacy. Painters, writers, educators were among them.

Scarcely an afternoon passed without informal groups congregating for cocktails, invariably a choice of martinis or Manhattans. To this day, the writer-environmentalist Marjory Stoneman Douglas, whose one-hundredth birthday anniversary was celebrated nationwide on April 7, 1990, prefers Manhattans to all other drinks.

The men met for the Houghton Fortnightly and weighty discussions, but the women were no slouches and at no loss for invigorating conversation of their own.

Several had marched as suffragettes, among them Florence Forbes Foster, whose husband, Nathaniel, sweetened the hours spent as a New Jersey patent lawyer by writing one-act plays that were published by Samuel French for little theater groups. Nat said that what he earned from this avocation paid for the family theater tickets. Needless to say, the Fosters were among the first marching to the Playhouse box office.

Soft-spoken Jannetta Sturtivant Reed, who sprang from the early Dutch who settled Manhattan Island, also had marched to get women the vote. Her husband, W. Maxwell Reed, wrote a string of books explaining science to children. He taught astronomy at both Harvard and Princeton before taking up writing and his "Stars for Sam" was one of the most popular in his "Sam" series. He knew his stars, but his spelling was atrocious so Jannetta took care of that end.

These people were following the pattern set forth at the turn of the twentieth century when Dr. John C. Gifford, the forestry expert, led a parade of academics down from Cornell University.

Among them was Charles DeGarmo, who held down the chair of pedogogy at Cornell after retiring as the president of Swarthmore College. His wife came first and purchased seventy acres in the Grove. Their son, Walter C. DeGarmo, became the architect of many of Miami's early buildings, and his son, Kenneth DeGarmo, an artist, is the third generation to live on a portion of the family land where he and his wife raised a family. For a time as a child, he lived in the beautiful home his father built for the family and which was lost in the "Bust." It is now in the process of being sold for more than a million dollars. The remaining four acres surrounding it are slated to be broken up into nine luxury residences. The developer is busy trying to remove the old trees and replace them with trees of "less canopy." Grove preservationists are fighting it.

In the 1950s, Dr. Delton Howard, following his retirement as head of Northwestern University's philosophy department, came to the Grove with his wife, Gertrude. She was the niece of former Governor Cox of Ohio, who had purchased The Miami *News* from Bobo Dean back in the 1920s. They fit right into the Grove scene, with Dr. Howard receiving once again his youthful nickname of Pegasus and entering into the spirited talk that made up the tenor of those days.

Life was not entirely conversation. There was music at the home of Dr. Franz Stewart and his wife, Ruth, who had trained at Julliard for a career as a concert pianist before her marriage. She continued her interest in music by arranging programs for her friends. Juan Bedetti, the Boston Symphony cellist, played frequently. For the general public, there was Civic Music, so popular as a series you had to wait for somebody to die to become a patron, and the University of Miami Symphony. The Lowe Gallery, with Virgil Barker as its first director, was started. His highly regarded basic textbook for students was called *American Painting: History and Interpretation*.

Coconut Grove and environs were not exactly a cultural desert, so there were plenty of people who could appreciate or, at least, comprehend George Engle's first offering, Samuel Beckett's intellectual treatise, *Waiting for Godot*.

A fashionable crowd from all over came to view the opening play and was flabbergasted. Due to inept advance billing, they came expecting a comedy. What they viewed was Bert Lahr and Tom Ewell talking interminably in a non-play that the British critic Kenneth Tynan declared had "no plot, no climax, no denouement, no beginning, no end," despite its effect of "pricking the nervous system."

Never mind. There were floodlights and national press coverage and enough celebrities like Joan Fontaine and Joseph Cotton to satisfy the people lined up outside to gawk. It was clearly the biggest event in Coconut Grove history.

Inside, the curtain was delayed for one full hour while diners were fed delicacies like pheasant under glass. Some never got their main courses, let

255

alone their dessert and coffee, but it was a night to remember on all counts. Many stayed late at the bar.

The man who had spent a million dollars "bringing Broadway to Coconut Grove" said mildly in the midst of fiery complaints, "Seems to me this has put Coconut Grove on the map."

In that first season Engle lured an extraordinary band of stage and film actors to the Grove, including Tallulah Bankhead, Billie Burke, Dolores Del Rio, Chico Marx, Edward Everett Horton, Cathleen Nesbitt and Maureen Stapleton. None was quite the hit that Victor Borge was. He was approaching three years of sell-out performances on Broadway, hamming up his piano act at the Schubert Theatre.

Engle cornered him and persuaded him to take a two-week break from Broadway and bring his act to Coconut Grove. The offer? The royalties from two oil wells and other valuable considerations. It proved the most profitable engagement of that or any other season for both men.

It was inevitable that after four years the oilman would tire of the responsibilities and headaches involved in producing theatre.

Some said Engle created the Playhouse in order to entertain people like Marlon Brando for dinner and produce a center for his own enjoyment.

Whatever the reason, it brought former President Harry S Truman and First Lady Bess, in one of her infrequent public appearances, to applaud daughter Margaret in *The Happy Time*.

George Engle changed the face of Coconut Grove single-handedly. The only official thank-you he ever received was the Grove Chamber of Commerce Golden Coconut Award and that was belatedly in 1965.

By that time he had turned his thoughts to the idea of building a monorail to transport Miamians from downtown to their homes. He died in 1977 in Fort Lauderdale, leaving that for others to bring about. He was one of Miami's outstanding dreamers, a creative man with ideas a little before their time.

Other qualified producers tried their hands at operating the Playhouse, but it never again achieved the stature of the Engle years. Today it is state-owned with a board of theater devotees.

Alfred Browning Parker, the architect who officiated at the resurrection of the old movie house made a comment as plans were underway to turn the Playhouse into a state-owned operation.

"They are going to have to clean the old girl up. People have used her without consideration."

He remembered the glory days when Engle doodled stars on a piece of paper to indicate the pattern he desired for the lobby carpeting. "He never stinted, not once," Parker said.

From the elegance of the Playhouse when it first bowed to the public, to the street theater of crowded sidewalk cafes in the 1990s, to the theater of the absurd that eventually sprang up at city hall, Coconut Grove became immersed in theatricality.

In the 1950s the City of Miami moved the city hall from the downtown courthouse to Coconut Grove. The Miami *Herald* called the vacated Pan American terminal building at Dinner Key an "inspired setting for the city hall of a city that is symbolic of the outdoors, of sunshine and climatic salubrity." It would also save the rent to the Dade County Courthouse which was beginning to run out of space and was pleased to lose the city as a tenant.

Miami paid the sum of one million and fifty thousand dollars for the home of the flying boats. Many Miamians considered it too far removed from downtown for a city hall.

City hall brought government to the settlement that had considered itself apart ever since losing its village government as the boom dawned.

It was Raymond M. Curtis, a highly civilized longtime winter resident of Coconut Grove (the M stemmed from Samuel Morse, from whom Raymond was descended) who pointed out that "we are losing our neighborhood."

The Grove was becoming calculatedly charming. Bert's Grocerteria became a real-estate office and Bert Albury retired and moved to North Carolina, thereby eliminating one of the favorite village meeting places. More and more, residents of the Grove turned their automobiles toward South Miami to run their errands as tourists and sightseers flooded the old village.

Disappearing were food markets, the hardware store, even the Florida Pharmacy, George Engle's fancy drugstore. In their place appeared boutiques, eating places and sidewalk cafes. High-rise condominiums began to appear where old houses had stood.

Raymond kept an apartment at The Lowell in New York and a summer place, the gatehouse of his late father Gerald's estate, up the Hudson in Garrison.

One of his pleasures was acting as an angel for Broadway plays. After his wife's death he shifted to horseracing and his horse My Dad George made it to the Kentucky Derby.

One day, accompanied by a friend, he came home to the Grove from the races with a great floral piece after his horse won and thugs were waiting for him inside his hedge. The next day, he signed a lease for the first of the bayfront apartments, called Sailboat Bay. When that was turned into the Mutiny, a spot of some questionable reputation during its heyday, he moved into a newer, taller condominium called Yacht Harbour just next door. Raymond always said it was better to live *inside* it because then he didn't have to *look* at it.

Times were changing and now danger lurked at the corner of U.S. 1 and Grand Avenue, as unsuspecting motorists were discovering. Stopped for a red light at that location, it became common fare for passing motorists to become victims of quick-moving thieves who reached in and grabbed purses or even gold chains and jewelry.

It was not generally known but a police lookout was placed atop the Coconut Grove Playhouse to keep an eye out for roving hoodlums with Molotov cocktails. Even along the shopping streets, merchants took to locking their doors during business hours and admitting customers only after inspection.

The threats came from all directions. Most alarming of all for many were the inroads being made by developers.

The day came when the developers of Mayfair in the Grove, a shopping mall entering the second phase of its development, went before the Miami City Commission to request half of one block of Rice Street in order to create "a pedestrian mall."

Kenneth Treister, a Coconut Grove architect-turned-developer, declared this move would "unite the Grove."

But David Tackett, then president of the Coconut Grove Merchants Association, retorted, "They are not trying to unite Coconut Grove. They are trying to build a fortress through which very little business will trickle into the rest of the Grove."

Marjory Stoneman Douglas pointed out: "We talk a lot of pretty pictures and we give away our shirts. Pedestrian malls in other cities are owned by the cities, not private developers. It does not all depend on giving up Rice Street."

Second generation Coconut Grove veterinarian Michael E. Marmesh was saying, "The Commissioners are asking us to go along with an increase in our taxes while giving away our property . . . I find it unconscionable that valuable publicly owned land is being given away . . . "

A city planner said, "Mall or no mall, Coconut Grove is going to have to keep pace."

The Grove lost Rice Street and gained a billionaire in developer Edward J. De Bartolo, who was in on the expansion of Mayfair with Treister and Joseph A. Garfield.

Based in Youngstown, Ohio, De Bartolo was the "largest developer of retail space" in the U.S.A. and said of Florida, "I love that state."

He could point to ten operating malls in Florida, five under construction and three on the drawing boards.

When he wasn't building malls, he was busy with associates and family in other properties which included the San Francisco 49ers, the Pittsburgh Penguins and horseracing.

Sharp operators had their eyes on Coconut Grove and as events unfolded, it began to seem that having city hall on one's doorstep was not that great a favor.

The arrival of a man named Monty Trainer on the scene had proved the opening wedge in the handing over of public lands to private interests. A former manager of the University Inn in Gainesville, Florida, he persuaded the city fathers to give him a long-term lease on a small restaurant named Jason's just north of city hall and proceeded to become one of the big wheeler-dealers in Miami. The restaurant included a marina which the city got from Billy Paul Kelly under threat of condemnation, claiming it for "public park purposes."

Without need for the usual permits, Trainer expanded the valuable waterfront site for the restaurant, which he re-named for himself. It became a hangout for politicians and police officers. Meals on the house were common and as time went on it also became the site of highly popular political forums on every level of government.

The affable restaurateur gave generously to causes and landed on important city boards. Needless to say he was a large contributor to political campaigns and quickly gained a reputation.

When he was indicted by a federal grand jury for tax evasion, there were those requesting that his case be postponed so he could travel to Europe on an important economic mission for the city.

Others protested after his indictment that he should not be required to give up some of these important civic posts.

In addition to his problems with the Internal Revenue Service, Monty Trainer, it turned out, had also been cheating the City of Miami out of its rent.

This was largely forgiven by his followers, who gave him a going away party attended by some of the commissioners, at which time he was presented with a state-of-the-art tennis racquet to help him while away the hours in prison. As it turned out, he was free in four and a half months.

One of Trainer's accomplishments had been to secure a long-term lease and when it came up for renewal there were protests from citizens and boatmen who saw his enlarging of the place as usurping public land. It was put to a vote and Trainer won, promising to make improvements on a large scale. Later, it was discovered his victory had been accomplished with a large turnout of black voters in the Grove. Trainer had promised to build a restaurant on a corner of Grand and Douglas where crime had been particularly acute and where black leaders were making valiant efforts to clean up the situation.

What Trainer did, instead, was sell his waterfront lease to a developer named Manny Medina, who immediately began the process of enlarging the operation. Today, Medina is the Grove's largest developer.

It has been a long time since local wags joked about Coconut *Grave* because not much happened there. Today, Coconut Grove is the "in" place for all Miami. The Coconut Grove Arts Festival, dreamed up by press agent Charlie Cinnamon to tout a showing of *Irma La Douce* at the Coconut Grove Playhouse during Zev Bufman's reign, draws more than a million people each February. Any Saturday night, the Grove jumps with movement and vitality as people wander the streets, sit at sidewalk cafes, engage in the sport of watching the world pass by.

Standing looking out through the slanting glass windows of

Stringfellow's, the newest "in" spot in Mayfair, as the sun is starting to go down, one can only be struck by how much it has all changed.

A gigantic hole next door is preparing to usher in still another shopping arcade where once the Variety Shop and the *patisserie* were village fixtures. When Free France fell in World War II, Groveites mourned with the baker, who drew the shades and sat in his flat up over the shop, giving vent to his sorrow. People went without their fresh bread and croissants until he was ready to open up again.

In 1990, another Frenchman, Marc Pietri, supervises this new entertainment center, CocoWalk, being built with foreign money. It boasts a large plaza surrounded by terraces, restaurants and, on upper floors, a motion-picture theater with as many as eight screens. It is costing forty-eight million dollars to construct.

Down the street and around the corner, the Grand Bay Hotel combines elegance and a five-star restaurant, along with Regine's, a penthouse inner sanctum for the jetsetters and celebrities who choose it for their stays. The quiet refinement with tea served in the lobby and dining with impeccable service pleases everyone.

Further north sits Grove Isle off the mainland where security is tight and works of art abound.

Everywhere in the Grove traffic is heavy and the easy times are gone.

School children from the century-old public elementary school were surprised one morning when their teacher marched them to Peacock Park to play. They were turned away for "lack of a permit." So many festivals are staged there that the parks department had to call a halt.

A street vendor slicing hot dogs outside the park declared himself a refugee from New York City, then added, "This place is getting to be a little New York."

Just down the street from Stringfellow's is the little Coconut Grove library, older than the city of Miami. Books had their beginning here with The Pine Needles Club. Canvas sacks of books were sailed up Biscayne Bay for the few readers at the mouth of the Miami River.

In a way it was because of that little library that so many had gathered that autumn night. Stringfellow's was jumping with a gathering to celebrate the upcoming 1989 Miami Book Fair International, the brain child of the

Miami-Dade Public Library and the Downtown Business Men's Association, now grown to the largest in the nation and spilling into the streets surrounding the Miami-Dade Community College, which plays the prime role in its execution.

At Stringfellow's, everybody has come to toast its success: booksellers and book lovers, community leaders like Monsignor Walsh and Judge George Orr, whose father, Alexander, helped build Miami and whose brother, Jack, played the role of state legislator on the side of desegregation, when he didn't have too much company. Later, he would be mayor of Metro-Dade County.

The First Lady, Barbara Bush, was due to talk at a downtown dinner preceding the Book Fair, her cause being to stamp out illiteracy. Doubtless, she and the Kirk Munroes would have had much in common.

Peter Stringfellow, a Londoner with night spots there and in New York, had embraced Coconut Grove at first sight. "I was looking for a sunshine city, not another tough city," he said. He chose the Grove over Marbella, Spain, and Los Angeles. People would always keep coming, keep changing things.

As the sun set, the burst of color outside drew attention away from the hubbub. Past and present merged.

Nowhere are there such skies as South Florida shows. Color that changes from pewter to violet, runs from lemon to coral, apricot to bronze— skies the color of magazine-cover baby's eyes one minute, shading, changing so that sunset is a piling up of mountains of color that give the lie to the fact that the land is flat. Those skies daily create hills and mountains.

The sky alone is changeless.

The Mix and the Mixups

Y OU HEARD THEIR PROTESTS FIRST in your own kitchen. The protests began "Them Cubans . . . " What they were saying was "they work longer hours for less money and are taking our jobs away from us. They are moving in on all the service jobs and we are losing out. The United States is giving them allowances and food stamps and low cost housing, but what about *us*?"

Dr. Jean Jones Perdue, whose longtime Miami Beach medical practice was followed by work among the elderly that won her national honors, remembers paying a first visit to the Claude Pepper Towers.

"It was built for the black elderly, who were displaced when Highway I-95 cut through their community, removing homes and displacing large numbers of permanent residents," she said.

A Virginian, she is the daughter and sister of physicians and came with her doctor-husband, the late J. Randolph Perdue, also a Virginian, to Miami Beach in the mid-1930s.

Dr. Jean's links with blacks goes back generations and she was appalled at what she found on that visit when she arrived to give the Invocation at a Thanksgiving celebration.

"The place was filled with Cubans," she recalls. "They had to provide a translator for the director, who spoke only Spanish, so that we could communicate. There were less than a dozen blacks in the whole place."

It wasn't until the mid-eighties that Dr. Jean, now in her late eighties and still occupied with various committees working for the care of the aging, found out why and how this had happened.

"When the Cubans came in and signed up for their allowances and

263

food stamps, they were immediately put on the list for low-income housing," she said. "People who had lived and worked for generations in Miami were not educated as to how to gain such access."

Uneducated blacks found themselves up against a new work force motivated by a burning desire to become self supporting, willing to take on any and all jobs available.

Former bankers and lawyers jumped at the chance to drive taxicabs and run elevators while their wives took their household skills into Miami homes and the clothing industry as seamstresses.

This all came at a time when blacks were finally making progress and proved doubly dashing to many in Miami. In the sixties, blacks had been coming into their own, assuming roles in the building trades and along the waterfront, behind the wheels of buses and in tourist positions. They had long ago cornered the market on servant-type jobs.

The sweeping Civil Rights Act of July, 1964, preceded by the new President Lyndon B. Johnson's call for a War on Poverty two months earlier, even before the Voting Rights Act of 1965, were victories. The Great Society, envisioned by President Johnson, poured millions into social and job programs.

Florida was blessed with two-term governor LeRoy Collins who took a steadfast stand against segregation. Even before the 1954 *Brown vs. The Board of Education* decision outlawing segregation in the nation's public schools, he was outspoken in his beliefs. But it was not until 1959 that two schools were integrated in Miami, and back in 1952 Dade County Auditorium was integrated only because Marian Anderson put her foot down about singing before a segregated audience, however admiring of her talents.

Three governors after Collins did little to assist in the matter of desegregation. It was not until Reubin O'D. Askew began the first of two four-year terms in January 1971 that any real action was taken in Florida. He established an affirmative action plan by executive order and brought blacks into the mainstream of government.

One of them was Miami's Athalie Range, the first black and second woman (Coconut Grove lawyer Alice Wainwright was the first) to become a city commissioner. Governor Askew appointed Mrs. Range secretary of the department of community affairs. There were others as well.

It wasn't all beer and skittles despite the gains for blacks. Ironically, one of the proposed tools for their improvement, urban renewal, created worse problems.

The construction of I-95 was the biggest contributor when longtime residents of Overtown were forced to sell their homes to make way for the new highway. The construction of apartments offered improved, modern facilities, but took away individual preferences and ultimately were left to deteriorate.

An elderly black woman later described what happened this way, "We lost Heaven."

Liberty City, born with high hopes, bore the brunt of displaced people seeking other living quarters. Blacks continued to move in and the boundaries of the area spread out.

The War in Vietnam killed the War on Poverty and disillusionment was strong. The assassinations of Martin Luther King and Robert Kennedy increased the disillusionment. Miamians watched as Los Angeles and Cleveland went up in flames. Protests and violence grew, as did the demand for drugs. Florida, with its inviting coastline, was becoming a main port of entry for the dope trade.

The right to demonstrate was high on the agenda for blacks, and in Miami, they chose a dramatic time to exercise it—just as Richard M. Nixon was giving his acceptance speech at the August 1968 Republican National Convention being held across the Bay at Miami Beach.

The National Guard was called to assist police in quelling what was first called a riot and later reduced to the term "civil disturbance."

It was Miami's first riot, but it would not be the last.

The disturbance of 1968 did not turn Nixon away from Miami. In the 1970s he purchased a home on Key Biscayne, close by his friend, Charles (Bebe) Rebozo, thereby bringing the winter White House to Biscayne Bay and providing a stream of headlines with Miami datelines.

This was hailed with joy by tourism officials. There was joy on other fronts as well.

Miami seemed to spring alive and find one voice in cheering the Dolphins and "the perfect season of '72." The football team won 17 straight games and went on to a Super Bowl victory.

The Los Angeles *Herald Examiner* called it THE BEST TEAM EVER the day after Super Bowl VII in which the Dolphins beat the Redskins. *Time* magazine put Dolphin Coach Don Shula on its cover. Miami named an expressway after him.

The Dolphins won two Super Bowls while Miami fans shouted "How sweet it is."

Jackie Gleason, who originated the phrase, had uttered the same message from Miami Beach, calling it "the fun and sun capital of the world" for the edification of beaming officials and for the envy of millions of TV viewers who wished they were there. As an unknown vaudevillian, Gleason had appeared at the downtown Olympia. When he died, his eclectic book collection would end up at the University of Miami.

Bringing Gleason to Miami Beach had been a coup for Hank Meyer, the night school student at the College of the City of New York, who came to Miami Beach seeking relief from hay fever in the late thirties. He found a five-dollar-a-week room at the Madrid Hotel and the second day after his arrival took a trolley and two buses to the University of Miami where he persuaded the late Franklin Harris to give him a scholarship in exchange for helping with public relations. Hank Meyer ended up with a Miami Beach street named after him.

In the 1950s, he negotiated with Arthur Godfrey to bring his ukulele to Miami Beach, actually Bal Harbour. Godfrey had such a wide audience that his radio and TV shows were considered number one in the field. The Miami Beach City Council changed the name of 41st Street to Arthur Godfrey Road out of gratitude. If by now you are gathering that Miami dotes on naming streets after living people, you are entirely correct.

The Decade of Progress bond issue went before the voters and passed. This meant giant steps for Dade County in the way of improvements in rapid transit, modern sewers, lights for streets and a new main library to take care of the expanding population.

Finally, Dade County and the City of Miami had gotten their acts together in the matter of libraries and, after decades of fighting for it, supporters took to the streets to drum up votes.

Libraries were voted in, just under the new Metrozoo, which was destined to become one of the most spectacular operations in the whole country, and today, Dade County has twenty-nine libraries in its system.

But despite these successes not everybody was happy.

President Nixon installed a helicopter pad and his immediate neighbors expressed annoyance at the noise created by aircraft landing with diplomatic pouches. They did not relish the increased traffic either.

Then, along the oceanfront, Key Biscayne residents of one twenty-seven-story condominium requested that the Weather Bureau's transmitter and antenna on top of their building be removed.

They claimed it was a threat to safety, emitted radiation and was unsightly besides. The United States Weather Bureau explained it was a necessary part of the hurricane warning system but, after failing to convince the high-rise residents of its importance, began to search for another spot for its signal system.

The high-rise dwellers with a view of the Atlantic admitted that they were also of the opinion that the apparatus interfered with their TV reception.

Miami had faced serious problems and come through. It seemed in 1973 when the Freedom Flights ended that it was now possible to look back at the integration of schools and the matter of providing education for all the Spanish-speaking children at the same moment with some pride. It was a period to savor. In the flush of victory the county commission declared the community bilingual and bicultural.

Nevertheless, life in Miami had been a roller coaster for some time now. Whenever the car was at the peak, the downside was just ahead. One was approaching and no one knew how long a slide it would be.

The financial markets provided the first lurch. Construction stopped as unemployment rose to more than twelve per cent. In Miami when the newest skyscraper, One Biscayne Tower, went bust, the visible skeleton against the blue sky brought back unpleasant memories of the 1930s Depression.

In the bare, unfinished building one early morning, Alvah H. Chapman, Jr., guiding force at the *Herald* and its parent, Knight-Ridder, called a meeting. He gathered more than two dozen leaders in business, government and the academic worlds and placed the situation before each of them. What could be done to revive the downtown which had suffered another blow?

Chapman had been behind such efforts to rally the business community before. Once he had spent months studying how the Greater

Miami Chamber of Commerce could be revivified. An incoming president, Lawrence Sheffey, had suggested it was either that or the group should be given "a decent burial." In 1971, an inner circle had met without fanfare and formed "The Non Group." It included leaders of all stripes.

Now, meeting in the unfinished building, Miami's business elite established a game plan as well as a new committee called the Downtown Action Committee to start things moving. It would operate under the Greater Miami Chamber of Commerce banner.

They all visualized an international center for business and wanted a striking name for the downtown they intended pushing. In competition, Hank Meyer produced it. It would be called *The New World Center.*

For all his efforts Alvah Chapman would one day have a street named for him. But that was in the future. Disappointments still lay ahead.

Bicentennial Park downtown had been exquisitely planned by Edward Durell Stone, Jr. Opened in 1977, it carried a built-in problem: people were afraid to use it.

A young man, arriving by bus, had walked into the park and been murdered before he could see the sights of the Magic City. The men running the food operation had been mugged and robbed the first night the park opened. Across the boulevard, a motel manager had been murdered. The park had become a haven for street people.

It was a time of concern for the whole country. Inflation was in the double digits. America's longtime friend in Iran, the Shah, had been forced out by the Ayatollah and in November, 1979, five hundred of his rabid supporters stormed the U.S. Embassy in Tehran and took sixty-three people hostage. The United States seemed powerless.

Jimmy Carter, the hapless man who had led the country through these years, would soon be uprooted by the next president, Ronald Reagan.

In Miami, the mood was about to turn ugly. On the night of December 17, 1979, four uniformed Miami police officers stopped a black insurance man, Arthur McDuffie, a former Marine, and beat him to death. McDuffie had no criminal record, carried no weapon and was savagely attacked and his borrowed motorcycle demolished. It was said he gave "the finger" to the police as he flew by.

Two months later, the whole community suffered a cruel blow when

Johnny Jones, the head of the huge school system, an admired figure and accepted as a symbol of black progress, fell from grace. He had held the mistaken belief that he could purchase more than eight thousand dollars worth of gold-plated plumbing fixtures for a vacation home with school board money. The county prosecutor charged him with grand theft. He was being called "a fallen angel."

This story when it broke was said by some blacks to be nothing more than a racially inspired attack. Blacks, who had been instrumental in the founding of Miami but whose names were then deleted from the voting rolls, were angry.

The city was a tinderbox. Fidel Castro would light the match.

In the spring of 1980 Castro and the Peruvian government became engaged in a dispute involving a group of Cubans who had sought asylum in Peru's embassy in Havana. Castro wanted them put out on the street. The Peruvians insisted they be flown to Lima.

In an unexpected move, Castro withdrew the guards and as many as ten thousand Cubans poured through the embassy gates.

Meanwhile, the Carter administration had made a fatal judgment call in the matter of airplane hijackings. When Americans hijacked planes to Havana, they were termed criminals by the United States. But when Castro requested that Cubans hijacking boats to the United States be treated as criminals, he was refused. Instead of prosecuting the arriving hijackers, the United States received them as freedom fighters.

Castro made no bones about it. If this practice continued he would see to it that more criminals were sent. He carried out the public threat a month later when he removed the guards from the Peruvian Embassy.

Miami paid the price for the federal government's mishandling of the matter. Castro opened the port of Mariel and announced that anybody desiring to leave Cuba could do so.

In Miami, the news was received with unrestrained joy by the exile community. Every boat of any size and shape was mustered by warm-hearted Cubans bent on picking up relatives and friends. They had not counted on being forced to return with thousands of the criminally insane from Cuba's prisons and hospitals. Castro was shipping them off for Miami to worry about.

None would be more out of pocket and inconvenienced than those in the charter boat business. Jackie Ott, the boy wonder of his father Alexander's water show in the early days of the Miami Biltmore Hotel, was such a one. The operator of Ott's Yachts, he was fined four thousand dollars and paid out an equal sum to the lawyer needed to extricate him from the clutches of the government.

"Everybody was gung ho and President Carter declared we would 'welcome them with open arms,'" Ott remembers, so he "assumed it would be okay to accept charters." Nevertheless, he took the precaution of getting clearance from both the Coast Guard and U.S. Customs.

The day after his vessels left Miami, the government lowered the boom and declared the warm welcoming of exiles ended. Getting back the vessels would take time and money.

The Castro maneuver sent streaming into Miami as many as one hundred twenty-five thousand Cubans. They landed at Key West and made straight for the Magic City where they were crowded into a hastily concocted Tent City, which hard-pressed Mayor Maurice Ferre ordered put into place under I-95.

Driving to work, Miamians were appalled at the sight of portable toilets and swarms of new residents to be looked after.

Actually some of those who came didn't find things to their liking that much. There were hijackings back to Cuba and that too proved fodder for the Castro preachments.

It was figured that about one hundred thousand of the exiles were decent citizens and, indeed, they have proved to be; the other twenty-five thousand hit Miami in a crime wave unsurpassed. Crimes around Tent City rose as much as four hundred per cent, it was figured. Everything from murder and rape to burglaries and street holdups became everyday occurrences.

The Council for Inter-American Security cautioned against permitting any "gap to develop between Cubans of the 1960s and those of the 1980s since this could have a disastrous effect on all concerned." It pointed out, somewhat unnecessarily, that "indeed, the Mariel exodus constitutes a challenge for the Cuban exile community, the people of South Florida and the federal government."

Cubans were welcomed by the United States government without question as to their credentials. When Haitians took to their often unseaworthy boats in an escape to freedom, they were either turned away out at sea or placed in the Krome Detention Center south of Miami. A cry of racial bias went up.

Governor Bob Graham, whose father, Ernest, had been a state senator from Dade County, was getting ready to sue the federal government to remove the Haitian refugees from the Krome Avenue encampment and come up with a sensible plan. The response was a plan to move some to Puerto Rico, talk of "interdiction," which meant intercepting them before they could land here, and sending them back home, even proposing Glasgow, Montana, as a spot to resettle them while the process of deciding their eligibility for citizenship went on.

It was a mess. Haitians arrived daily. As many as thirty-five thousand spread out over forty or so blocks in the northwest section. The Immigration and Naturalization Service had lost control of the situation. The U.S.A. had lost control of its borders.

The question was being asked, "Must Miami be penalized for having a convenient coastline for this stream of illegal aliens?"

Monsignor Walsh, now the leading expert on Cuban and Haitian refugees, was saying, "Once a person is here and allowed to remain, he should receive equal treatment of eligibility of services. It makes no sense to have different sets of eligibility for Soviet Jews and Indo-Chinese and Haitians and Cubans on the other hand."

A lot of caring people were asking how the Coast Guard could arrange to turn back refugees in boats too unseaworthy to make the return trip, having made it to the golden shores of old Miami by the seat of their pants, so to speak. The Coast Guard had no instructions from the Secretary of State or any other official.

"Because we are black they do not want to accept us," the Haitians were saying. Meanwhile, dengue fever was discovered among some of the recent arrivals.

On the practical side: What to do with the creaky boats after the Haitians dumped them? A spokesman for Public Health, Walter Livingston, said, "Nobody wants to take the responsibility." Sometimes, after rescuing the pitiful crews, the Coast Guard burned the boats at sea. Sometimes the Florida

Marine Patrol handled them and, once in a while, the Dade County Parks and Recreation Department took on the job. One observer called the boats "floating septic tanks." One twenty-four-foot wooden tub came in under sail with one hundred and ninety-nine people aboard and was still over at Bear Cut Beach a week later while residents of Key Biscayne complained vigorously.

"If we put a towline on a boat because it is overloaded and it needs assistance, we are responsible," said a Solomon-wise Coast Guardsman. "If the boat washes ashore, it is the Florida Marine Patrol's responsibility."

Weather watchers could almost feel the storm coming. When it hit, it was 1926 again. Only this storm was human anger.

The first squall struck in April as the Cubans were in the midst of joyously welcoming their families: Johnny Jones was found guilty by an all white-jury. The big blow came three weeks later when an all-white jury in Tampa acquitted the four Miami police officers in the senseless beating death of Arthur McDuffie.

The riot that followed was bloody. It reached from Overtown and Liberty City even into the black neighborhoods of the Grove. Eighteen people died and more than four hundred were injured. One white motorist was dragged from his car and beaten to death by a crowd. Miami police were on a war footing. Curfews were imposed.

Marvin Dunn of Florida International University and Bruce Porter of Brooklyn College co-authored *The Miami Riot of 1980* and in it pointed out that whereas previous riots had been designated "property riots," the McDuffie riot was a matter of blacks "attacking white people." More riots were to come.

In 1982, the Overtown riot came as the result of another killing of a black man by a police officer.

The Super Bowl '88 disturbance was the most sorrowful for the planners whose preparations had been so extensive that they had even arranged for classes in courtesy for taxi drivers (a long overdue move, Miamians felt).

The circumstances were startlingly like those of 1980. Refugees, this time from Nicaragua, were flooding to Miami in numbers great enough that they were being housed at the city-owned Bobby Maduro baseball stadium putting the dream into action. Black Haitian refugees were being turned back by the thousands, but the Nicaraguans were welcomed, though Miami officials sensibly had sent a representative to Texas immigration centers to beg the Nicaraguans not to come.

Days before Game Day, a Colombian-born police officer, William Lozano, on patrol in Overtown, stepped into the path of a racing motorcycle and opened fire. The shot killed the motorcyclist, Clement Lloyd. His passenger, Allan Blanchard, died in the crash.

The explosion that followed was quite within view of those Super Bowl guests staying at the Omni International Hotel, geographically nearby but light years away in point of reality.

A black football player in the Super Bowl leaned across a balcony to view the flames lighting up the sky and said somberly: "This is no different than anyplace else. It's the same all over."

A year later, Miami leaders were applauding when the Lozano jury returned and found the police officer guilty of negligence for shooting Lloyd— and there was no riot!

Hispanics were claiming that the verdict was an accommodation to avoid a black uprising.

Blacks were showing hurt annoyance that everybody assumed they would riot if the verdict went against them.

Miami still had a long way to go in the field of human relations.

Dreams For Sale

IN THE SUMMER OF 1981, downtown Miami was choked with traffic, parking was impossible and guaranteed to get worse. Dust rose from new skyscrapers being erected—to the tune of one billion, five-hundred-million-dollars, it was gleefully reported. Sometimes the sum named was two billion, one hundred million dollars, depending on who told it.

Fred Grimm, reporting the scene for the *Herald*, likened the street scene to "Londoners in a blitz" and interviewed the foreman of a roofing gang, one Mike Gowdy, who was working over at the new five-hundred-million dollar government complex close by the County Courthouse.

Gowdy admitted he was sweltering. "The buildings cut off the wind and it's one hundred degrees up there—and no air blowing . . . During the day this is just like any other town to me—but at daybreak, when you go up there and see the sun come up, Miami is like a picture postcard."

When the business day began, neck-tied men in business suits ducked in and out of air-cooled offices and restaurants, to the rhythm of machines at work, pounding, shrieking, clanking and, in between, horns honking and cars screeching to sudden halts.

They were tearing down the old Bandshell where once Caesar LaMonaca's free concerts brought out listeners under the Miami moon and stars; where President Franklin Delano Roosevelt escaped death when Mayor Anton Cermak of Chicago took the bullet intended for him, and where President-elect Dwight Eisenhower had come to campaign.

Make way for a rebirth, a renaissance, a new world.

The curtain was going up once again on the city building drama, back

275

where it had all started after Julia Tuttle enticed Henry Flagler into bringing his Florida East Coast Railroad to the mouth of the Miami River. Not since the boom of 1925 had there been such concerted action in this spot.

Giants of industry were applying their touch to planning giant buildings and calling them megastructures, a word that had not yet reached the dictionary. Megalopolis was in the dictionary and meant a "great city." So was megacephalic, defined as "having a large head."

Megastructures were supposed to solve all Miami's problems and make it *The New World Center.*

The Mayor of Metropolitan Dade County, Stephen P. Clark, was saying that what was happening at the mouth of the Miami River "didn't just happen" but had been a combination of "an aggressive business community working in tandem with receptive local government." He was right about the business community being aggressive.

Longtime residents had been avoiding the decaying downtown while their own outlying communities grew. What was happening seemed on the preposterous side. But as plans for the Southeast Bank building and Theodore Gould's Miami Center turned into actual buildings beginning to rise, amusement turned to awe and finally concern.

Property owners were asking questions. Who would pay for all this? Who would live in all these apartments?

As though in answer, the first month the condominiums at Miami Center were offered, fifty million dollars was plunked down from the floor plans alone.

Maurice Ferre, about to campaign for a fifth term as mayor, was busy assuring wary voters that the downtown development would create a tax base to relieve homeowners carrying an increasingly heavy burden for services in an area gone wild with people pouring in.

Demonstrating every bit as much ebullience as his long ago predecessor, Ev Sewell, who dreamed of making Miami "a second Atlantic City," Mayor Ferre envisioned "a world-class city." The son of a Puerto Rican millionaire, he had come to Miami in the 1950s to study at the University of Miami and had married the Venezuelan-born Mercedes Malaussena, whose father's Brickell Avenue estate adjoined that of the Ferres. After his marriage, he went into politics, which he clearly enjoyed.

A master plan for all the bayfront was being urged and it brought the Florida East Coast Railroad back into the picture as in the very beginning. The city filed suit to condemn thirty-two acres owned by the FEC separating the two parks, Bayfront and the newer Bicentennial, toward the north. After prolonged litigation, the courts required the city to pay twenty-three million, three hundred and fifty thousand dollars to the FEC.

It was a victory for native-born lawyer Toby Prince Brigham, representing the railroad.

Behind the scenes it was said that the true motivation behind the condemnation was the desire of the longshoremen of the Port of Miami on Dodge Island to shut down the competition from the profitable, non-union port operated by the FEC.

Plans for the south end of Bayfront Park were being formulated.

Noted sculptor–landscape artist Esamu Noguchi, in partnership with Shogi Sadao, who shared office space with him back in Long Island City, would receive as a fee two hundred and fifty thousand dollars for preparing sketches and economic studies for redoing that section of the park. The plans included a walkway along the bay, an amphitheatre and two sculptural fountains.

The local firm of Pancoast/Albaisa was in on the deal. That meant that architect Lester Pancoast, great-grandson of John Collins, who built the first wooden bridge to Miami Beach with Carl Fisher's help, was continuing the line. He and Sadao had been classmates at Cornell.

Everyone connected with the ambitious plans for the transformation of Bayfront Park would suffer frustrations in carrying them out. Years would pass and Noguchi would die before the city of Miami would complete his plans. Congressman Claude Pepper would also die, and, in a burst of emotion, the city commission would attach his name and that of his late wife, Mildred, to the historic old park. Sad disappointment at changing the familiar name was expressed by many who had invested their lives in Miami, but nobody was listening.

What to do with the statuary and placques grouped about Bayfront

Park was a question. Consider: the busts of Jose Marti, Bernardo O'Higgins, liberator of Chile, and Cecelio del Valle, Honduran politician-writer, among others.

When it came to tampering with The Torch of Friendship, the statue of Simon Bolivar and the Cuban Salute installations, nobody would agree to move any of them.

The Dade County War Memorial, it was suggested, might be appropriately ensconced at the American Legion Park, but the Veteran's Council said thanks, but no thanks.

It had in mind enlarging the monument to include soldiers from every war the United States fought instead of just World War II heroes.

Plans were afoot to blow up the Public Library.

Opened with a sense of pride in July, 1951, it was slated for the scrap heap despite public outcry. County commissioner Beverly Phillips proposed utilizing the edifice as a "Y" exercise center for businessmen, but arts-conscious planners of the New World Center scoffed at such a proposal.

In the works was a billion-dollar Metrorail system financed in part by federal and state funds, stretching from just south of Dadeland Mall north across the Miami River to the Brickell station, thence through downtown Miami to Overtown, then west along Seventy-ninth Street through Hialeah to west of Okeechobee Road. It was rising now all along U.S. 1, and workers were calling it Stonehenge South. Already there were whispers of cost overruns.

In connection with it there would be a downtown People Mover which would run overhead at a maximum speed of twenty-five miles per hour with a capacity of fifty-five passengers. It would link the Government Center with downtown as well as the "Brickell office corridor" to the south and the Omni shopping complex to the north.

When it all came together it would mean that Miamians would ride along Biscayne Boulevard and look down over Bayfront Park and out over the water, one reason for knocking down the library and moving the books to a grand new library.

The new library would share a plaza with the Center for the Fine Arts, voted into being by the county commission, and a museum for the Historical Association of South Florida. It was being called a Cultural Center and every

278

distinguished architect in the nation had been vying to get the job of designing it. Their proposals were heard at a series of public hearings in which a commission-appointed board listened to and questioned the architects.

Miami architects were hungry for the opportunity to be heard and when New Yorker Philip Johnson, who won the Cultural Center assignment, addressed them at the old Main Library there was standing room only. They expected some space-age design and what they got was a Mediterranean enclave raised up from Flagler Street by a picturesque ramp. The nimble-witted Johnson had provided a return to George Merrick's dreams of what a city should be. The younger architects felt cheated.

Mayor Maurice Ferre was saying "this definitely puts Miami on the map" as he watched Theodore Gould's Miami Center I rising at Ball Point. It would contain a two-hundred-million-dollar bayfront hotel-office-condominium complex set on 8.46 acres.

Beth Dunlop of the *Herald* was saying: "When the contractors leave, Ball Point will be virtually shrouded in brown travertine marble."

Over at Miami Beach, city fathers were showing signs of apoplexy over the action at the mouth of the Miami River.

Since the 1950s, the Beach's popularity as a tourist haven had faded and it was ending up as home base for the retired, some of modest pocketbook. Many of them had settled in South Beach and it was there that the Mariel boatlift criminals found and terrorized them. Once these people had called Miami Beach paradise.

Ironically, it was a City of Miami official, Cesar Odio, who steered the Mariels to the Beach by providing a fleet of buses to give the new arrivals being housed in Tent City outings to show off the beauty of the area.

The elderly were at everybody's mercy because there was a mammoth redevelopment program slated for South Beach with a three-hundred-sixty-million-dollar bond sale scheduled to be done in two phases. That was at a standstill for the moment, while neither new buildings nor repairs were on the agenda.

Meanwhile, Miami Beach was looking hard at its redevelopment program and realizing that as things were shaping up it could become a bedroom community, a mix of residents or maintain the tourist quality. "It could turn into the Coral Gables of Dade County," Leonard (Doc) Baker, Executive Vice President of the Miami Beach Chamber of Commerce, was saying.

Once Lincoln Road had been called the Fifth Avenue of the South, but that was no longer true. Fifth Avenue had moved up to Bal Harbour.

Everybody was fighting mad the last week of summertime. One woman, who came before the city commission dealing with its budget, grabbed the microphone and yelled: "I'm tired of being Mrs. Santa Claus."

The commission was yelling at the high-powered Steve Muss, who had poured millions into renovating the Fontainebleu and had been given the job of redeveloping South Beach. It had been five and a half years of planning and meeting and nothing had happened because of high interest rates. Now, the commission was saying fish or cut bait and it was talking about the one-billion-two-hundred-million-dollar redevelopment plan. Commissioner Mel Mendelson, said, "They've loaded everything on the wagon and they have no horse to pull it."

Mendelson was pointing across the bay to Miami: "Look what they're doing, it's unbelievable. That's private enterprise. This isn't, and we're dying."

It seemed like a time for Miami leaders to sit back, take a good breath and look back on some extraordinary achievements.

Just in time for Thanksgiving, 1981, *Time* magazine published another cover story on Miami, asking the question: *Paradise Lost?*

Inside the magazine, page after page of photographs and well researched text offered the complete story of crime, drugs and refugees.

Miami's history was sketched, citizens spoke out against the problems besetting the Magic City and in most cases they proved the severest critics of the scene.

Only a week before, the Miami *Herald* had spread out on page one of its huge Sunday paper the sad facts about Miami with headlines that said: *How the World Sees Us; It's Frightful.* Excerpts from major newspapers told the story of what was coming to be known as "the roaring eighties."

A pertinent point was made by Charles Chai, a University of Miami political science professor, engaged in a study of Miami's power structure, when he said: "It's like looking at a patient who is ill. Everybody has their own ideas of what's wrong with him. Everybody. But nobody's brought out a stethoscope. Nobody's done a blood test."

Mayor Clark said the "image problem had reached a crisis" and called an emergency meeting of all the tourism officials, most of whom were furious at the newspapers for not reporting "good news," and asked for eighteen million dollars to create "an image of a community fighting back."

In the *Time* article a businessman and former county commissioner, dumping the sand from his shoes and preparing to move to North Carolina with the growing colony of displaced Miamians, said, "I've been through two wars and no combat zone is as dangerous as Dade County."

In the end, *Time* did Miami a service.

There wasn't a thing in the story that those reading the local newspapers over the summer of '81 could not have perceived for themselves, but in *Trouble in Paradise*, which is how the magazine headlined its inside nine-page story, it was laid out for the world.

It hit Miami with a tearing impact and it was as though veils were suddenly removed from eyes unwilling to see. The *Time* story was too big and too glaringly accurate to do anything but point up the fact that slogans weren't good enough this time.

The frustrated police, who had been speaking out right along, and the frustrated news media, which had been trying to do the same while being accused of "overplaying" the scene, and the frustrated citizens, who felt confused and leaderless, were now all given roles to play. The rallying cry at last had to be: *We are all in this together.*

It was a time for speaking up and speaking out and a lot of people in both high and low places were engaged in doing just that.

Janet Reno, the first woman state attorney, had been saying patiently for some time, "It's a matter of the police, the schools, the community, the criminal justice system as a whole beginning to work together. There are no certain, sure solutions. The solution with people working together is going to be a far-reaching one."

The metro commission's Tourist Development Council, hastily reassembled, this time asked for a "tourist police force" and a "tourist ombudsman" to help solve acute problems for tourists.

It was a change of tune and a time for cheering until the council also asked for one hundred thousand dollars for a survey to find out what tourists liked and didn't like.

The idea for a survey came back like an old sigh and caused one policeman on the street to ask if it wouldn't be more to the point to increase the pay and number of police officers.

The day before Thanksgiving fifty influential merchants and business leaders met to write their own blue print for eradicating crime. They elected astronaut Frank Borman of Eastern Air Lines and Armando Codina as co-chairmen.

The group re-affirmed Governor Bob Graham's and U.S. Senator Lawton Chiles' call for action from the federal government and the suggestion that President Reagan "come and see for himself" the acute problems.

"Miami's For Me"

WORKING ON ITS IMAGE WAS SECOND NATURE to Miami. Thanks to the instant picture provided by worldwide television, Miami's riots had been fully observed, as had the bodies of murder victims from the dope wars raging as "cocaine cowboys," using sophisticated weapons and organized along paramilitary lines, went about their business of killing.

The streets of Miami were being viewed as unsafe all over the world, not precisely the image Miami had in mind. *The Wall Street Journal* pointed out in the early eighties that "Miami's only organized response to its image problem so far is a proposed advertising campaign with the slogan, 'Miami's For Me.'" It was being aimed at Miamians, the advertising spokesman explained, because, "This place needs a little shot of *esprit de corps.*"

Miamians had always had *esprit de corps.* Remember Dr. James Mary Jackson, for whom Jackson Memorial Hospital was named? His first question when he arrived in Miami two weeks before Flagler brought the railroad to join the wilderness to the rest of the U.S.A. was, "When does the next boat leave?"

A week later, he had changed his tune and wrote his wife, "There is a spirit about this place, the people are young and active and ambitious and hopeful. You feel it is a land of promise."

A new slogan, "Miami. See It Like A Native" won an award, but feminists declared themselves offended by the posters displaying the rear view of a well-proportioned female with snorkeling equipment.

So twenty-three thousand copies of the posters were put through the shredder by order of the metro commission. It was a perfect way to call attention to the posters because it created a scarcity. Telephone calls came all the way from Germany and England from people wanting copies.

Jokers reconstructed another poster, only the well-stacked, young lady this time was packing a pistol and the words read, "Miami. Siege It Like A Native." This one was for home consumption.

Another underground poster read, "Miami. It's A Riot." A metro commissioner received one in the mail and hung it on his wall.

Miami had not lost its love for slogans.

Jacques Decornoy, editor-in-chief of the French newspaper *Le Monde*, wrote what he thought of Miami. He called it "a society at once turbulent and stagnant" and pointed to "the waltz of the monied interests and, on the same spot, the outcasts of fortune."

He added, "The television broadcasts practical information—the telephone number to call in case one discovers an unidentified body."

Newspaper editors came to refer to certain kinds of stories as "only in Miami." There were plenty of those around.

Dade Medical Examiner Dr. Joseph H. Davis had begun renting a refrigerated truck for corpses since the "cooler" in the morgue could hold only thirty.

Mother Teresa of India came to town to feed the hungry and homeless in the name of her Missionaries of Charity and established a hostel for the bagwomen who slept in the parks and under the expressways.

While Archbishop Edward A. McCarthy was preparing to say Mass at St. Francis Xavier Catholic Church before proceeding with the blessing at the nearby mission, the crowds arriving outside were being set upon by thugs. A teacher was thrown to the ground and robbed of her expensive camera; others lost gold necklaces and purses. These practiced street robbers were fast as lightning and, in a few split seconds, had accomplished their mission and were off.

A policeman arriving on the scene asked, "What's going on here? Wouldn't it be something if that woman, who never hurt a flea, got beat up or shot down here?"

Then there were the heart-warming occurrences, just the right antidote to the tides of cash flooding Miami from the drug markets.

A rental car employee found a wallet with twenty-five thousand dollars in it and rushed after a Brazilian banker who was departing for home, in order to return it.

Another employee found an attache case on the counter with fourteen thousand dollars in U.S. and Argentine money and was able to find the owner and return it.

Still another visitor from Argentina, an elderly woman, dropped her money belt containing twenty thousand dollars as she left a Miami Beach bus. A second elderly woman turned it over to the police. Her name was Dora Schiff and when the story was reported she said she got a number of calls telling her what a "damned fool" she was.

It was not what the Chamber of Commerce would have wanted, but Miami developed its own following. When television brought Miami to the screen again, it was no Jackie Gleason, but a cops-and-robbers show, *Miami Vice*, pitting Miami police against an array of homicidal drug traffickers. The show zoomed near the top of the ratings, and Miami's reputation was made. Tourists, especially those from overseas, flocked in.

Miami was "the new Casablanca," exciting, exotic, all sunlight and glitter, and everybody wanted a piece.

"Europeans," said Matt Spetalnick, the Miami bureau chief of the Reuters news agency, "are fascinated by the scene and are not thrown off by the drugs and crime."

Don Wright, who was twice awarded the Pulitzer Prize for his cartoons which originated in the Miami *News* and spread to two hundred newspapers around the world, called Miami a "wacky town," but he uttered the words with affection.

Where else would a bunch of fifth graders rise up to lobby Donald Trump to rescue the dying Miami *News*, Miami's oldest newspaper? They wrote letters pleading with the billionaire to purchase the Cox newspaper which began life as the *Metropolis* and whose life was now entangled with the Miami *Herald* and which died a sad death in December, 1988. The fifth graders at Leisure City Elementary School were accurate in viewing its demise as a community loss.

"If you want sustained stability, don't come to Miami," said Bob Graham, once the governor, now a United States senator and always a Miami native. "But if dealing with change is a challenge, Miami is for you."

Miami, U.S.A.

One remembers his father telling Miamians at the start of World War II,
"I predict a great change in the method of living hereabouts."

Some Of My Best Friends
Are Ethnics

Y OU NEEDED A GLOSSARY to get around the burgeoning international city of Miami.

Tri-ethnic meant that there were three separate worlds, circling away within the New World Center being created by events and with a big shove from the political-economic power base.

Numero Uno were the Hispanics; in second place were White Anglos; and third, where they always seemed to end up, the Blacks.

"Who decided to call us Anglos?" people asked.

The answer usually came back: "The *Herald.*" The morning newspaper in this climate of turmoil seemed to be losing friends on all sides despite its *El Herald* edition for Spanish-speaking readers.

A third generation Miamian, Dr. John C. Nordt, declared he was beginning to feel more "anonymous" than "Anglo" and wondered if an arrangement could be made whereby he would be known instead as an "English-speaking white?" Miami had always been attached to the Caribbean, even in the beginning. Now it was being Cubanized.

Some displaced natives of Miami cracked jokes: "Will the last American leaving Miami please bring the flag?"

It was a bumper sticker and on T-shirts and awfully American, somehow, quite in the tradition of soldier jokes, but it inflamed some Cubans. They were Americans, too, and, to say that just because Miamians had been born in North America that only they could lay claim to being Americans was unseemly, arrogant and misleading.

It had happened, it was enriching Miami both financially and culturally, and all that was needed now was to figure out how to arrange to have a trio of inner worlds touch each other. Perhaps humor would do it?

The problem of course was that different cultures enjoyed different kinds of humor. Cultivating a common bond in humor was proving ticklish.

A woman flying two flags over her high building was on the receiving end of verbal abuse every time she took one or the other down. They were, of course, the American flag and the Cuban, and they were flying on a prominent corner, Twenty-seventh Avenue and *Calle Ocho*.

An ex-Marine was livid. "It's a slap in the face to all Miamians," he said. "Cuba is a communist country."

The owner, an Arab-American of Palestinian extraction, now married to a Jew, said only, "There's not enough flag waving in this country."

Later, President Bush would come along and correct that.

There were times when one yearned to mount a soap box to deliver humorous remarks, but the appropriate moment never quite materialized.

Ralph Renick, one of the first to interview Castro and hold reservations about his intentions, arrived at a solution. He joined a Joke Club.

Humor did seem to be lacking in the entire scene although at one point Manny Diaz, during the early 1980s when he was serving as executive director of the local Spanish-American League Against Discrimination (SALAD), told the *Christian Science Monitor* that "in ten years we would all be chuckling" over such matters as the bilingual referendum. Passed by the metro commission in a moment of good cheer, it declared the county bilingual. The voting public thought otherwise and rescinded it, requiring in a referendum that all county business be conducted in English. The whole issue proved a stumbling block to smooth relations, an unnecessary piece of business raised in good will, but ill-advised.

Jorge Valdes had the right idea when he became the first Latin appointed to the metro commission.

The first thing he did was tell everybody they did not have to say "Horhay," the pronunciation for Jorge. "Just call me George," he said.

The second thing he did was invite Emmy Schafer, who had spearheaded the anti-bilingual ordinance, to sit down over luncheon.

He even sent roses along with the invitation, and the Russian-born head of the Citizens of Dade County United was impressed. "He's not obnoxious or arrogant or loud and he has a nice appearance," she said.

Here are some other terms that called for study in a period of re-education for Miamians.

White Flight meant people leaving in droves. The *Herald* did a poll and discovered that forty-three per cent would like to leave, leave behind the murders and rapes, the repeated burglaries, the change of life styles that prevented evening walks, the bars on the windows, the running into Spanish-speaking salespeople who appeared to make no effort to speak English, the crowds.

Some were forced to leave because they could no longer pay their taxes, which were rising astronomically.

One saw the old names turning up in obituaries, dying away from their old homes. Those who fled were every bit as displaced as those waves of refugees flooding Miami.

The late Richard Merrick, riding down Coral Gables' Miracle Mile on his motorcycle, which he enjoyed as a break from painting and teaching art at the University of Miami, barely avoided a collision with a car full of exuberant young Latins. One rolled down the window of their air-conditioned car to yell, "Yankee go home."

Artist Richard Merrick *was* home. His father, the Reverend Solomon Merrick, had built the very first house in Coral Gables, and his late brother, George Merrick, used the name of the old home for Coral Gables, the city he founded.

Richard, a lovely man, enjoyed the humor of the situation.

"To pretend to have a second national identity is like claiming to be descended from the Bourbons, pure escapism. Nationality is not comparison shopping . . . "

That was how Wilfred Sheed, in a piece called *The Subject of Ethnics*, would have reacted to Miami. Odgen Nash put it this way in his poem *Goody for Our Side and Your Side Too,* which begins "Foreigners are people somewhere else/Natives are people at home" and ends this way: "You may be native in your habitat/But to foreigners you're just a foreigner."

Capital Flight meant all that money flooding Dade County from South and Central America, from South Africa. There was much investment from France, Germany, and Japan. Choose your favorite country.

It certainly made a circular motion and more than anything seemed to be saying that the whole world was in disorder. Might as well sit tight and keep your powder dry.

More than that, watching the exodus from Miami and then watching the influx of newcomers, whether they came in leaky boats from Haiti or on jet airplanes from Rome or Cairo, one was struck with the fact that there is no hiding place.

Black Flight meant that Miami was suffering the loss of some of its native sons and daughters because of lack of professional opportunity and that constituted as great a tragedy as *White Flight* and more, since black leadership was so sorely needed.

Some like Charles F. Johnson, Jr. decided to return.

A Miami native who graduated from Booker T. Washington, he headed for Howard University, and ended up with a fine job in Chicago after serving in a helicopter unit in Vietnam.

At IBM, he became the first black marketing representative in a Chicago branch. He stayed there seven years until he began to get a hankering for home.

In Chicago, he was a recognized somebody, serving on boards. What would it be like to return to Miami? He did it in 1977, packed up and headed for Miami with his wife, Carol, and children, Charles, then 6, and Danielle, 4. He had no job, only this hankering—and an understanding wife. "What was pulling me?" he kept asking himself.

He found out back home. "Here I realized that what was bothering me away from Miami was I felt obligated to return. What appeared a foolish decision was the only one for me."

At the funeral of his grandmother, Annie Coleman, in the summer of '81, he found out something he'd never known. She had started the first library in her community and had talked D. A. Dorsey into giving land for it. "It gave me a wonderful feeling. At her funeral I learned exactly why I came back."

His first job was working as a link with the black community for a savings and loan. This led him into starting his own company called Johnson Associates.

290

Then there is Newall J. Daughtrey, who was appointed executive director of the Community Revitalization Board, to deal with relief programs for the areas torn up by the May 1980 rioting. Daughtrey served as administrative assistant to a state senator before becoming Opa Locka's city manager. He took a year's leave of absence to accept the new job.

He's a former Marine sergeant who spent more than a year in Vietnam and is married to a school teacher, Jean. They have a married daughter, Cherita. Daughtrey spoke up after the riots: "All of us are guilty. We allowed this situation to come about. So now we collectively have to bring about changes."

His forebears have been in Florida "for a hundred years," he says, and he's made his choice. "You can be part of the problem or part of the solution. I choose the latter."

Sociological terms like tri-ethnic act as greater dividers at a time when the realization that all men are brothers—and women sisters if you prefer—is of prime importance.

Let's talk about the first Hispanic woman to be appointed to the Florida Circuit Court, Maria Marinello Korvick. She was fifteen the day she left Cuba and twenty-one the day word came that her father had died before a firing squad, accused of conspiring with the CIA. He received no trial.

That was the day she decided to become a lawyer like her father, whom she describes as "a very idealistic man." She says: "His death made me think of the value of life and the importance of receiving due process."

Judge Korvick at age thirty-five made it from immigrant law student with a small child to Circuit Court judge in eight years.

Miami Hispanics, encouraged to become citizens by the U.S. government, claimed political power in the mayoral runoff election of '81 when fifty-six per cent of the Latins voted, to the thirty-seven per cent of the white non-Latins. Happily, forty-eight per cent of the blacks turned out, which helped re-elect Maurice Ferre for a fifth term as mayor of Miami, giving him ninety-six per cent of the black vote.

At the swearing in, Ferre made a stirring speech. Prayers were in both English and Spanish, but there was only one flag. The Mayor said, ". . . this is not a *patria* . . . I totally reject the notion of a municipal fatherland . . . Cuban power is there, but it does not rule Miami . . . "

291

The Cubans had run away from Castro, but now they were running for office in Miami and teaching long-time Americans about voting power. In the next election, Cuban-born and Harvard-educated Xavier Suarez became mayor of Miami.

In the 1989 scramble to grab the late Claude Pepper's seat in the House of Representatives, Ileana Ros-Lehtinen, who had bowed out of the Florida State Legislature in order to run, beat out Brooklyn-born lawyer Gerald Richman. She spent nine hundred eighty-seven thousand, ninety dollars to accomplish it and it was a bitter campagn, beginning with Republican party chairman Lee Atwater declaring that it was "a Cuban seat."

When Richman declared it was not a Cuban seat, not a Jewish seat, but an "American seat," the fur began to fly with Ros-Lehtinen calling it a slap in the face at her Cuban lineage and refusing to debate. It cost Richman five hundred fifty-one thousand, eight hundred fifty-two dollars to lose, but many thought he did it gracefully.

There was a good laugh among those in the know when the Ros-Lehtinen victory was announced in headlines by the *Herald*, calling her the first woman from the area to make it to the United States Congress. Ruth Bryan Owen of Coconut Grove, daughter of William Jennings Bryan, the Great Commoner, had beat her to it all of half a century earlier.

Streams of refugees have poured into Miami since the Cubans arrived: Nicaraguans, Colombians, Jamaicans, Salvadorans, Guatemalans, Venezuelans, Peruvians, Ethiopians, Cambodians, Lebanese, and Ukrainians to name a few, all with their own uniqueness.

Germans, Japanese, Mexicans, Chinese and citizens of the Arab countries have joined the march to South Florida.

At La Gorce Country Club, French is frequently heard and this is becoming true at Key Biscayne as well. Michael Lewis, publisher of *Miami Today*, a lively downtown weekly newspaper, attended a recent birthday party on the Key where guests sang "Happy Birthday" in five different languages, including Italian.

It would appear that during all the struggles with tri-ethnic problems, Miami had turned multi-ethnic and is on its way to becoming cosmopolitan. One can hope.

When Manny Medina was being unsuccessfully fought by the residents of Coconut Grove in the early phases of his bold moves as a developer, he was quoted in the newspaper as saying, "Let them go to Kendall."

In a letter to the editor, the last recourse when frustration builds too high, one woman wrote that she had lived in Coconut Grove for forty years and understood that Medina lived on Star Island in Biscayne Bay.

Going to Kendall would be no privation, mind you. Twenty years ago, it consisted of fields of strawberries and tomatoes. Today, it is a thriving, politically active community with its own newspaper, *The Kendall Gazette*. Gloria Brown Anderson, a former managing editor of the deceased Miami *News*, reports that it now exceeds the downtown tax base by one hundred million dollars.

"Kendall is where the pot has melted," she says. "Colombians live next door to Puerto Ricans who in turn live next door to Germans and French. There appears to be no ethnic tension. Venezuelans, Nicaraguans, Salvadorans live side by side. On my staff I have a political refugee from Panama, a Nicaraguan biologist who does type setting, a Guyanese bookkeeper. A Jamaican handles advertising."

Community newspapers are popping up all over, so it is not surprising to find a new publication, *The International Asian-American*, taking to the streets to serve the estimated eighty thousand Asians spread over Dade, Broward and Palm Beach counties. The first issue coincided with the start of the 1990 Chinese New Year, sometimes referred to as the Lunar New Year because Korea and Vietnam also observe it. Thais, Filipinos, Burmese will all be served. Speaking in different languages, the newspaper will attempt to "speak in one voice."

Speaking in one voice would be restful and indeed devoutly wished for, but there is no clear evidence that such a state of being is in the cards anytime soon.

Not one voice. The Tower of Babel is more like it.

The world saw the Pope saying Mass in the rain and was moved by the sight and, indeed, it was said that all of Miami carried an afterglow from his presence.

But there were some problems.

Pope John Paul II first met with President Reagan at Vizcaya and, understandably, there were no outcries over that meeting, but early the next

293

morning there were wrinkles to be ironed out at the Center for the Fine Arts where a group of influential Jews selected from around the country were scheduled to meet with His Holiness.

Things hit a snag when some Jews declared themselves unwilling to meet the Pope since he had met with Kurt Waldheim.

Brenda Williamson, on the staff of the center, had been coping with the Secret Service, but now she had a calligrapher to contend with as well. Because of the dignity of the occasion and the enormous hope the instigators had poured into the planning, the calligrapher had been assigned to make individual programs with participants names inscribed. Brenda was up until 5:00 A.M. getting things sorted out.

Meanwhile, the Roman Catholics were having their problems with complaints that the Pope was not giving Cuba enough recognition. Cuban Catholics had a request: that the Pope visit the Shrine of Our Lady of Charity of El Cobre, a statue that had been spirited out of Cuba and now graces a shrine close by Mercy Hospital. Miami Archbishop Edward A. McCarthy resolved the matter by placing the statue in his residence chapel where the Pope would pray during an overnight stay.

Perhaps we had better go back to the dictionary and read that the word *ethnocentrism* describes "the emotional attitude that one's own race, nation or culture is superior to all others."

How about Wendell Willkie's "One World" concept?

Don't look now, but it's closing in on us.

Any doubters have only to turn to Mikhail Gorbachev, the man who rewrote history and opened a new century before its time.

Like an old-fashioned trolley overflowing with passengers and the word Freedom emblazoned as its destination, it came clanging in and things will never be the same.

Governor Bob Martinez, recognizing all this, appointed a twelve-member commission in February 1990 to make a study of how the exile community in Miami would react to Castro's fall from power, should it come.

"The impact will be here, not in Georgia, not in Texas," he wisely pointed out. "If we are not prepared we will have a debacle."

Others were thinking that things might even quiet down for a bit.

State of the Art

VOGUE MAGAZINE ASSIGNED Stephen Birmingham to write about the Miami eighties boom and he called it "the biggest and most exuberant in the history of Florida booms: blue skies, lacy white clouds, pink nights, music from great cruise ships in the bay, Gucci Cadillac Sevilles skimming across airy causeways, and buildings—tall glistening-white buildings rising everywhere."

Birmingham also called South Florida "the capital of capital." That coincided with a New York detective's evaluation when he said there was "more money in Miami banks than in Geneva." He added, "bills of every denomination everyplace, in closets and automobile trunks and money belts. You wouldn't believe it."

Publications from home and abroad were giving reason to be optimistic about Miami's place in the sun.

The distinguished Italian architecture and design magazine *Abitare* pointed out in a lavish issue devoted to the Magic City, with mentions of other South Florida locations, that "Miami is the city where Spanglish is spoken . . . and has a mixed population of 35 per cent Anglo, 19 per cent coloured and 48 per cent Hispanic."

Miami was chosen for the third issue of the magazine's "American trilogy, following second-to-none Chicago and imperial Washington." The introduction described Miami as "the *Americanissimo* product of entrepreneurial individualism . . . Enthralling and incoherent . . . A city that has barely been created, a city yet to be created."

The editors and photographer who came to Miami to fill the magazine

295

with arresting art and story used the words "strong . . . stunning . . . kaleidoscopic in nature." The words brought no hurt to tourist officials.

Tourism was on the mind of both business and government. Merrett Stierheim was primed and ready to go as the new president and CEO of the consolidated Greater Miami Convention and Visitors Bureau. The former county manager, who had performed for nine years through some dark times, then left for a change of pace as head of the Women's International Tennis Association, was back. He had traveled the world and was feeling "very bullish on Miami."

Twenty-seven years of government service lay behind him, beginning as a graduate intern with the City of Miami, fresh from the Wharton School with a master's degree in his hand.

How could he reconcile the 1985 Growth Management Act passed by the state, feeble though it appeared to be, with a drive to bring in new people, particularly when the world was already flocking to Miami's golden shores?

"Tourism is a clean industry," he said eagerly. "The alternative is growth. Tourism is the solution to having people come who need jobs and housing and work. No pollution in tourism."

Government was reassessing itself and, even as he was receiving the outstanding Public Administrator Award of the Year 1989, J. A. (Tony) Ojeda was saying sadly that it was no longer "fashionable" to train for government service and that the big challenge for those who had done so was to find imaginative ways to come up with the funds needed to give the people what they demanded without paying taxes.

Cuban-born Tony, who assisted the new manager, Joaquin Aviño, was under strong attack from proponents of the arts demanding he spend more time and money on them. On the other hand, some other citizens were suggesting that the one and a half per cent tax on public buildings for the purpose of creating art should have been put to the vote of the taxpayers.

President Edward T. Foote invited a group for luncheon to meet the new head of the University of Miami's Department of Art and Art History and his opening remark at the Faculty Club was that "art and public money don't mix comfortably."

Walter Darby Bannard had come from Princeton to join the faculty and his words hit like the cool breeze from the Gulf Stream on a summer morning.

296

Particularly was this so when he described how the work of Horatio Greenough was received in 1830 when the U.S. Congress commissioned him to make a sculpture of George Washington for the rotunda.

"Greenough, in accordance with the classical high art fashion of his time, made a twelve-foot-high, semi-nude Zeus with a George Washington head on it," Bannard explained. "The public hated it. It was defaced by graffiti and eventually removed amid much controversy."

Miami has had its share of hated art works from the bestowing hand of the Art in Public Places Trust and it is probably too soon to count on the removal of any of them.

An unforgettable art statement occurred over a two-week period in May, 1983, when the Bulgarian artist Christo placed 6.5 million square feet of bright-pink fabric over some Biscayne Bay islands, enlisting the assistance of a retinue of individuals and spending a fortune to execute *Surrounded Islands*.

A film entitled *Islands* tells the story of how this was all accomplished. Environmentalists protested vigorously, others jeered, but in the end it created what Miami loves best—attention, and all over the world. Christo predicted this "major work" would cause "the true friction that makes the true energy of my art." Another friction emerged. Christo was asked for a six-figure cash "flowback" from government officials.

What it turned into was a community event of absorption and high fun with hundreds of volunteers pulling ropes and wading in water. When the goal was accomplished, the buildings and bridges within view of the scene were filled to overflowing. People who couldn't even see *Surrounded Islands* gave parties.

They were instructed by those in the know that they were experiencing an art lesson.

Thomas Hoving had said back in the beginning of the seventies when the Art in Public Places movement was being born that Miami couldn't go far wrong since it was coming from nowhere.

Tom Wolfe, summoned by Northern Trust Bank to address an early morning breakfast crowd of twelve hundred, told it the way it was: "Art in America is a religion and money is God." Art, it turned out, was also good for business.

Certainly that was the case with David L. Paul, who arrived in town to rescue a fading savings and loan and in six years proceeded to make himself an indispensable member of both the downtown establishment and the partying circuit. His good works included symphony and hospital.

His parties were fabulous—and he collected art. Big art for big bucks: Ruben's "Portrait of a Man in Armor on Mars," purchased for thirteen million, two hundred thousand dollars, for example. A highlight of one of his parties was to fly in six chefs from Europe (who became disgruntled when they were forced to eat in the pantry) and the cost of this caper was another six figures.

Anyone with a finger in the air to test the currents might have predicted that this Paul was headed for a fall. After federal regulators took over CenTrust, it was said that David Paul had used the savings and loan as his own private "piggy bank."

Paul's comment after the failure and just before being removed from his golden office was, "I got an awful lot of intellectual stimulation out of it. I had a lot of fun." CenTrust had risen to being the largest savings and loan in the Southeast, mainly by investing one billion dollars in high-risk, high-yield securities known as junk bonds.

A year earlier, asked by the fashion and gossip weekly *W* about Miami, he had said, "Miami has no roots. Whatever you want to do here, you can do."

No roots?

Tell that to Bill Graham, born on the family houseboat at Pennsuco, who helped create a state-of-the-art town, one envisioned by Ernie Graham's three sons: Philip, the late publisher of the Washington *Post* and *Newsweek*, Bill and Senator Bob. Not everybody gets to build his own town. Miami Lakes, the only personally developed place of any size since George Merrick, is there in place, well run and well regulated.

At the passing of Paul, who had made it into the inner sanctums of the Non Group, but was turned down by the trustees of the University of Miami, there was much comment by key players in the city-building game.

Former Mayor Ferre, out of power politically, had this to say: "He's a super salesman, a gambler, and Miami is a place where people are awed by money as a status symbol of achievement."

Alvah Chapman, the former World War II bomber pilot, was more succinct: "People come and go. This is a big city. David made some contributions but if he's not here, so be it. The community will continue to deal with concerns."

Without a doubt the concerns will be around. So will the changing colors in the CenTrust Building.

Designed by I. M. Pei, the forty-seven story CenTrust Building has become a skyline signature, with patterns of changing color to fit different occasions.

They show to great advantage when the Junior League puts on its Miami Magic evening each year, with people moving around downtown, and on those occasions Dr. James M. Jackson Hutson says he feels excited at the sight of downtown and hopeful about the state of the world.

Dr. Hutson is the grandson of the Dr. Jackson whose name adorns Jackson Memorial Hospital. Like his grandfather who wrote to his wife before the railroad, Dr. Hutson finds "a spirit about this place."

"When I see the downtown area I can't believe it," he says. "When I was a kid you could shoot a cannon down Flagler Street and it wouldn't hit anybody. I was born in 1922 and we played in Trinity churchyard because it had paving for skating and bicycling. The expressway is in my front yard now, but we have our house and our trees and I would never let anybody run me out of Miami." Dr. Hutson adds, "The sky is prettier than anywhere else in the world."

CenTrust isn't the only downtown building, and the fifty-five-story Southeast Financial Center, an eye-catcher by night and by day with its graceful lines and ambient quality, helps set the spectacular stage that is nighttime Miami. The best way to see downtown at night is gliding in on a yacht, but a rowboat will do.

The lights of Bayside Marketplace gleam to the north on the land reclaimed from the FEC and turned into a gallery of shops and restaurants that has brought people back to downtown at night. A gamble, everyone wondered if Miami would conquer the fear of downtown enough to leave suburban homes. The evidence is clear in the people that jostle along the walkways, under the ceiling fans and among the vendors.

Across the boulevard, Freedom Tower, downtown's most distinguished landmark, restored after a period of wide neglect and now

299

brilliantly lit against the night sky, carries memories of the vanished Miami *News*. Renamed, the building had welcomed tens of thousands of refugees fleeing Cuba and bent on starting new lives in Miami.

Now a Saudi sheik is restoring it. Nothing strange about that. There are sheiks all over the place and you don't pronounce it the way it was done in the days of Rudolph Valentino. You say it "shake," and sheiks have been shaking their money all over the place.

Aman al-Dahla is the sheik involved and Zabid Ramlawli is his man on the Tower job. More skyscrapers are planned.

One day, Miami Beach awakened to the fact that some of its buildings from the 1930s fell into the Art Deco category and with determination set about creating an Art Deco District in South Beach, which saved a number of old, small hotels and resulted in the organization of the Miami Design Preservation League. The whole movement created another tourist attraction. Miami Beach, once fading and fearful, is now energized with the young who flock to the old retirement hotels, remade into night spots with sidewalk cafes that beckon visitors, both foreign and domestic.

Helping change the face of Miami Beach where he was born is Mitchell Wolfson, Jr., heir to half the Wometco fortune, which his father earned from movie houses and television. Wolfson's fancies have led him into the art world, where he has made a considerable splash, and at the Beach he has purchased a warehouse in which to store the objects picked up all over the world. He has become a kind of godparent for all of Miami with his huge contributions.

Micky, as he is generally known, is one of those who has said that "Miami has not yet found its soul" and he is busily attempting to assist in the evolution. He is a Miami authentic who, at the age of fifty, has left behind five years of service in the State Department and is indulging himself adding to his fifty-thousand-piece collection of decorative and propaganda arts. Since he maintains a residence in Italy, it is not surprising that he recently purchased a castle in which to share his museum with the Italians.

Grace Glueck in the New York *Times* had this to say about the Miami Beach native in a full-page spread, "That he expresses himself in the grand manner of William Randolph Hearst and J. P. Morgan, with a little of Andy

Warhol thrown in, has not escaped notice in Miami, a city that dotes on extravagance."

An authentic shine was placed on the Miamis with the arrival of the Miami City Ballet, directed by one of the greats of the dance world, Edward Villella. A two-part *New Yorker* piece by Arlene Croce ushered in a period of high recognition for Villella that included his being given the prestigious Capezio award before top drawer figures at New York's Lincoln Center.

Back at Miami Beach the old Lincoln Road movie theater, the Lincoln, had undergone a transformation and was now a home for the New World Symphony, a training orchestra attracting world-wide attention and headed for a Paris appearance in its third season.

When a New Year starts in Miami it is upbeat. All the way, upbeat. Ushering in the year 1990 was no different.

The Orange Bowl Parade marched along Biscayne Boulevard with national TV cameras grinding away. Viewers watching the parade had stars in their eyes. Smiling faces from Germany and Belguim and France gazed up at the floats with childlike joy. Soft air. Laser beams. Beauty. What a way to start the New Year.

New Year is the time for admiring the Magic City, and after the revival of the 1980s, downtown shines.

All over Miami people were glad to turn the corner and come out into a new decade. Historical Plymouth Church in Coconut Grove was chosen by NBC to be shown over the world as part of Christmas. Former President Nixon was due to visit his friend, Bebe Robozo, who was planning to sell his Key Biscayne Bank to a wealthy Panamanian. And downtown, in a secure basement, Panama's General Manuel Noriega was tucked away into a holding place as plans for his trial proceeded. One of his lawyers was losing a fight to change the zoning on an old Coconut Grove house in order to run his office in a residential zone. He was meeting resistance from homeowners and would fail.

Driving along the glittering highway that Brickell Avenue has become amounts to an eye-blinking experience. Where a few short years before waterfront homes had claimed the view of the bay and where the Miss Harris

Florida School helped educate young ladies, an international banking center has erupted. Some of the buildings are outlandish, but as a scene they present a shining display of commerce and prosperity. A Parisian friend of taste declares it "restorative and beautiful."

Is it not a fictional note that the great-grandson of William Brickell should have been sent from Maryland, where he lives with his wife and three daughters, to have his share in the rebirth of the Magic City?

James Bain Brickell, Jr., was the man chosen by the Rouse Company to serve as project manager in the building of Bayside Marketplace. He came and went with only a few family friends being the wiser, spending week nights at the Inter-Continental Hotel, looking out over the same view as his forebears, turning his eyes inland to the broad highway named for his family and now a shining row of buildings, all glass and gleam.

A lot had changed since Old Man Brickell purchased those six hundred and forty acres on the south side of the Miami River. His great-grandson wondered if it was really true that Ponce de Leon had sailed in searching for the Fountain of Youth.

We do know that the discoverer sailed down Florida's east coast to Key West. Did he stop off for a quick test of the waters of the Devil's Punchbowl?

Looking out the window of the fifty-fourth floor of the Southeast Financial Center, Bill Colson has his eye on other matters. "On a clear day you can see all the way to Fort Lauderdale," he said dreamily.

Even on a murky day he is seeing far beyond Fort Lauderdale. The distinguished trial lawyer, a leader in all areas, paints a rosy picture for the city of his birth.

"We have an absolute foundation for being one of the top financial centers in the world, right along with London, Paris, Singapore. We have location. Climate. No matter what the immigration situation is, we sit like Rome at the bottom of Italy—in place."

ENDWORD

I look at the eighty-year-old Dade County pine tree rising against the blue sky and think that it has a bit more than one year on me and that I hope very much we manage to hang in there together until the end.

My son tells me that it could become a threat in a hurricane and its days are numbered. The day is coming, he tells me, when we will have to cut it down.

I receive the news calmly but begin saluting the old friend first thing each morning and the last thing at night.

After all, we have been together for a long time, that tree and I.

I remember burying our second daughter and choosing a plot in Woodlawn Cemetery because two Australian pines on it reminded me of the trees that held up the hammock on which she and her sister spent carefree hours. I remember how hurt I was when I returned to put flowers on her grave and discovered the trees had been removed.

My husband consoled me by saying, "It will all be gone in a hundred years." That was the summer of 1944 when the world stopped for a little bit, the summer our child was killed before reaching her fifth birthday.

Imagine all the pines that have fallen since then in order to create rising towers for the millions of people who have come to live. Imagine the changing scenes created by their coming.

What would the captain of the *Lady Lou* have thought of the fact that Miami welcomed three million passengers on cruise ships alone last year? Seventy years ago, the captain was insisting, "It's not the money I want. It's the people."

Today, Miami has both, but sometimes in the rush toward richness and power, observing the string of glitzy events, the sociological, economic and political problems, I stop and think that the beauty of the place is being short-changed.

There is no doubt that we have short-changed our fragile environment. Plundered it, more than not.

In writing a new section to accompany the edited original work, it was necessary to go back and scan what I had written in 1953. I was struck by the fact that many of the same patterns emerge despite the upheavals.

Change is part of life, but human nature has trouble with change. Margaret Fuller said, "I accept the universe" and when told of it, Carlyle muttered, "Gad, she'd better."

I accept the bars on my old study, transformed into a dower house for me by my children, and rejoice in the air-cooled temperature on summer's hottest days. I cherish the yellow elder, the golden hibiscus, the plumbago and the bilbergia moved long ago from the Barnacle.

I do miss the presence of birds sent flying by the bulldozers. I miss the courtesy sometimes lacking in the present-day climate. But when I ask myself what word I associate with Miami, I come up with "home."

That was the word Dr. Jean Jones Perdue spoke for Miami, too. So did Metro Mayor Clark.

No surprises to find Finlay Brooks Matheson giving a top-of-the-mind synonym for Miami with the same word. It was his great grandfather, William J. Matheson, who responded to his son Hugh's urging to "come see Coconut Grove." Young Finlay is the kind of investor who considers the environment in his undertakings. At home on Biscayne Bay, as are all Mathesons, he restricts his own three sons to remaining in port over weekends, out of consideration for the speed demons and weekend boaters who know nothing of the rules of the road.

Somehow it was touching to me, after all the talk and searching out of individuals, to have a leading community figure, Leslie Pantin, Jr., say immediately "home."

He was eleven when his family came here from Cuba. There was no culture shock for him because they had always visited Miami and for the first months stayed in a Miami Beach apartment with maid and all the comforts.

Later, when going back to Cuba was obviously not going to happen, his late father plunged into community life and earned a reputation as a "bridge" between Miamians and Hispanics. It's nice to know that the first word that comes to his namesake's mind when he hears "Miami" is "home."

Miami has become home to close to two million. Growth management aside, *¡Saludos Amigos!*

BIBLIOGRAPHY

ALLMAN, T. D. *Miami: City of the Future*. Atlantic Monthly Press, 1987.

BALLINGER, KENNETH. *Miami Millions*. Miami, Franklin Press, 1936.

BEACH, REX. *The Miracle of Coral Gables*. New York, Currier and Harford, 1926.

BLACKMAN, E. V. *Miami and Dade County, Fla., Its Settlement, Progress and Achievement*. Washington, D.C., Victor Rainbolt, 1921.

BROOKFIELD, CHARLES M., and GRISWOLD, OLIVER. *They All Called It Tropical*. Miami, Data Press, 1949.

COHEN, ISIDOR. *Historical Sketches and Sidelights of Miami, Fla.* Cambridge, 1925.

CORY, CHARLES B. *Hunting and Fishing in Florida*. Estes and Lauriat, 1896.

DIDION, JOAN. *Miami*. Simon and Schuster, 1987.

DORN, MABEL. *Under the Coconuts in Florida*. South Miami, South Florida Publishers, 1949.

DOUGLAS, MARJORY STONEMAN. *The Everglades, River of Grass*. New York, Rinehart, 1947.

FAIRCHILD, DAVID. *The World Grows Round My Door*. New York, Scribner's, 1947.

FISHER, JANE. *The Fabulous Hoosier*. New York, McBride, 1947.

FONTANEDA'S *Memoir*, translated by Buckingham Smith. Coral Gables, Glade House, 1945.

GIFFORD, JOHN C. *The Everglades and Other Essays Relating to South*

Florida. Miami, 1911.

HANNA, ALFRED JACKSON, and HANNA, KATHRYN ABBEY. *Florida's Golden Sands.* New York, Bobbs-Merrill, 1950.

HOLLINGSWORTH, TRACY. *History of Dade County.* Miami, 1936.

HOOVER, J. EDGAR. "New Tricks of Nazi Spies," *American.* October, 1943.

HUDSON, F. M. *Beginnings in Dade County.* Coral Gables, Tequesta, Historical Association of Southern Florida, 1943.

KLEINBERG, HOWARD. "Miami: The Way We Were." The *Miami Daily News Inc.,* 1985.

LAWRENSON, HELEN. "Damn the Torpedoes!" *Harper's.* July, 1942.

LUMMUS, J. N. *Miracle of Miami Beach.* Miami Beach, 1944.

MORRIS, ALLEN. *The Florida Handbook.* Peninsula Publishing Co., 1988-89.

MUNROE, RALPH MIDDLETON, and GILPIN, VINCENT. *The Commodore's Story.* Ives Washburn, 1930.

NASH, CHARLES EDGAR. *The Magic of Miami Beach.* Philadelphia, David McKay, 1938.

PARKS, ARVA MOORE. *Miami: The Magic City.* Continental Heritage Press Inc., 1981.

PETERS, THELMA. *Biscayne Country,* 1981.

PRATT, THEODORE. *The Barefoot Mailman.* New York, Duell, Sloan & Pearce, 1943.

REIFF, DAVID. *Going to Miami.* Little, Brown, 1987.

ROBERTS, KENNETH. *Florida.* New York, Harper's, 1926.

———. *Sun Hunting.* New York, Bobbs-Merrill, 1922.

ROMANS, BERNARD. *A Concise Natural History of East and West Florida.* New York, 1976.

SIMPSON, CHARLES TORREY. *Florida Wild Life.* New York, Macmillan, 1932.

SMILEY, NIXON. *Knights of the Fourth Estate.* E.A. Seemann, 1974.

———. *In Lower Florida Wilds.* New York, Macmillan, 1920.

STOCKBRIDGE, FRANK PARKER, and PERRY, JOHN HOLLIDAY. *So This*

Is Florida. New York, McBride, 1948.

TEBEAU, CHARLTON W. *A History of Florida*. University of Miami Press, 1971.

TRAPP, MRS. HARLAN. *My Pioneer Reminiscences*. Miami, 1940.

WAIT, LUCITA. *Fairchild Tropical Garden, The First Ten Years*. New York, Ronald Press, 1948.

WHITED, CHARLES. *Knight, A Publisher in the Tumultous Century*. Dutton, 1988.

WILLOUGHBY, HUGH L. *Across the Everglades*. Lippincott, 1897.

WOLFF, R. P. *Miami, Economic Pattern of a Resort Area.*, University of Miami, 1945.

WPA *Guide to Miami*. American Guide Series, Bacon, Percy and Daggett, Northport, N.Y., 1941.

WYLIE, PHILIP, and SCHWAB, LAURENCE. "The Battle of Florida," *The Saturday Evening Post*. March 11, 1944.

NEWSPAPERS AND PERIODICALS

Abitare.
The Christian Science Monitor.
The Economist.
Geo.
The Kendall Gazette.
The Miami Daily News.
The Miami Herald.
The Miami Metropolis.
The Miami News.
The Miami Review.
Miami Today.
The Miami Tribune.
New Miami.
The New York Times.
Newsweek.
South Florida.
Time.
The Washington Post.

Index